Zambia
Pathways to Excellence

Adonis & Abbey Publishers Ltd

24 Old Queen Street,
London SW1H 9HP
United Kingdom

Website: http://www.adonis-abbey.com
E-mail Address: editor@adonis-abbey.com

Nigeria:
No. 39 Jimmy Cater Street,
Suites C3 – C6 J-Plus Plaza
Asokoro, Abuja, Nigeria
Tel: +234 (0) 7058078841/08052035034

British Library Cataloguing-in-Publication Data
A catalogue record for this book is available from the British Library

ISBN: 978-1-913976-07-1

Zambia
Pathways to Excellence

Chisanga Puta Chekwe

Table of Contents

Abreviations and Acronyms

AfCFTA	African Continental Free Trade Area
AIMS	African Institute for Mathematical Sciences
AMWU	African Mineworkers Union
ANC	African National Congress
CDC	Constituency Development Committee
CIP	Citizenship by Investment Programme
DFATD	Department of Foreign Affairs Trade and Development (Canada)
DMMU	Disaster Management and Mitigation Unit
DPP	Director for Public Prosecutions
DRC	Democratic Republic of Congo
FISP	Farmer Input Support Programme
GDP	Gross Domestic Product
GPI	Global Peace Index
HDI	Human Development Index
IBA	Independent Broadcasting Authority
ICT	Information and Communications Technology
IDRC	International Development Research Council (Canada)
IEA	International Energy Agency
IEC	Independent Electoral Commission
IMF	International Monetary Fund
KAS	Kitwe African Society
LAZ	Law Association of Zambia
MMD	Movement for Multiparty Democracy
MPLA	People's Movement for the Liberation of Angola
OAU	Organisation for African Unity
OECD	Organisation for Economic Cooperation and Development
PCR	Polymerase chain reaction
RAA	Rhodesian Athletics Association
SADC	Southern African Development Community
STEM	Science, Technology, Engineering, and Mathematics
UHI	Urban Heat Island effect
UNDP	United Nations Development Programme
UNESCO	United Nations Educational, Scientific and Cultural Organisation
UNICEF	United Nations International Children's Emergency Fund
UNIP	United National Independence Party
UNISA	University of South Africa
UPND	United Party for National Development
WEF	World Economic Forum

WTTC	World Travel and Tourism Council
WRI	World Resources Institute
ZANC	Zambia African National Congress
ZCID	Zambia Centre for Interparty Dialogue
ZIPAR	Zambia Institute for Policy Analysis and Research
ZNBC	Zambia National Broadcasting Corporation

Preface

Events in Zambia can move very rapidly. One minute, it is a one-party dictatorship with no hope of getting out of the economic hole it has dug for itself. The next minute, it is a shining example of democracy and one of the fastest-growing economies in the world. Before you know it, the country has a debt crisis and is reported by The Economist as 'slouching' toward abject failure. Zambia has experienced all these in the space of thirty years. It is not just the country's dynamism, however, that makes it a challenging subject to study.

The country is also frustratingly casual about exploiting the natural advantages it has over many other nations. These advantages go beyond the peaceable nature of Zambians and include an abundance of natural resources and good weather. Zambian intellectuals are often baffled by their political leaders' willingness to shun what they see as common-sense solutions to challenges.

Less thoughtful critics even go as far as arguing that independence may have come too soon for Zambia, suggesting that the country would have been better equipped had it remained under British rule longer. These critics are mostly young people who never experienced colonialism. After reading this book, they should understand that the purpose of colonial rule included a commitment to keeping 'natives' uneducated on account of their skin colour. They will also discover that many colonial 'achievements' were not designed to improve black Zambians' lives. To the extent that they existed, the benefits of colonialism can be likened to bread crumbs from the master's table.

Both advocates and critics of the country should find this book informative. The hope is both sets of readers will, on occasion, see their views addressed in an evidence-based manner.

The book has been written in an accessible fashion. Footnotes have been used only in instances where it is felt that the reader may wish to pursue further study of a particular issue or where the proposition made is novel or not self-evident.

This book seeks to provide a unique explanation of how the trauma of colonialism has held the country back. But it goes further and shows how Zambia can increase collective confidence and thrive, despite this trauma. To do so, Zambia must acknowledge the colonial experience but must not become unduly obsessed with it.

Zambia needs to transition from a victim to a survivor intent on thriving. To do so, Zambians must learn about their achievements in both pre-colonial and post-colonial times. A cultural re-examination is also essential to ensure the best traditional Zambian values are incorporated into modern Zambian life.

Zambia is a relatively young nation which has a long way to go. The country has made many mistakes. Yet, Zambia is infinitely better off than she was before independence. It is now time to turn her into a shining example of success.

Acknowledgments

This book would not have been possible without the support of my wife, Jean, who gave me the space to write, and the encouragement of people who have harboured goodwill for Zambia all their lives. The sentiments of these people have persuaded me that Zambia has what it takes to be a great nation.

Sadly, my main inspiration, my mother, Grace Kambole, passed away before I started writing this book. Throughout the writing of the book, I was constantly reminded of her disappointment at the Zambian leadership's failure to do what she considered obvious to address the country's challenges. Given her educational background and the fact that she had spent her entire working life in the private sector, it is not surprising that she favoured greater utilisation of the private sector in resolving the country's challenges.

About eight months after my mother's passing, her cousin, Flavia Musonda Musakanya also died. FMM, as she was known, was a tough lady who seemed to delight in achieving the near impossible. In her early forties, she was left alone to fend for herself and family when her husband was incarcerated as a political prisoner. By all accounts, she ran the family business splendidly during the five long years that Valentine Musakanya was away from home.

Mrs Musakanya often talked about her desire to write a book about her experiences as a detainee's wife. That book was not written but I benefited from her insights and analysis of Zambian politics as we discussed her proposed project.

Less than four months after Mrs Musakanya's passing, her brother-in-law, Francis Herbert Kaunda, the soft spoken former head of the Fortune 500 Zambia Consolidated Copper Mines Ltd, passed away. Over the years, I spent many hours with Mr Kaunda discussing the Zambian economy. More recently, I spent a considerable amount of time discussing his second book, 'Things to Remember not to Forget', which outlines Zambia's challenges as a newly independent country. His plan was to write a sequel, but that never came to pass.

Mr Kaunda possessed a unique knowledge of the mining industry and metal marketing. He offered a unique perspective that helped me analyse issues more cogently.

2021 started off promising to be as tragic as 2020. At the end of February, Andrew Sardanis, passed away. Mr Sardanis had more confidence in the Zambian people (although not necessarily in the government of the day) than any person I know. He understood the impact of colonialism more than most, and saw through the myth of race. I enjoyed the many discussions I had with him, starting in my pre-teen years and ending in March 2019, the last time I saw him. I was enormously impressed by his quick wit and intellectual consistency. I have read his trilogy of books on Zambia, and learned a great deal from them.

Andrew Sardanis was a born teacher who enjoyed nurturing budding entrepreneurs and simplifying complex issues. When he served as head of Zambia's Industrial Development Corporation (INDECO), he took the opportunity to teach business skills to as many of his protégés as possible.

One of these protégés was Greene Mumba Simpungwe, a family friend whose uncle once attended school with my late father. Mr Simpungwe was destined to die within 24 hours of Mr Sardanis' passing. Both Sardanis and Simpungwe were excellent resources in the quest to understand the interaction of business and politics in modern Zambia.

I am grateful to all these people and many more who cannot be named now.

CPC
Burlington, Ontario
29 March 2021

Foreword

A scion of one of Zambia's old political families, Chisanga Puta Chekwe has produced a book that draws on his upbringing, experience, and wide-ranging research to analyse and critique his homeland. He does this from the vantage point of a son of the soil, born and raised in Chingola on the Copperbelt—Zambia's mining heartland—and a member of the diaspora, based in Ontario, Canada. A lawyer and Rhodes Scholar, he has held several positions in business, government, and philanthropy, including deputy minister in the Ontario Government, chair and CEO of the Ontario Rental Housing Tribunal, country manager of First Quantum Minerals in Zambia, and executive director of Oxfam Canada. In addition, he is a prolific writer, having authored books on the historic 1964 post-apartheid general election in South Africa, where he was an election observer. His other books include: *Getting Zambia to Work*; *Staying Ahead: Due Diligence in Residence and Citizenship by Investment Programmes*, and *Cobra in the Boat: Michael Sata's Zambia*, a critical account of Zambia's fifth president's government.

This eclectic background was put to good use in this provocative book that laments Zambia's failure, thus far, to fulfil its abundant potential. "A rich country, poorly managed" is one of his characterizations, a situation he attributes in part to its failure to fully address the legacy of its traumatic colonial past, which he documents at some length. He views the low self-esteem that still persists among Zambians more than fifty years after independence from the British as one of the causal factors of the country's current troubles. The racist stereotypes of the colonial era, with its cruelty, neglect, and injustice have, he argues, left an indelible mark and undermined confidence at all levels of society. He critiques the widely-referenced economic policy failures, and the lost opportunities in agriculture, tourism and mining. His solutions are not necessarily original—investing in people, access to capital, policy consistency, good governance, and the rule of law—but what is perhaps different is his emphasis on the cultural shift needed to produce more discipline and self-confidence. "The country needs to behave more like a survivor determined to thrive and less like a perennial victim destined to fail," he opines.

Not everyone will agree with Chekwe's views and advocacy, but his thoughtful commitment to the land of his birth, his evident frustration with its current situation, combined with his wide-ranging recourse to research, deserves to be read, digested, and debated.

Robert Liebenthal
Development Economist
March 2021

Introduction

A tale of two victims

From 1991 to 1997, I served as an adjudicator on the Ontario Criminal Injuries Compensation Board. When I became the board's chair and chief executive officer, I continued to adjudicate cases because listening to the compelling human stories made me a better leader.

The board's mandate was to compensate innocent victims of violent crime. Throughout my tenure, one-third of all cases before the board were related to sexual abuse. Listening to more than four hundred such cases, I developed a better understanding of the impact of trauma on human beings.

Typically, sexual abuse reorients victims and saps their confidence, making it impossible for them to rely on past achievements for reassurance. Their past almost disappears, and they see their life only in the context of the abuse. Victims of sexual abuse almost always consider everyone else as better than they are, leading to unnatural admiration of other people, even those who may remind them of their assailants. Unless professionally addressed, the loss of confidence and other consequences of abuse can cripple the victim for life. Victims who are fortunate enough to get professional help have a very high chance of overcoming the debilitating effects of sexual abuse. Recovery also depends on the degree of trauma and its impact. Unfortunately, victims do not respond to trauma in the same way, as the two stories below demonstrate.

One of the most horrifying cases of childhood sexual abuse I adjudicated involved a father who routinely raped his pre-teen daughter. As if that was not bad enough, the perpetrator acted in concert with his wife, the child's mother, to physically restrain the victim during the assaults. Mary V (not her real name) eventually escaped her home and made a life of sorts for herself. She, however, felt held back by her childhood experiences, suffering flashbacks, loss of confidence, and episodes of depression. She also went through a period of self-mutilation and, at some point in her adult life, blamed herself for the assaults. By the time she entered her thirties, Mary V found it difficult to function, overwhelmed by feelings of worthlessness and fatigue. It was at this point that she approached the Criminal Injuries Compensation Board for help.

Mary V's trauma was evident at the hearing. Thanks to the assault she suffered, her educational attainments were limited. On the face of it, the lack of education did not prevent Mary V from presenting outwardly as a regular member of the middle class. There was, however, a mismatch between her outward appearance of normalcy and her ability to function. She had limited confidence and assumed that just about everyone she met was better than her and consequently looked to others for solutions to the challenges she faced. Despite these challenges, her therapist was confident she would function fully and control her life in due course.

In another case, the victim had taken control of her life before she showed up for her hearing at the board. Jane S (not her real name) arrived in Canada with her mother, aged five. The two-member family emigrated from Jamaica in search of a better life. Two years later, after settling well into their lives as Canadian residents, Jane S's mother met a man who proposed to her. The man was in love with Jane S's mother and appeared keen to adopt Jane S. The marriage took place, and the new family appeared happy until about five years later when Jane S started putting on abnormal weight. The ensuing medical examination revealed that Jane S was pregnant. Further inquiry found that Jane S's adoptive father had been sexually abusing her for years. He had won her silence by persuading her that what he was doing was a Canadian tradition that could not be talked about it, as doing so would tear the family apart. In those days abuse within families was treated differently than today, and police involvement yielded no criminal charges as the matter was considered a domestic issue. Jane S did, however, undergo a therapeutic abortion, receiving emotional support from her mother.

Shortly after Jane S's return from the hospital, her mother's stance changed. She accused Jane S, who was about 13, of provoking her husband and causing him to rape her. Jane found it impossible to continue living with her parents, so she ran away from home and lived on the streets for a few weeks. Being a clever girl, she quickly realised that she was vulnerable to further exploitation on the streets and set about looking for a job and accommodation. She found a job as a server in a restaurant, took a room in a boarding house, and sought and discovered a programme that would enable her to complete middle school. According to the file, Jane S was quite successful as a student. But the details in the file had no comprehensive information on Jane S's educational endeavours after elementary school and ended with Jane S exploring night school for her secondary education.

On a rainy morning in Toronto, I was in one of the hearing rooms at the board, waiting for my next case, when a well-groomed and slightly nervous handsome young woman walked in and asked if she was in the right room. I did not immediately connect this woman to the application before me, so I asked for her name. She was relieved to learn she was in the right place. I was amazed at the incongruity between the victim's picture I had conjured up in my mind after reading the file, and Jane S in person. Even at that early stage in the hearing, I suspected she had completed her high school education.

Given the preponderance of the documentary evidence about the historic sexual assault and the fact that her claim was unchallenged, I told Jane S that she need not go into the details of the violent crime committed against her as I was more interested in the impact that the crime had had on her life, and would find evidence in that regard particularly helpful. When Jane S, now in her early 20s, concluded her evidence, I asked her, out of curiosity, what she was currently doing. With justifiable pride, she said, 'I am hoping to graduate with a BSc degree in Social Work from the University of Toronto next summer.'

Despite her ordeal, Jane S thrived. She regained her confidence and found a way to move on and contribute to society. I can only hope that Mary V was also able to overcome the trauma and regain her confidence eventually.

CHAPTER ONE

Historical Background

J ust as individuals can be traumatised by extreme events, nations can suffer greatly from extreme factors that disrupt their lives and force them to adopt a new way of living. As with most countries recently liberated from colonialism, Zambia has suffered traumatic events that have deeply affected its collective and individual psyche. This chapter seeks to explain the genesis of Zambia's trauma.

Carve them up

At Portugal's instigation, German Chancellor Otto von Bismarck convened the Berlin Conference of 1885. The purpose of the gathering, which included 13 European countries and representation from the United States, was to establish a formal treaty for the colonization of the African continent. Agreements were reached over existing conflicts between the participating powers, resolutions were passed to end slavery on the continent, and, more sinisterly, the huge territory known as the Congo Free State was assigned to King Leopold II of Belgium, in his personal capacity.

This conference further established the principle of 'effective occupation' which required colonising powers to demonstrate political and administrative control of their territories without regard for indigenous borders. It was on this basis that spheres of influence were allotted. Not surprisingly, the principle accelerated the infamous Scramble for Africa, characterized by unrestrained colonial adventure, while simultaneously diluting, and, in some cases, eliminating indigenous governance models.

Zambia gets its wings

The butterfly-shaped territory now known as Zambia was designated a British colony. At about the same time, the king of the Lozi kingdom (one of the major pre-colonial Zambian kingdoms), Chief Lewanika, was deceived into signing a concession that gave the British South Africa Company, led by Cecil Rhodes, an excuse to invade the kingdom. Initially, the company's interest in the region appeared innocuous, as Rhodes was mostly concerned with arresting the Belgian advance on mineral-rich Katanga. He was not successful as by the time he reached the Lozi capital of Lealui, Katanga had already been taken. Nonetheless, Rhodes' emissary to Lewanika's kingdom, Frank Lochner, managed to get an important concession from Lewanika.

The Lochner concession gave the British South Africa Company the perpetual right to mine, trade, and build railways in Lozi-controlled territory. Explicitly excluded from this concession was central Barotseland. In return, the kingdom would have British protection, the appointment of a British resident administrator, and an annual salary for Lewanika. When BSAC became embroiled in conflict with the Ndebele nation, the concession lapsed. If Lewanika had hoped to preserve the kingdom's independence through concessions such as these, his hope must have been dashed, as in 1911, Barotseland was incorporated into Northern Rhodesia.

The Lochner concession was followed by seven years of company neglect and failure to live up to written promises. Lewanika himself often complained that the BSAC failed to modernize his kingdom and provide financial security for the Lozi aristocracy. Be that as it may, the Lochner concession was an important milestone in the development of modern mining in Zambia. Under this concession and further agreements signed in October 1900 and August 1909, Lewanika ceded to the BSAC a monopoly of commercial and mining rights within the territory he claimed fell under his jurisdiction. As indicated earlier, the portion of territory occupied by Lozi people was excluded from commercial exploitation by the BSAC. The rest of the territory, which, according to Lewanika, included present-day Copperbelt Province, was open for business.

It appears, however, that the Copperbelt Province did not fall within Lewanika's jurisdiction, his claims to the contrary notwithstanding.[1]

---

[1] Stephenson, J.E. Chirupula's Tale, London, Geoffrey Bles, 1937

Seeds of discontent

The copper mines developed on the Copperbelt generated huge profits, which were remitted overseas. To remain profitable, the colonial authorities needed to guarantee a steady supply of labour. They could not do so if potential members of the mining workforce had an alternative life in rural areas. Therefore, the colonial government introduced taxes and prevented local farmers from selling cattle and crops in the 'European' market. In addition, they expelled indigenous farmers from fertile land and placed them in overcrowded and unproductive reserves. The result was that local farmers became low-paid workers on the Zambian Copperbelt and in South African mines. The expulsion of indigenous farmers from fertile land, which over time resulted in significant loss of farming skills, would later lend credence to the claim that indigenous Zambians made poor farmers.

The first major reaction to the low wages and brutal working conditions was a spontaneous strike in which six men were killed and twenty-two wounded in 1935. According to Jane Parpart:

> Most studies of the strike have accepted the Russell Commission's conclusion that it was basically a spontaneous reaction to a tax increase and was dominated by Bemba-speaking miners.[2]

But Parpart cautions that while one cannot equate the 1935 strike with the better-organised strikes of the 1940s and 1950s, it was much more than 'the protest of the desperate'. The strike suggests that deeper changes which signalled growing worker consciousness among black miners on the Copperbelt were occurring. The evidence gathered by Parpart suggests that by 1935, most miners had developed some awareness of their common interest as a group. Their grievances centred on abusive racial exploitation. They complained of racism, which made it impossible for miners to identify across racial lines even when they had common interests.

The 1935 experience increased debate about the viability of a union for black workers, especially at the Nkana, Mufulira, and Roan mines. Thus, in February 1948, a union branch was formed at Nkana. The

---

[2] Parpart, Jane L, Labor and Capital on the African Copperbelt, Philadelphia, Temple University Press, 1983

executive committee elections resulted in the patrician Lawrence Chola Katilungu assuming the union's presidency and Simon Kaluwa and Philip Simwanza elected secretary and treasurer respectively. The Nkana committee members worked hard to spread the word and encourage unionization. Three months after the Nkana union branch was formed, Mufulira had an executive committee and 300 members. Roan hesitated as some of the leading black miners there continued to work toward a multiracial union. By June 1948, Roan was on board with a few keen members of the works committee and 150 black workers deciding to form a union. Toward the end of 1948, Nchanga established a branch. The total membership in all four branches stood at 5,000. In March 1949, the four branches came together to form the African Mineworkers Union (AMWU), with more than 7,000 members.

As black workers' power was being consolidated through the AMWU, Northern Rhodesia was prospering, with the bulk of the benefits going disproportionately to the white settler community. These settlers looked to their counterparts in Southern Rhodesia, who were more numerous and powerful, and began talking of territorial amalgamation. This effort was opposed by both black Northern Rhodesians and the Colonial Office in London. The latter could not accept a situation that would undermine the flow of money from Northern Rhodesia to London, while the former were wary of stronger association with Southern Rhodesia, whose mining companies treated black workers even more appallingly than the Copperbelt companies. At least the Copperbelt companies had stabilized their skilled black mineworkers, who were now accepted as a settled workforce in urban areas.

Church commissioned by Kongo King

The stabilized mine workforce was supported by the black petty bourgeoisie developing in the towns. The two groups worked closely to establish welfare associations whose principal objective was to protect African interests in the towns. Inevitably, the associations became political and in 1946 convened to discuss territory-wide political issues. These discussions resulted in the formation of the Federation of African Societies, which became the Northern Rhodesia Congress in 1948; the forerunner of the African National Congress. The African National Congress served as the principal training ground for politicians who eventually steered the country to independence.

Before colonialism

One of the myths promoted by the colonial enterprise was that the indigenous peoples of Zambia had no civilisation or history to speak of until colonialism came along. Even more absurdly, the same claptrap is disseminated about the entire African continent despite an abundance of evidence to the contrary.

In fairness, this disregard for history is not confined to obvious sympathisers of colonialism, such as members of the privileged Zambian white ghetto who seem to have dedicated their lives to misunderstanding everything about the country they live in. It can also be found among indigenous Zambians who have uncritically accepted the colonial assessment of their history and capabilities. Ironically, some white Zambians (as opposed to white Zambian ghetto dwellers) have a much more refined appreciation of Zambian history than many of their black compatriots. They know and appreciate that the kingdoms and societies brutally conquered by colonialism and turned into dependencies did have culture and refinement worth noting.

Zambian Khoisan

While the Berlin Conference is seen by many as the beginning of Zambian history, the country has a history that precedes this disastrous conference and the Kongo/Lunda-Luba migrations,

The Khoisan were the earliest modern humans to live in the territory now known as Zambia. They were brown-skinned hunter-gatherers who lived a nomadic life with stone-age technology. Khoisan existence in

Zambia continued uninterrupted until the fourth century, when Bantu people started to migrate from the north. The Bantu had more developed technology, mostly in the form of iron and copper tools. They also had weapons that they used to effectively subdue the Khoisan and settle on their land, introducing agriculture in the process. By the eleventh and twelfth centuries, a more sophisticated society was emerging, creating opportunities for long-distance trade, primarily in the export of ivory and importation of cotton. With their relatively advanced tools, copper mining was introduced. The value of this commodity is perhaps underlined by the fact that the first currency used in the country was a copper cross.

An ethnic group that came with the Bantu migration of the fourth century and settled in the country's south was the Mbara. Unlike other Zambian ethnicities and cultures that claim the Lunda-Luba kingdom as their place of immediate origin, the exact origin of the Tonga, descendants of the Mbara, is still a subject of speculation. The Southern Province of Zambia is home to 1,300-year-old iron age settlements. The best known of these is Ingombe Ilede, which translates as 'the sleeping cow' in the Tonga language. The name comes from the cow-like shape of a fallen baobab tree near the famous site where the Mbara settled. Archaeological excavations suggest that Mbara art exhibited in their pottery bears an uncanny resemblance to today's traditional Tonga art.

Another difference between the Tonga and the other Bantu groups in Zambia is the absence of a formal traditional aristocracy. The late anthropologist and Tonga culture enthusiast, Elizabeth Colson, observed that although ritual office existed in small neighbourhood communities, political office was embryonic or non-existent until the British government recognized headmen and chiefs.

Zambezia

The Northern Rhodesia independence movement often looked to the territory's past as it planned the future of independent Zambia. An early decision concerned the country's name once British colonial rule came to an end. This was certainly an important matter for the radical wing of the African National Congress, led by Simon Mwansa Kapwepwe and Munukayumbwa Sipalo, which broke away to form a new political party in 1958.

The radicals wanted their new party to bear the name of the future country, so they settled on Zambia African National Congress (ZANC). When deciding what the future country should be called, Whittington Sikalumbi, a veteran campaigner for independence, suggested Zambezia, after the southern African kingdom shown on medieval Portuguese maps of the region. Simon Kapwepwe, one of the founders of the independence movement, who later served as vice president of the republic, thought 'Zambezia' was too cumbersome. He, therefore, truncated it to the more euphonious 'Zambia'[3]. There was, however, much more than euphony at play in choosing a name connected to the ancient kingdom of Zambezia. Over a thousand years ago, Al Mas'udi, an Arab writer from the Hejaz, a region in the west of present-day Saudi Arabia, travelled down the East African coast, gathering information from sailors and merchants about the region. From this information, the book, The Meadows of Gold and Mines of Gems, was born.

In the book, the author described a large African state near the mouths of the Zambezi River governed by a king whose authority rested on elections and whose mandate was to 'govern the people with equity.'[4] Few countries in the world were concerned about equitable governance in 900 AD when Zambezia thrived.

The Kongo kingdom

While Zambezia inspired the name of the newly independent Zambia, for the most part, the country owes its cultural and historical heritage to the Kongo kingdom, a 129,499 square kilometre empire in the western part of central/southern Africa that was founded in 1390. The kingdom stretched from modern-day Gabon in the north to River Kwanza in the south, and from the Atlantic in the west to River Kuango in the east.

By all accounts, the Kongo kingdom was wealthy and well organised. The wealth came from agriculture, copper mining, ivory, and textiles. Agricultural proceeds came from communally owned farming land in the villages. This produce was shared among families and the surplus was used to pay taxes. Towns, on the other hand, relied on indentured labour

---

[3] Sardanis, Andrew. Africa Another Side of the Coin, New York, I.B. Tauris, 2003
[4] Davidson, Basil. Which Way Africa, London, Penguin Books, 1967

to farm plantations. The most popular currency was Nzimbu (cowrie) shells gathered from coastal waters within the kingdom.

Although the territory had a powerful king, much of the monarch's power was delegated to aristocrats known as the Mani, who occupied key positions in the kingdom. For example, each of the kingdom's six provinces was administered by a Mani governor who received orders directly from Mwine Kongo, the king. One of the more important functions performed by these provincial leaders was collecting taxes on behalf of the king. Orders to the provincial leaders were issued from Mbanza Kongo, the territory's capital where the king resided. By the sixteenth century, Mbaza Kongo's population had exceeded fifty thousand inhabitants. The population for the entire territory was estimated at three million.[5]

Enter the Portuguese

When the Portuguese arrived in Kongo in 1485,[6] they found a well-organised society with a centralized monarchy and powerful noble class. There had been an earlier landing in 1482[7] , which did not result in immediate Portuguese settlement. Written accounts from the early Portuguese about the kingdom describe a well-developed system of taxation that allowed the aristocracy to maintain a luxurious lifestyle. These accounts are consistent with oral history.

Diogo Cão is generally recognised as the first European to land at the mouth of the Nzeri River (incorrectly called the Zaire River by the Portuguese) in 1482. This encounter, although initially challenging, led to many Portuguese wishing to settle in the kingdom, especially after word of the country's wealth spread. Portugal also saw an opportunity to spread Christianity, which was relatively easy because the indigenous religion was not too different from Christianity. The ancient Kongolese believed in their god, Nzambi, who was the highest of all spirits. The earthly representative of Nzambi was Ng'anga Kongo, who acted as a spiritual adviser to the king.

Understandably, Christianity would have been seen as simply a new medium of communication with Nzambi. Thus, King Nzinga accepted the faith, was baptised, and then given the new Christian name of João

---

5 Gondola, Ch. Didier. The History of Congo, London, Greenwood Press, 2002

6 Tanguy, F. *Imilandu ya Babemba*, Oxford, Oxford University Press, 1948

7 www.britishmuseum.org/pdf/KingdomOfKongo_TeachersNotes.pdf

on May 3, 1491. Despite the king's conversion, not everyone was enthusiastic about the adoption of Christianity as the Kongo's religion. Mpansu, the heir apparent who was sidestepped in favour of his Christian brother, Mubemba (aka Mbemba), and the then Ng'anga Kongo were not in favour of christianising Kongo, and were prepared to challenge the Portuguese in this regard. Unfortunately for them, because of the alliance between the Portuguese and the newly converted Christians, they found themselves in a minority that was quickly defeated. According to oral history, Mpansu and Ng'anga Kongo warned their compatriots of an ominous future should the Portuguese continue influencing events in the Kongo.

Mbemba Nzinga

Since the Portuguese and Kongolese got along peacefully, at least initially, under the strong leadership of Mubemba, now known as King Afonso l, this warning seemed farfetched and even ludicrous. Indeed, the relationship with Portugal seemed to be beneficial to the Kongo nobility, who acted as middlemen in the slave trade perpetrated by Portuguese traders. It did not, however, take long for the highly intelligent and erudite Afonso to see that the slave trade posed an existential threat to the kingdom. For a start, there was the question of the acceptability of slavery as practised by the Portuguese. Under Kongolese law and practice, no one could be held captive forever. For this reason, the people the Portuguese saw as locally owned slaves were in fact indentured labourers who were routinely freed as the various debts for which they were held were deemed paid. The Kongo kingdom had expanded by conquering neighbouring territories and taking 'slaves' as reparation. In due course, however, many of these 'slaves' regained their freedom and were often absorbed by the royal family and other members of the nobility.

Afonso also understood that the increased use of Portuguese-owned slaves outside the Kongo, mainly to work the sugar plantations in São Tomé, threatened Kongolese population growth. The King, who wrote and spoke Portuguese, sent several letters to his Portuguese 'brother king', government officials and bishops in Lisbon, and the Vatican between 1509 and 1541. In these letters, Mbemba complained about the depletion of his country's population through slavery. He also complained that the ability of Portuguese agents to deal directly with the local population in the sale of goods (and creating a new class of independently wealthy nationals) had greatly undermined the power and influence of the king.[8]

Unfortunately, Afonso's letters of distress to the King of Portugal elicited only casual and dismissive responses.[9] For example, repeated requests for priests, doctors, religious paraphernalia, and even a boat to transport them were met with demands for payment in the form of slaves. Since there were not enough potential slaves in his kingdom, the king was forced to raid neighbouring territories to secure captives. It is possible that, at this time, Mbemba may have allowed those enslaved within his country and thus protected by Kongo law to be sold.

To minimise the likelihood of slaves being exported illegally, Mbemba placed restrictions on the trade in 1526.

The beginning of the end

Although subdivided into six provinces, the Kongo kingdom was highly centralised with all critical decisions taken in the capital, which was also the main beneficiary of national wealth. The Mani and all who held office in the provinces looked forward to promotions and a base at Mbaza

---

[8] See for example letter of October 18, 1526. www.genius.com/Nzinga-mbemba-afonso-i-letters-to-the-king-of-portugal
[9] www.britishmuseum.org/pdf/KingdomOfKongo_TeachersNotes.pdf

Kongo. The prospect of this kind of promotion was a reason for diligence in collecting taxes and remitting them to the capital. The downside of the system was that provinces were deliberately kept underdeveloped.

It was this reality that the Portuguese exploited in the province of Soyo, where traders started trading directly with local officials, making the latter wealthier and more independent-minded. Soyo had the main embarkation points for slaves awaiting Portuguese ships, which were often late. This delay in the shipment of human cargo created an opportunity for slaves to be diverted by local officials for work in the province. Inevitably, this strengthened the Soyo economy and reduced the province's dependency on Mbaza Kongo. The strengthening of the Soyo economy and the corresponding weakening of the central government may well have marked the beginning of the end for the Kongo kingdom.

Afonso was greatly discouraged by the responses he received from Europe. Although he continued to be appalled by the illegal kidnapping of his people, he appears to have given up on getting any kind of help from either Portugal or the Vatican. In 1542, two years after writing his last letter to European leaders, Mubemba Nzinga, King Afonso l, died. Twenty five years after Afonso's death, an outbreak of violence was instigated by a group known as the Jaga. It is unclear who organised the Jaga, but the most accepted reason for their invasion was a desire to break King Alvaro's slave trade monopoly. Having just been installed as king in 1568, it is unlikely that Alvaro was fully prepared for the invasion.

Alvaro Nimi a Lukeni lwa Mbemba was an unlikely successor to the throne. His father was an unknown nobleman who died prematurely, leaving behind a widow who consummated a second marriage with King Henrique I. When Henrique died fighting on the eastern frontier, his stepson Álvaro was his regent. It is not clear how Alvaro became king, given that there were other more traditional candidates for the role. This lack of clarity led many to conclude that Alvaro was not a legitimate ruler.

The invasion of the Yaka, referred to as the Jagas by the Portuguese, which took place shortly after Alvaro became king, is said by some to represent a protest against Alvaro's alleged usurpation of the Crown. Whatever the case, the Yaka, an ethnic group in the present-day southwestern Democratic Republic of the Congo, posed a huge threat to both Alvaro and the kingdom. At one point, the Yaka fought so ferociously as to force Alvaro to abandon Mbanza Kongo, the capital, and flee to an island in the Nzere River.

From this place of temporary exile, the king sought help from Portugal to restore him to the throne. Portugal responded by sending an expedition of 600 soldiers, mostly from the colony of São Tome. This was not however, a completely altruistic gesture. A condition of their support was an undertaking of vassalage from Alvaro and regaining control of the Portuguese community in Kongo by building a fort, ostensibly to protect them. There was strong opposition to these demands by both the Portuguese in Kongo and Kongo nobles. As a result, these particular demands were not accepted.

Nonetheless, Alvaro did permit the Portuguese to settle in Luanda, paving the way for the creation of the colony of Angola. The Portuguese colony in Luanda was formally established in 1575. The Portuguese quickly abused their new status as colonial masters of Luanda by launching raids into Kongo to gather slaves and seize tracts of territory.

The first full military assault on Kongo by the Portuguese occurred in 1622. On that occasion, Portugal discovered, to its horror, that Kongo was still a state to be reckoned with. Kongo inflicted enough casualties on the invaders to cause them to temporarily retreat. The friendly and mutually beneficial relationship with Portugal that King Afonso l had so assiduously nurtured was clearly over. The Kongolese must, at this point, have rued their decision to assist Portugal in Angola by sending an army to rescue the Portuguese governor Paulo Dias de Novais when he lost the war against the nearby kingdom of Ndongo in 1579. Thanks to help such as this, Portugal became stronger, and in 1622 sent a large army that incorporated Mbundu archers and Imbangala mercenaries famed for hyper-violence and cannibalism to invade southern Kongo. With a 10 to 1 ratio of Portuguese soldiers to Kongolese soldiers, the Portuguese claimed victory at the Battle of Mbumbi.

New evidence suggests that Kongo, with the help of its new Dutch allies, was able to regroup and inflict defeat on the Portuguese at the Battle of Mbandi Kasi. This victory led to the ouster of the Portuguese governor of Luanda and, more importantly perhaps, the return of Kongolese subjects who had been taken as slaves.[10] It now appears that

---

[10] Thornton, John, A Re-interpretation of the Kongo-Portuguese War of 1622 According to New Documentary Evidence, The Journal of African History 51, No.2:235-248, 2010

after the Battle of Mbandi Kasi, Kongo began the process of re-occupying lands previously absorbed by the Portuguese. At this time, Kongo conceived a plan to attack Luanda and drive the Portuguese from Angola. That plan was eventually realized in 1641, later than originally anticipated.

But we shall go back to 1622, which saw the death of the young Mani Kongo Alvaro III, who had no heir apparent but had ambitious uncles who had eyes on the Crown and instigated a great deal of tension and controversy. The Electoral College responsible for choosing kings was aware of this and decided to avoid internal strife by opting for King Pedro II, widely regarded as a virtuous man and a model Christian. Pedro had served in the provincial government of Mani Kongo Alvaro III Nimi wa Mpansu as Marquis of Wembo and later as Duke of Mbamba.

Pedro had just ascended to the throne when the governor of Angola, João Correia de Sousa, sent an army into Kongo on the pretext that he had the right to choose the Mwine Kongo. Sousa also accused Pedro of having harboured runaway slaves from Angola during his tenure as Duke of Mbamba. Thus, the stage was set for the battle of Mbumbi. As we now know, the Kongolese loss at Mbumbi was reversed at Mbandi Kasi, partly because of Dutch support for Kongo. It should not be surprising then that Kongolese nobility in general, and King Pedro in particular, started to entertain thoughts of a formal alliance with the Dutch. Widening the distance between Kongo and Portugal was of interest to local Portuguese residents who feared getting caught up in the anti-Portuguese fervour. Pedro however behaved like a statesman and lived up to his reputation as a model Christian. He drew a distinction between the state of Portugal and the local Portuguese community in Kongo, which had remained loyal during the war. Pedro did what he could to protect Portuguese life and property within the kingdom, to the consternation of detractors who quickly gave him the sobriquet 'King of the Portuguese'.

The behaviour of the local Portuguese community did nothing to assure King Pedro that Portugal as a state could again be trusted to unreservedly respect Kongolese sovereignty. He, therefore, continued with his efforts to ally with the Dutch. Specifically, Pedro wrote to the Dutch Estates General, proposing an alliance between Kongo and the Netherlands to completely drive the Portuguese out of Angola. Thus, in 1641, a combined force of Kongo and the Netherlands took Luanda, forcing the Portuguese to withdraw further into the interior. That, however, was not the end of the Portuguese, who in 1648 retook Luanda. This victory emboldened Portuguese governors of Angola, who were anxious for revenge against Kongo. The victory also presented an opportunity to satisfy the Portuguese demand for slaves. As part of the new slave trade policy, attacks were mounted on Dembos, small, semi-autonomous states separating Angola from Kongo. Since both Kongo and Portuguese Angola claimed authority over the Dembos, the aggressive slave trade policy was destined to lead to a full-scale war.

When this policy was implemented, King Garcia II was monarch of Kongo, having installed himself in 1641 when his brother Alvaro died under mysterious circumstances. Antonio I Mbita (also called Mvita wa Nkanga) was elected monarch following the death of King Garcia II, and ruled from 1661 until his death at the Battle of Mbwila on October 29, 1665. Antonio I's foreign policy was similar to that of King Garcia II as it focused on driving the Portuguese out of the region.

When Antonio I took the throne, Kongo and Portugal had been in an intermittent state of war for more than forty years. Respite in hostilities typically took place only after decisive Kongo victories. Despite these victories, the Portuguese did succeed in retaking Luanda when Antonio ascended to the throne. Portugal's return to Kongo's southern border caused considerable anxiety for the new monarch, who responded by plotting a new war against the Portuguese with a new alliance. Since the king felt he could no longer rely on the Dutch, he sent emissaries to Spain to enlist the country's help. The mission failed as Spain was either unwilling or unable to help. The Portuguese got wind of Antonio's plans and intensified their plans to take control of the small kingdom of Mbwila. The opportunity to do so came when a succession dispute between Mbwila's king and his aunt emerged. The former was supported by Kongo, while the latter was egged on by the Portuguese. To resolve the dispute, the rivals descended upon Mbwila with their armies. The Battle of Mbwila proved to be the worst military defeat suffered by Kongo, resulting in the death of hundreds, including King Antonio, who led a contingent of four hundred swordsmen into the battle. King Antonio I was decapitated during the battle and, with what came to be seen later as typical European duplicity, had his head buried with royal honours by the Portuguese, while his crown and sceptre were taken to Portugal as trophies.

Antonio I died without an heir apparent. Matters were further complicated because his seven-year-old son, who could have taken over from him, was either killed or captured at Mbwila alongside other nobles. The lack of an heir apparent and the absence of visible successors to the throne put the ruling House of Kinlaza and the opposing House of Kimpansu on a war footing. The ensuing civil war was so devastating, it guaranteed the effective end of the once-glorious Kongo kingdom.

Two hundred years earlier, an ancestor of the House of Kimpansu had warned that Portuguese influence in the kingdom would lead to disaster.

The Lunda/Luba Empire

Significant migration from the Kongo kingdom appears to have started before the death of King Antonio I, so that by the end of the sixteenth century, descendants of King Afonso I were abandoning the Kikongo language for the Ciluba (Chiluba) language spoken in the emerging Luba Empire.[11] The new kingdom was founded by King Kongolo Manyema around 1585. At its peak, the state had about a million people paying tribute to its king. Luba kings were, unfortunately, not always benevolent. One in particular, Kapopo, had a bad temper and a reputation for killing perceived opponents. Kapopo was feared even by his children, one of whom, Mukulumpe, persuaded his siblings to leave the royal court and establish a settlement further east, north of the Lwalaba River. Thanks to good governance established by Mukulumpe, the settlement grew rapidly and subsequently became the Luba capital, Kalilunga.

One day, a man brought a message to the king about a woman with elephantine ears. When the woman was brought before the king and asked where she had come from, she pointed to the sky and was understood to have claimed that she came from heaven. That was not in fact what she meant. She meant to say her father was Lyulu, which also means heaven. She later told the king that she was Mumbi Mukasa, the beautiful girl mocked by her many siblings because of her elephantine ears. Since she was of royal lineage, a member of the Crocodile clan, or *Abena Ng'andu*, King Mukulumpe decided to marry her.

---

[11] Tanguy, F, *Imilandu ya Babemba*, Oxford University Press,1948

The marriage was a happy one, at least in the early days. Certainly, both the king and Mumbi were thrilled when they had their first son, Katongo. F. Tanguy, the Jesuit teacher and historian, identified three other children: Nkole, Chiti, and Chilufya Mulenga, a girl. Traditional history, however, makes reference to three other sons: Chimba, Kasongo, and Kanongesha. Tanguy left these children out of his account because they probably came from another mother, King Mukulumpe having had more than one wife.

In any event, the children were trained in statecraft and given territories to govern. This gave them a measure of independence from Mukulumpe, allowing them to govern without the daily supervision of their father. One of the decisions taken in this fashion was the construction of an elevated observation point from which approaching enemies could be seen. Unfortunately, the tower was not on firm ground and it collapsed, killing many people. Mukulumpe was furious when he heard the news. His cabinet, which had always resented the elevation of the sons to the status of governors, egged the king into taking drastic action. In so doing, they cited other wrongs done by the boys. They advised the king that the boys' ultimate goal was to seize power from him. The magistrates, known as ba Cilolo, also issued dire warnings of the danger Katongo, Nkole, and Chiti posed to the kingdom.

The king was suitably riled and summoned his sons for an explanation of the alleged misdeeds. He then decided that severe punishment of one of the children would serve as a warning to the others. Thus Katongo, the eldest of the siblings, had his eyes plucked out. His life changed considerably, spending most of his time indoors reciting poetry and playing musical instruments, including talking drums.

In the meantime, his brothers Nkole and Chiti fled from the kingdom. In a demonstration of vindictive implacability reminiscent of his father, King Kapopo, Mukulumpe laid out a plan to kill his exiled sons. He ordered his soldiers to dig spike traps on the road to the palace and then camouflage them. After that, he sent an emissary to Nkole and Chiti to assure them that all that was required to put matters right was for them to come back and beg for forgiveness, which would be readily given as long as they came at night, not during the day. Katongo learned of his father's plan and set about to warn his brothers. He composed a stanza which summarised the plot and sent it to his brothers as soon as they were within earshot. The message basically warned the brothers to be on the lookout for signs of recent digging. Nkole and Chiti followed their brother's advice, avoiding sites with freshly dug soil, and eventually arrived at the palace. Before arriving at the palace, however, Katongo briefed his siblings on the goings-on in the kingdom and the approach to take when speaking to the king.

Mukulumpe was shocked to hear their voices when they announced their arrival. The boys sounded contrite and the king told them to seek his audience the following morning.

Perhaps it was the shock of realising how close he had come to killing his children, but the following day he declared he had forgiven them and they could live in the kingdom as noblemen. The royal peace that followed was, however, uneasy because the king continued to be suspicious of his sons. The main source of tension appears to have been the king's fear that either one of Nkole or Chiti could foment a rebellion capable of resulting in the ouster of Mukulumpe and the installation of one of them as the new monarch. While Mukulumpe accepted that he would one day cease to be king, he did not want his sons to succeed him.

Thus, Mukulumpe's harassment of Nkole and Chiti continued, culminating in the graveyard incident when Mukulumpe ordered Nkole, Chiti, and their subjects to clean up the graveyard at a time when he knew that most of these denizens would be tired from other work. The inhabitants of Nkole's territory complied with the order, but Chiti disobeyed what he considered an unreasonable order motivated by the king's insecurities and inability to truly forgive his sons.

Nkole's assessment was correct as shortly afterward, Mukulumpe arranged for a group of thugs, apparently led by his wife, to attack Chiti's subjects. The group was, however, unsuccessful in intimidating Chiti and easily repelled, with many of its members suffering grievous injury. In response, Mukulumpe sent in his army, with devastating consequences, leading to Chiti fleeing the territory.

After this victory, the king summoned Mumbi Mukasa, told her that her children were insane and inclined to destroy the kingdom. The king then expelled Mumbi from the kingdom and banished her to a small village, where she died from depression.

Although Nkole was not harassed, he began to worry about his future in the kingdom. Therefore, he went to Chiti's hiding place and suggested they leave the kingdom altogether. Chiti immediately agreed, and the two brothers started working on the logistics of the journey. When word got out that Nkole and Chiti were planning to leave, many of their subjects expressed a wish to go with them as they were also concerned by the king's temperament and his poor treatment of the brothers and their mother.

Inevitably, the king also got wind of these plans. His response was surprising. He feared that if Nkole and Chiti left the kingdom bearing grudges, they too could die from depression as their mother had done. Whether he acted out of understandable paternal instincts or more complex reasons to do with Luba spiritual beliefs is unclear. What is known is that he summoned his sons to the palace for a final blessing and parting gifts, which included an elephant.

Shortly after this blessing, Nkole and Chiti left the kingdom with many people and commenced their trek toward the east. The elders of the group included Ng'andu aristocrats such as their brothers Chimba, Kasongo, and Kanongesha. Other Ng'andu aristocrats were Kankomba-we-Lala, Kalubila, Mutale Mukulu, Chileshe Mukulu, Chimboola, Mashete, Kalulu wa Mawanga, Mfungo, Nkweto wa Chilinda, Nkweto wa Chisungu, Mumena, Mumbi Mfumu. There was another group of the Luba aristocracy in the group. This group included a woman called Chanda, accompanied by her brother, Papwa Mung'ombe, and her two children, Chintu wa Mikumbi and Mwenga. Kopa, Mungulube, Chibesakunda, Kabinga, and Kabanda were also in the caravan. Chilufya Mulenga was keen to join the caravan but was prevented from doing so by Mukulumpe, who needed her to remain, marry and bear a grandchild to succeed him.

One of the more conspicuous members of the caravan was a man called Luchele Ng'anga, a skilled medicine man with a very light complexion. Many accounts of Zambian history suggest that Luchele Ng'anga had Portuguese ancestry and was probably a descendant of Mubemba Nshinga, later King Afonso I. When Diogo Cão first arrived in the Kingdom of Kongo, his crew reportedly included a 15-year-old cabin boy. Using original records from various sources, the late historian and journalist, Peter Forbath, artfully blended fact and fiction into an epic tale centred on the life of the cabin boy in Kongo. That boy went on to marry into the royal family. His child, born by Mubemba's sister, subsequently travelled to Portugal to study for the priesthood. Despite being in the priesthood, he too married upon his return to Kongo. Luchele Ng'anga is believed by many researchers to belong to this ancestral line.

In any event, Luchele Ng'anga was a member of the multitudes who joined the trek to find a new homeland for a new nation led by Abena Ng'andu. It took many days to reach Kashengeneke, where the party crossed the 560-kilometre Luapula River. For most of its course, the river forms part of the boundary between Zambia and the present-day Democratic Republic of the Congo.

The first person in the party to cross the river was Chiti, who almost immediately sighted a large evergreen tropical tree known as mupundu, named after the tasty plum-like fruit it bears. Chiti then threw a spear into the tree and boasted as follows:

Nine mutanshi wasabwike bemba
Nine Ntalasha matanda
Nine Mukulumpe wamwene ubwikalo.

The basic translation of these lines is that Chiti was the first to cross the big river and found a nation. Other noblemen followed Chiti's example and stuck their spears in the tree. The exception was Nkole, who was preoccupied with storing grain. Having crossed the river first, Chiti declared himself king, Chiti Mukulu (the big tree), even though he was younger than Nkole.

Although Chiti claimed to have cut the umbilical cord from the Luba motherland, he fervently hoped his new nation would replicate the more successful aspects of the Luba kingdom, such as succession and the ability to absorb foreign leaders and even governments. Chiti was confident he had the skills to do so. These skills were soon put to the test as his people encountered the Lunda, who had already settled in the area. Although the Lunda and the newly minted Bemba nation had similar ancestral origins, Chiti nonetheless found it necessary to challenge and conquer them. After that, he installed one of his brothers as Mwata Kazembe, king of the Lunda.

Having thus taken over the Lunda state and incorporated its royalty into the Bemba ruling class, the matter of succession to the throne now had to be addressed. Until 1500, the Luba lineage was strictly matrilineal. After that, kings could be succeeded by their children or grandchildren. For this reason, Mukulumpe had, at the commencement of the great trek, ordered Chilufya Mulenga to stay at home when her brothers left the kingdom in search of new territory to settle in and govern.

Mukulumpe needed Chilufya to stay home and give him a grandchild to succeed him.

Around 1700, after crossing the Luapula, the Bemba built a large settlement called Isandulula-fyalo, a name reflecting the suitability of the land for human settlement. They then set about aggressively populating the land. But Chiti and Nkole also realised that a stable aristocracy with a credible succession system was necessary to guarantee the kingdom's future. They needed to ensure that Abena Ng'andu continued to rule.

These thoughts were probably provoked by Chiti and Nkole's saudade memories of their sister Chilufya Mulenga. They needed her to give them a nephew who would assume the throne in the event of Chiti's death. Indeed, her children would play a huge role in consolidating the aristocracy as they could succeed Nkole and Chiti's other brothers.

A plan was therefore hatched to send a party to King Mukulumpe's court to rescue Chilufya. The persons chosen for this task were Kapasa, Mwangata, Sompe, and Mumba-Ng'ombe. As the quartet approached the court, they ran into a woman who gave them the most recent intelligence about Chilufya Mulenga. According to this source, Chilufya was isolated from most of society and kept in a house without an entrance. The only way to get to her was through a removable roof that had alarm gongs called *Indibu*.

Thanks to the warning, Kapasa, Mwangata, Sompe, and Mumba-Ng'ombe were able to hatch a plan to rescue the king's sister without detection. They gathered leaves and got hold of a ladder and some baskets. The ladder was used to get them onto the roof, where they carefully inserted leaves in the gongs. They then placed the silent gongs in baskets. Having thus secured the house, they called Chilufya's name till she woke up, and told her they had come to rescue her and take her to her brothers. The escape was successful, but the journey back was not easy. The following morning, after walking throughout the wintry night, Chilufya's feet swelled up and she had to take a rest. Kapasa then suggested that Mwangata, Sompe, and Mumba-Ng'ombe go ahead and report the good news to the king, while he stayed behind to look after Chilufya and allow her to continue the journey at a less stressful pace. Mwangata, however, insisted on staying behind as well. It is possible he suspected Kapasa of having amorous intentions toward Chilufya.

It was net hunting season when Mumba-Ng'ombe arrived at Isandulula and found the king seated on a stool at the head of the gathering. Mumba-Ng'ombe was too cold and numb to narrate how he and the rest of the quartet sent to rescue Chilufya had travelled. Chitimukulu noticed this and offered him a stool by the fire. Once rejuvenated, Mumba-Ng'ombe told his story, and as he was doing so, Sompe arrived in rather better shape than Mumba. For this reason, Sompe was able to greet the king appropriately in accordance with tradition.

After getting the brief, the king gave Mumba the stool he was sitting on and his smoking pipe as gifts. To this day, the descendants of Mumba and Sompe take the stool and pipe whenever they make official visits to Chitimukulu. Eventually, Chilufya and Kapasa also arrived at court to much jubilation. The Chitimukulu line was now secure as in due course, Chilufya would marry and bear heirs for the king. That time was not as far off as Chiti and his brothers imagined because, after a couple of months, it became clear that Chilufya was already pregnant.

Chitimukulu took this discovery badly and pressed Chilufya for the identity of the child's father. Chilufya eventually relented, pointing the finger at Kapasa. This breach of trust could not go unpunished and Chitimukulu responded by expelling Kapasa from the prestigious Ng'andu clan. He banished him instead to a different clan known as the *abena Membe* or *abena Mulombwa*. According to Chitimukulu, no one with an uncontrollable sexual appetite deserved membership in the elite Ng'andu clan. To this day, the stereotype for the Membe clan includes hyper sexuality. Chitimukulu's ire with Kapasa did not prevent him from genuinely rejoicing when Chilufya gave birth to a boy, who was also named Chilufya.

Chiti's Luba people, now known as the Bemba, were restless. Despite the suitability of Isandulula for human habitation, they were still interested in further exploration to find even better land. But leaving Isandulula was never going to be an easy decision. In the end, the solution was offered by Luchele Ng'anga, the light-skinned descendant of Kongo King Mbemba Nzinga. Luchele suggested that he go fishing using Ibende and if he succeeded in catching any fish using that method, they would all leave Isandulula. He did indeed succeed, and the Bemba set off once again.

It appears the Bemba set up several temporary settlements during this trek. Inevitably, there was both friction and bonding during the long hours and days of travel. The effect of this was to further refine the Ng'andu clan and to spread the new Bemba nation, as the common punishment for those who erred was to expel them from the main clan, freeing them to establish new clans and settlements. For example, at one stopover, the women went into the bush to pick mushrooms which they later cooked. A woman named Chanda picked a huge amount and saved some in a traditional pot for future consumption.

After eating and resting, the trek set off once again. During this portion of the journey, one of Chilufya Mulenga's children complained of hunger and cried for food. Recalling that Chanda had picked a huge amount of mushroom and believing that she must have saved some, Chilufya asked if she could spare some food for the hungry child. Chanda denied having any food left. Unfortunately for her, while the group was crossing Luchindashi River, one of Chanda's children got stuck in the mud and, in an attempt to free herself, spilled some of the mushrooms her mother had asked her to carry. This was done in Chilufya's view, who took the matter up with the king, accusing Chanda of parsimony. Chitimukulu's judgment was swift. He concurred that Chanda's parsimony rendered her unfit for membership in the Ng'andu clan and expelled her from the clan. He also expelled her children, commanding them to not follow the rest of the group but instead settle where they were and establish a Bemba outpost governed by one of Chanda's children, Chintu wa Mikumbi. The exiled were henceforth to be known as the Mushroom clan on account of their love of mushrooms.[12] They would, however, remain Bemba citizens, and to ensure that this was not forgotten, Chitimukulu planted a tree in the *Bena Bowa* territory that was never to be cut as it would serve as a reminder of Bemba sovereignty over the area.

The trek proceeded eastward, where the Bemba encountered the Lala people. It appears this contact was entirely peaceful with the Lala being impressed by the visible military might of the Bemba. The Lala quickly understood that the Bemba could be an important ally. This was perhaps the primary reason the Lala begged Chitimukulu to give them a powerful person to rule over them. They believed leadership provided by a Bemba royal would strengthen the Lala. Chitimukulu obliged by asking Kankomba, later known as Kankomba we Lala, to remain with his people as ruler of the Lala.

The next stage of the trek took the Bemba northeasternly, until they encountered the Nsenga people, who received them well for fear of

---

[12] Ibid page 12

being vanquished by the Bemba, who were proficient in the art of war and territorial acquisition. This happy state developed into a personal friendship involving frequent exchanges of gifts between Chitimukulu and Mwase, the Nsenga monarch. The Bemba had established a settlement called Chibambo, near Kateng'oma River, not far from Mwase's palace. Quite often, Mwase visited Chitimukulu there to deliver gifts.

Mwase's queen, Chilimbulu, was a very attractive woman in whom Chitimukulu soon developed an interest. Chilimbulu appears to have welcomed this attention. One day, she volunteered to take the gifts to Chitimukulu, ostensibly to save Mwase the trouble of travelling to Chibambo. That was a fateful decision. As soon as Chitimukulu set his eyes on Chilimbulu, he decided to marry her and keep her at Chibambo. Three days later, Mwase set out to find his wife. After entering Chitimukulu's settlement, Mwase quickly spotted Chilimbulu and attempted to remove her from Chiti's court. But Chiti would have none of this, and he intervened. The intervention was tragic as one of the poisoned arrows in Mwase's quiver pierced Chiti's left arm. The poison moved quickly in Chiti's body, and in short order, His Royal Highness was dead.

Chiti's death did not alter the balance of power in the region as the Nsenga had no strategy to take over the Bemba settlement. Instead, they retreated to their own area, allowing the Bemba to mourn Chiti in relative peace. Nkole decided that the Bemba should leave the settlement because of the terrible thing that had happened to their monarch. He wanted a new area with suitable land for the burial of Chiti. Thus, the Bemba were on the move again. The next destination turned out to be Mwalule, where Chiti was embalmed in accordance with traditional Kongo practices[13] and, a year later, interred.

After the mourning period, Nkole raised an army to avenge Chiti's murder. The ensuing battle was quite savage and resulted in the death of Mwase, his wife, and many Nsenga and the destruction by fire of Mwase's village. Many Nsenga were captured as indentured labourers to work for the Bemba state until Mwase's 'debt' was deemed settled. Gratuitous violence included the dismemberment of Mwase's body, turning Chilimbulu's skin into ilamba, and placing it in the royal archives.

---

[13] https://ahc.unesco.org

Ngoni Migrations from the south

The Bemba continued to conquer and expand their nation. Their victories were relatively easy ones until they encountered the Ngoni, who hailed from the south.

In the early nineteenth century, Zwangendaba kaZiguda Jele Gumbi, king of the Ngoni for over thirty years, led a group of followers north, through Mozambique and Zimbabwe to Zambia, using Zulu warfare tactics to conquer and integrate local peoples. Zwangendaba's party crossed the Zambezi River into Zambia on November 20, 1835. The Ngoni were intent on capturing as much territory as possible, but their advance was halted by the Bemba. The price paid by the Bemba in this endeavour was immense and included the death of royals such as Makasa Kalulu, the ruler of the Mpanda territory.

Makololo Migration

Five years before the Ngoni crossing into Zambia, an army from the Tswana-speaking Bafokeng region of South Africa, known as the Makololo, led by a warrior called Sebetwane, invaded Barotseland and conquered the Lozi, who had also originated from the Luba/Lunda empire. The Makololo ruled until 1864, when the Sotho clique was overthrown following a Lozi revolt. Twenty-one years after the successful Lozi revolt, German Chancellor Otto von Bismarck convened the Berlin Conference of 1885.

Impact of the Berlin Conference

The Berlin Conference committed to ending slavery on the African continent. Although this commitment cast European nations in a positive light, it, in practice, did little to enhance the protection of the human rights of the indigenous people of the continent, as Edmund Morel's work revealed.

Morel was a French-born British journalist, pacifist, and politician who started his professional life as a shipping clerk. In this role, he, from time to time, travelled to the Belgian port of Antwerp to oversee the loading and unloading of ships. While carrying out these duties in the late 1890s, Morel made a horrendous discovery: the Congo Free State exported tons of raw rubber to Belgium, but little was shipped back to Congo except guns and ammunition. The quick-witted Morel worked out that the natives needed to collect the rubber only did so under duress. He said, 'I had stumbled upon a secret society of murderers with a king [as an accomplice].'

This discovery changed Morel's life. He devoted himself to learning more about human rights abuses in Congo. In 1901, he resigned his position at the shipping company and began a campaign, through newspaper articles, speeches, and books and pamphlets, to discredit and expose Leopold's egregious abuses of the basic rights of the people under his rule. As a result of Morel's activities, the British government sent Roger Casement, a diplomat, to the Congo Free State to investigate. Casement, whose own investigations revealed evidence of murder, mutilation, floggings, forced labour, and hostage-taking, found Morel's concerns to be justified. In 1904, after publishing his report, Casement joined Morel in forming the Congo Reform Association, which is now recognised as the first significant international human rights movement of the twentieth century.

Leopold's attempts to counter the evidence provided by Casement and Morel were largely ineffective as public opinion turned decidedly against the Belgian monarch. When the British and United States governments realised that the evidence could not be ignored, they applied sufficient pressure on Leopold and forced him to surrender the Congo Free State to the Belgian government in 1908. But not all was lost for the tyrant. He received a huge cash payment and other benefits from Belgium for 'his great sacrifices made for the Congo.' It is doubtful the people of Congo would have gone along with the idea of compensating Leopold for committing atrocities against their kin. But, as with the Berlin Conference, the Congolese were not consulted.

The impact of the Berlin Conference went beyond the egregious violation of human rights. Long after the imperial powers had withdrawn, one major consequence remained and became part of the African landscape. As a result of the Berlin Conference, new political boundaries were drawn, leading to the partitioning of African ethnicities and nationalities across freshly fabricated states. Thus, most new countries became instant candidates for civil war as groups of people who had previously belonged to different nationalities were now obliged to co-habit and obey a new order that governed without their consent. In many of these countries, order was maintained only by imperial brute force. The perennial question of the time was: What would happen after the withdrawal of the imperial order? Would the different ethnicities miraculously come together and settle on a new governance model? Or would they violently vie for cultural and political supremacy?

This question was less pressing in Zambia where the discovery of huge copper ore deposits attracted many migrants from different parts of the country and led to the creation of the multi-ethnic Copperbelt region. This forged a new identity from the indigenous Lamba culture and other cultures that found their way there. Zambia's Copperbelt Province remains the most integrated of all of the country's provinces. Although the point is often lost on politicians, particularly those not raised on the Copperbelt, the denizens of this remarkable region do not necessarily identify with indigenous ethnicities. They are urbanites who consider themselves to be Zambians first.

This background prompted Copperbelt-born and raised Edgar Lungu to propose removing ethnic identity details from the country's National Registration Card, which every citizen aged 16 and over is obliged to have. Unfortunately, President Lungu's call was seen in entirely political terms and rejected out of hand by many with a vested interest in promoting ethnic identity. President Lungu understood that the promotion of indigenous ethnic identity is dangerous and can undermine national unity. It is perhaps not surprising that the President made his call after visiting Rwanda and hearing credible accounts of the 1994 genocide that claimed an estimated 900,000 Tutsi and moderate Hutu lives. How was this possible? How did the perpetrators commit such heinous crimes over a period of only 100 days?

As President Lungu discovered, the simple answer is that every Rwandan citizen was required to carry an identity document that stipulated the holder's ethnicity. All that Hutu militia manning roadblocks during the genocide did was ask motorists and passengers for identity cards. Possession of a Tutsi identity card meant instant death.

Despite this danger, one paramount chief responded to the President's call by opining that 'a person is known by their tribe and the village.' A remarkable statement to make in a modern republic. Most urbanites beyond the first generation are not necessarily known by their 'tribe' and village. They consider themselves indigenes of the towns and cities they were actually born in. They subscribe to the Copperbelt culture and see Zambia through that prism, not their alleged villages and ethnicities. Moreover, Zambian law does not make membership of a village and an indigenous ethnicity a precondition for citizenship. There are many Zambians of British, Greek, Indian, and South African origin. None possess a village or a chief in the way demanded by the paramount chief.

Many opponents of the Lungu proposal confused acceptance of ethnic diversity with the official promotion of ethnic particularism. Chiefs' roles would not end with the implementation of the Lungu proposal. Traditional ways of life would continue and people would still be able to identify themselves informally as belonging to particular ethnicities. What would change is the National Registration Card would cease to be a potential vehicle for discrimination. There would be less risk of people being denied jobs or services based on the ethnicity revealed on the National Registration Card.

The Berlin Conference guaranteed ethnic diversity as a result of the arbitrary borders it imposed. These boundaries endured after Zambian independence because it was impractical and dangerous to go back to the old borders. Upon independence, like most African countries, Zambia was between a rock and a hard place in this regard. As a result, the Nukwe ethnic group, for example, is split between Angola, Namibia, Zambia, and Botswana. The Chewa, split between Mozambique, Malawi, Zimbabwe, and Zambia, are another example of arbitrary boundary drawing.

It is estimated that 40-45 percent of the African population belong to ethnicities that have been partitioned by a national border.[14] Zambia has been fortunate that ethnic partitioning has not led to civil war. A study by Stelios Michalopoulos and Elias Papaioannou found a correlation between devastating civil war and the partitioning of ethnic groups. Furthermore, the study showed that these conflicts have a cascading effect as they tend to embroil adjoining areas where the non-split ethnicities reside.[15]

Creating new African states with a proclivity for civil war resulting from partitioning is unlikely intentional. After all, the creators of these new countries wanted sufficient state order to allow for trade. Thus, the partitioning was more likely a consequence of ignorance than ill intent.

Robert Arthur Talbot Gascoyne-Cecil, third Marquess of Salisbury, was elected to the British Parliament in 1853 as a Conservative Party member. He served as prime minister three times, for a total of 13 years. As his periods of service as prime minister indicate, Lord Salisbury was a key player in the Berlin Conference. His observations are useful in determining whether the participants at the Conference deliberately designed states that would be prone to civil war. Europeans had almost no knowledge of African ethnogeography. We must also remember that the bulk of the continent's non-coastal areas remained unexplored by outsiders before the Berlin Conference. Lord Salisbury's observations on the matter evince ignorance rather than willful intent caused ethnic partitioning and other aspects of the irrational boundaries drawn by the Europeans.

The British Prime Minister said:

> We have been engaged in drawing lines upon maps where no white man's feet have ever trod; we have been giving away mountains and rivers and lakes to each other, only hindered by the small impediment that we never knew exactly where the mountains and rivers and lakes were.[16]

---

[14] The Long-run Effects of the Scramble for Africa, www.voxeu.org, January 06, 2012
[15] Ibid
[16] Ibid

CHAPTER TWO

A Traumatised People

Since formal colonisation of what is now Zambia only lasted seventy years, the argument is often made that the country ought to have recovered quickly from whatever ills arose from imperialism. This argument is disingenuous. It is not too different from the argument that victims of sexual assault ought to recover quickly because the actual assault typically takes only a tiny portion of their lifespan.

The period of formal colonisation may have been relatively short, but its impact was great. The colonised found their way of life completely changed. Their history was suppressed, their diet was changed, the value of their culture was deliberately understated, and the new system of education and official segregation encouraged feelings of inferiority in their minds, to the delight and benefit of the colonisers. At independence, Zambia found herself in a multifaceted dilemma. The impact of colonialism was massive and devastating. Going back to pre-colonial status and thus recognising the traditional kingdoms and granting full power to the monarchs of these kingdoms was not an option as it would result in the immediate breakup of the new state. This is the fear the Organisation of African Unity aimed to address when it formally proclaimed in 1964 that existing colonial borders should be accepted.

Independent Zambia was modelled on a European state but only had a handful of persons with sufficient knowledge and education to manage that kind of state. On the other hand, those with knowledge of managing a traditional Zambian kingdom became largely irrelevant because Zambia would not be run as a traditional kingdom. Indeed, it could not because the new country was home to remnants of different kingdoms. The best the country could do was cherry-pick surviving parts of the traditional society amenable to incorporation into the new state.

Thus, Zambia had to build new European structures and rebuild aspects of a pre-colonial society destroyed by European adventurism.

Education

Colonialism apologists sometimes argue that the British brought education to Zambia and we should all be grateful. This argument misses the larger point, however: colonialism halted the progress of the traditional societies that fell under the British banner. Before their withdrawal from Zambia, the British, in an effort to influence post-colonial development, promoted an elite class that they thought could be trusted to guarantee the new nation's development along British lines. But this exercise was relatively unsuccessful because it came too late. At the time of independence, Zambia simply did not have the capacity in the form of highly educated men and women to manage the affairs of a modern post-colonial state.

The country's little capacity came disproportionately from the white settler community due to immigration policies which blatantly favoured white British nationals. Consequent to these policies, the white settler population rose from 22,000 in 1946 to 37,000 in 1951. By 1964, the white population had reached 70,000 (a 6,000-drop from a peak of 76,000 in 1960) out of 3.4 million people.

On its face, the Northern Rhodesia economy, based on copper mining and agriculture, was quite sophisticated. Unfortunately, the African population expected to manage this economy was woefully unprepared for the task. For example, until the 1950s, the country only had three secondary schools which admitted black boys. As for black girls, only Chipembi offered secondary school education.

Concerning human resource capacity, the new nation's situation at independence was quite dire. This is well summarised by Andrew Sardanis, the Cypriot-born Zambian patriot who set the standard for modern Zambian entrepreneurship and campaigned for her independence. He said:

> We had only one black engineer, three black doctors and three black lawyers and some 90 other black university graduates, working mainly as teachers and senior civil servants. We had 884 men and just 77 women qualified at School Certificate level, some 4,000 at [Grade10] level, mainly working in the civil service, and a few thousand junior teachers, junior clerks and policemen and semi-skilled workers with just elementary school education (standard IV or VI).[17]

---

[17] Sardanis, Andrew, Zambia The First 50 Years, London, I.B. Tauris & Co Ltd, 2014

While most Zambians are aware of these facts and generally go out of their way to mitigate the consequences of this particular aspect of colonial history, British white settlers, existing in a social ghetto, are generally unaware of the relevant data and persist in promoting the myth that colonialism brought education to Zambia. Sadly, many in the Lusaka-based diplomatic corps tend to get their information from this uniquely uninformed segment of the population.

About a decade ago, I met a German diplomat who told me the British, for all their faults, deserve praise for building the University of Zambia. She was shocked when I told her that UNZA, as the University is known, is a post-independence creation. It was built after an aggressive fundraising campaign by Zambian patriots who wanted their children to have better educational opportunities than they had had. This desire for widespread education in post-colonial Zambia is perfectly understandable, given the country's educational experience under British rule. Toward the end of the colonial era, the British government spent five times more on the education of white children than it did on the education of black children. That was the closest the colonial government came to closing the gap in education spending between European children and African children. As Snelson pointed out, the total amount spent on educating black children between 1924 and 1945 was £875,000, the bulk of which came from the poll tax paid by indigenous Northern Rhodesians. In comparative terms, the government spent £40 per white child in 1945 and £1 and six shillings per black child. Therefore, it is not surprising that at independence in 1964, Zambia only had 'one black engineer, three black doctors, three black lawyers, and some ninety other black university graduates,' as Sardanis said. Snelson describes this as 'an inexcusably tiny store of educated manpower on which to draw for the development of a new state.'[18]

And yet, this is the store of educated manpower that the new state had to draw on, given that it could not go back to traditional methods of education that produced skills relevant to a society that no longer existed.

---

[18] Snelson, PD, *Educational Development in Northern Rhodesia,1883-1945*, Lusaka, Kenneth Kaunda Foundation 1990

Learn and be frustrated

Despite these obstacles, the Black elite who obtained a good education soon found another hindrance: their education guaranteed neither employment nor respect.

Valentine Shula Musakanya, described by the Guardian newspaper at the time of his death as, 'the most talented Zambian of his generation'[19] attended St Francis Xavier College, better known as Kutama College in Southern Rhodesia (now Zimbabwe), for his secondary education. He was an outstanding student who found the philosophy of the Marist Brothers who ran the school most agreeable. There was no compulsory manual work at the school which emphasised individual responsibility. The school's philosophy stood in marked contrast with the ethos of colonialism which discouraged the intellectual advancement of natives. The environment at Kutama allowed Musakanya to thrive intellectually.

Musakanya graduated from Kutama with solid performances in Latin, English, Physics, and Chemistry. The results encouraged him to pursue a career in science, starting as an electrician at Nchanga Mine where his father worked at the time. This seemed plausible, especially given the mining companies' recent commitment to 'African Advancement'. Musakanya started at the highest level of African Advancement as a Grade Nine electrical apprentice, and paid a handsome salary of £26 per month.

Unfortunately for Musakanya, black people could not, by law, become apprentices despite the African Advancement policy. Although possessing better qualifications than most Europeans of his age entitled to participation in the apprenticeship programme, Musakanya was obliged to transfer to the Leach Plant as an attendant. His predecessor there was a European and this fact seemed, in the eyes of the mining authorities, to satisfy the requirements of the African Advancement policy. But the work was so below Musakanya's abilities and expectations, that he could not stomach more than one day in this role. He quit the mining company a day after being appointed Leach Plant Attendant.

Although Musakanya's ambition to become an electrician was thus thwarted, the discrimination he suffered turned out to be a blessing in disguise. He joined the public service and read Philosophy and Sociology

---

[19] Hall, Richard, the Guardian Newspaper, London. August 1994

as a long-distance student with the University of South Africa. Then, as Northern Rhodesia transformed into a less intolerant society, Musakanya received a one-year scholarship to study administrative law at Cambridge University.

After serving as one of the first black district officers in Northern Rhodesia, Musakanya was seconded to the British Foreign Service as vice-consul to Belgian Congo, as the Democratic Republic of Congo was known. One of his more challenging tasks was extricating British mercenaries trapped by United Nations forces during the 1960-1963 Katanga crisis. MI6 executive Daphne (later Baroness) Park, who was based in Leopoldville, the Congolese capital, deeply admired his level-headedness and unusual intelligence.

After independence, Musakanya became the first secretary to the cabinet and head of the Zambian civil service. For every Valentine Musakanya, however, there were many Zambians whose careers and hopes died suddenly as a result of colour-based discrimination. Andrew Sardanis made the following observation about black labour in Northern Rhodesia in the 1950s:

> I do not know how many black workers the mines employed. A few thousand I would guess. Most of them had no skills to speak of except for a few drivers and clerks. Racial discrimination in skilled trades was total. The European Mineworkers Union made sure of that and managed to hold it until the end of the decade. So blacks were recruited for unskilled manual work and the policy was not to train them. But they learned by experience and performed well in jobs that officially they were not supposed to be doing.[20]

Pre-independence Zambians' ability to learn from experience is as remarkable as their thirst for formal education, which they obtained, when circumstances permitted, largely through long-distance learning. Although education by correspondence was relatively inexpensive and not racially discriminatory, the low salaries paid to black workers ensured that only the most determined could successfully take this route. Black Zambians unable to pursue study by correspondence sometimes joined security services, such as the army and the police, where a certain amount of formal training had to be given, even to black citizens.

---

[20] Sardanis, Andrew. Africa Another Side of the Coin, New York, I.B. Tauris, 2003, page 24

Great dreams

Edward Festus Mukuka Nkoloso is best known for his efforts to establish a Zambian space programme. Most foreigners considered him eccentric, dismissing his efforts to establish the programme as a silly dream. But Mukuka Nkoloso's ability to dream also reveals an intelligent and entrepreneurial spirit. This is a man who may well have achieved great things had he had the opportunity to pursue advanced education.

In his early twenties, Mukuka Nkoloso was drafted into the first battalion of the Northern Rhodesian regiment to fight in World War II. He was evidently a successful soldier who learned as much as possible in the army where he subsequently gained promotion to the rank of sergeant.

When the war ended, Nkoloso worked as a translator for the Northern Rhodesia Government, before becoming a grade school teacher. He then opened a new school, which was reportedly closed by the colonial government. This appears to have been the immediate catalyst for his involvement in nationalist politics in general and the civil disobedience campaign. The campaign focused immediately on ending the exploitative Central African Federation but later centred on demands for independence. Mukuka Nkoloso was a visible leader in organising strikes, boycotts of establishments practising the 'colour bar', and challenging the authorities. He was arrested and imprisoned in 1956 for a year. Upon the formation of the United Independence Party in October 1959, Nkoloso became a senior security official in the new party.

A year later, he founded what a 1964 *Time* magazine article described as the 'unofficial' Zambia National Academy of Science, Space Research and Philosophy. Nkoloso carried out several experiments designed to familiarise his future astronauts with weightlessness. While he had neither the money nor the equipment to run a modern space agency, Nkoloso seemed to understand the main issues in space exploration. As was the case with many of his contemporaries, Nkoloso taught himself as much as he could, building on the primary education he received from the Lubushi School in Kasama, and his experiences in the army. He was thus quite comfortable reading Latin texts and analysing the Cold War. Imagine what this man would have done had he had the opportunity to acquire a good tertiary education! It is a matter of regret that Nkoloso's immense talents were not put to better use after independence. He died on 4 March 1989 at the age of 70.

Nackson Bwanali Longwe was lucky to receive a secondary school education and, after a stint in the government, obtain a management job with a private company led by an anti-racist executive. Longwe took advantage of his time as a civil servant to study for a degree by correspondence. Like his friend, Valentine Musakanya, Longwe excelled in his studies and obtained a Bachelor of Arts degree from the University of South Africa. The civic-minded Longwe served as a councillor with the local municipality and, in 1963, at the age of 29, became the first black mayor of the Municipality of Chingola. During his tenure as mayor, Chingola earned the title of 'Cleanest Town' in the territory. He was, by most accounts, an exceptionally effective leader of the town. Sadly, Zambians generally seem reluctant to give him due credit when they reminisce about the 'good old Chingola' days, preferring instead to assume that the town must have been led to glory by a foreigner.

The education obtained by people such as Longwe and Musakanya did nothing to promote traditional Zambian values and teach skills that would have been critical in the pre-colonial era. Instead, it focused on the requirements of British society. Thus, recipients of this education were likely to know more about the Battle of Hastings than the Battle of Mbandi Kasi. Moreover, the new education system complemented the earlier policy of expelling indigenous farmers from fertile lands and placing them in largely overcrowded and unproductive reserves, leading to significant loss of indigenous farming knowledge and capability.

Second-class citizens

The loss of indigenous skills contributeted to black Northern Rhodesians becoming second-class citizens in their own land. Society was re-organised in such a way as to make indigenous skills irrelevant and to constantly remind these citizens that they were considerably less than their white counterparts.

The consequence of colonialism, possibly by design as the colonial administrators must have foreseen this, was denting indigenous self-confidence and reducing self-esteem and self-acceptance. Virtually all major symbols of Northern Rhodesia told black citizens that they belonged to the 'loser' community, though they could perhaps redeem themselves (partially) by imitating white settlers. Undermining indigenous confidence was considered necessary because it is near impossible to subjugate a free and confident people. Few cases illustrate the devaluation of black Northern Rhodesian life more than that of Elliot Mulenga. On 3 April 1940, during the second African Mineworkers Union strike, seventeen unarmed Africans were killed and sixty-three seriously wounded by shots fired by white-led law enforcement officers. Elliot Mulenga was initially shot in the arm and received treatment at the mine dispensary. After his treatment, he returned to support his striking colleagues. This time he was stabbed with a bayonet and disemboweled. Mulenga died on the spot.

There was neither remorse nor apology for this savage killing. Instead, the white authorities considered this to a practical way of intimidating Africans. The message was that there was a price to be paid for 'foolishly' daring white authorities. Far from frightening the African mineworkers' leadership, however, this brutality served only to strengthen their resolve to fight for what they believed was a just cause.[21] At the very least, demanding better pay was considered an act of sedition by the colonial authorities. Five years after Mulenga's traumatic death, Archibald Elwell, a welfare officer with the Kitwe Municipal Council, spoke as a guest at a Kitwe African Society meeting. In response to one of the questions, the honest and enlightened Elwell suggested that African workers could earn more money by forming trade unions. This response made absolute sense to the African audience but not to the district commissioner, who learned about it from an informer. The district commissioner was so shocked by Elwell's remarks that he called for the meeting's minutes from the KAS chairman, Godwin Mbikusita Lewanika who declined after consulting with Elwell.

Elwell was accused of making seditious remarks, suspended from his Council job, and transferred to the less politically volatile town of Livingstone, before being sent back to the United Kingdom. The trauma represented by the Mulenga and Elwell affairs affected every African (and many white liberals) regardless of educational attainment. In some ways, the daily racist humiliations were more intense for educated Africans who were obliged to interact with Europeans because of their work and status.

John Mupanga Mwanakatwe was the first indigenous Zambian to obtain a university degree. In January 1949, he received his Teachers'

---

[21] Chileshe, Jonathan H, Robinson Chisanga Puta Chekwe: Zambia's Trade Union Stalwart, www.chekwe.com

Diploma Certificate from Adams College in South Africa, where he had been in residence for two years. He had also managed to accumulate credits for the University of South Africa (UNISA) Bachelor of Arts degree during that period. With the encouragement of his Rhodes Scholar mentor and English tutor, Raymond Keet, Mwanakatwe enrolled for the Bachelor's degree as an external student. Before completing his degree, Mwanakatwe was appointed a teacher at Munali, Northern Rhodesia's most prestigious secondary school for black boys. His intellectual acumen and strong work ethic guaranteed success in his teaching role and as an external student of UNISA. It surprised few who knew him that he served briefly as acting principal of Munali and that, later, he became the first black head of a secondary school in Northern Rhodesia.

Mwanakatwe became a politician and lawyer, but it is his experiences as the principal of Kasama Secondary School that we shall draw on to illustrate how education failed to guarantee protection from the humiliations of colonial racism. The following passage in which Mwanakatwe describes an encounter with a white telephone repairman is from Mwanakatwe's autobiography, *John Mwanakatwe: Teacher, Politician, Lawyer*:

> He suspected that the fault might have been with telephone wires in the office so he walked into my office. I was marking exercise books. He told me that he wanted to talk to the Bwana. In those days, Bwana was a word of respect for a white man-originally a Swahili word for a gentleman. Therefore I told him that I was the Bwana. However, he insisted that he wanted to talk to the Bwana who was in charge of the school.

> It was quite clear to me at that stage that I was speaking to a pathological racist. In the circumstances, I felt that firmness was totally justified. I therefore shouted at the top of my voice, 'Look young man, I am the Bwana here. I am in charge of this school'. To my surprise, the technician walked out of my office. His African helpers [who had been] outside the office during the altercation joined the technician and they drove away. The telephone line was not repaired.

Henry George Mumbi Shikopa is another Munali graduate and victim of gratuitous colonial racism. Shikopa joined Mwaiseni Stores in 1958, a year after the launch of the company. In light of his relatively high level of education, Shikopa became a manager, a responsibility that included collecting the day's takings and depositing them with the bank. The practice at the time was not to allow Africans in the banking hall but instead to let them do their banking through a recess on the sidewalk and a hatch. In his book, *Africa: Another Side of the Coin*, Andrew Sardanis narrates how this worked out for Henry Shikopa:

> We agreed with Henry that he would go straight into the banking hall.
>
> After a few days I noticed that he took a long time to return from the bank. When I asked why, he suggested that I should go with him and see for myself. I dropped him at the entrance, did some other business and sometime later returned to collect him. Henry was still in the line. I stood back and watched. The teller was inviting every white customer who came in to jump the queue. Henry would be given attention only when there were no white customers in the banking hall. My patience was exhausted when the teller gave a nod to an eight-year-old girl to do the same. She wanted to cash a £2 cheque for mummy, I discovered later. I moved up.
>
> He was here first,' I said, pointing to Henry. The teller was stunned. This was not the etiquette he had been accustomed to. The manager, John Angel, was called. He invited me to his office and admonished me not to 'let the side down'. But Henry was never made to wait again.

A few years after independence, Henry Shikopa served as the managing director of the Mwaiseni chain of supermarkets. Andrew Sardanis was permanent secretary in the Ministry of State Participation and chairman of the Industrial Development Corporation. In these capacities, they were invited to lunch with the Barclays Bank Zambia board of directors. John Angel, the bank manager in the Chingola story had been promoted to the head office, and he was the one who met Sardanis and Shikopa at the door. After Angel introduced himself, Shikopa responded, 'Oh! I know you from Chingola. Many times I felt like jumping over the counter and punching you in the face.' Sardanis reports that Angel took the remark in good spirit.[22]

---

[22] Ibid, page 74

Not all race-inspired humiliations could be mitigated by a white compatriot. More often than not, the victims of these humiliations found novel ways of either ending the humiliation or getting around it.

For virtually the entire colonial period, shopping centres in Northern Rhodesia were segregated. Africans could only shop in areas designated 'second class' trading centres. The whites, of course, went to 'first class' trading centres. When a black customer needed something unavailable in the second class trading area, they were permitted to shop in the first class trading area as long as they did not actually enter the shop. Instead, they were served from the backyard through a hatch in the wall.

Robinson Chisanga Puta (aka Shi Bwalya Chekwe), a former teacher at Mindolo Primary School near Kitwe, vice president of Harry Nkumbula's African National Congress, vice president of the African Mineworkers Union, architect (with Jameson Chapoloko) of the huge 1955 pay increase for African mineworkers which would qualify many of them for the vote under Northern Rhodesia's restricted franchise law,[23] found a novel way of highlighting the absurdity of the rule preventing Africans from entering white-owned stores.

Robinson Puta required a bed and had to go to the Nchanga co-operative store to buy one. A white sales lady told him to go to the hatch outside the shop to make his order. Robinson obliged. He then told the lady he wanted to buy a bed, was told the price, and paid. Upon receiving the money, the sales assistant asked him to enter the shop to collect the bed. Robinson declined the offer to go inside the shop and insisted that the bed be given to him through the hatch where the money had passed!

A few years later, Puta left the mining industry to start a business that thrived in pre-independence and post-independence Zambia. His stores were noted for the respect staff showed to all customers. Before independence, he served as a director at Rhodesia Railways and president of the Northern Rhodesia African Traders' Association.

At the same time that Robinson Puta was trying to end the absurd practice of forcing Africans to pay for their goods through hatches, there was also a prohibition on black people's consumption of hard liquor. The only way to get around this prohibition was to acquire an 'exemption certificate'. As determined by the colonial government, Africans deemed

---

[23] Parpart, Jane, Labour and Capital on the African Copperbelt, Philadelphia, Temple University Press, 1983, page 144

to have attained a 'suitable' social standard could obtain the exemption certificate. Obtaining the certificate required an application to the District Commissioner, who had the power to grant or deny the application. A notice to this effect was published in the government gazette and a certificate issued to that effect if the application was granted. This certificate had to be presented each time the 'lucky' native wanted to buy hard liquor.

Here is a description of how two of Andrew Sardanis friends circumvented the hard liquor prohibition law:

Picanniny Donnas

No self-respecting 'native' would apply for an exemption certificate, unless he wanted to buy a shotgun, for which it was also a requirement. Two 'native' friends of mine followed an entirely different route in order to secure their supply of liquor. John Makasa and Bill Mporokoso used to have it flown up to Balovale on the weekly Beaver flight from Meikles store in Bulawayo, Southern Rhodesia, whenever they could afford it. John was the local supervisor for Nortons, a British company that had trading stores in Balovale and Kabompo. He would place the order by mail, signing himself as John McArthur. Bill, the head clerk at the Boma, used to sign as Bill McPollocks. It was not a case of impersonation or fraudulent misrepresentation. It was simply a matter of phonetics. The pronunciation of the word McArthur in the vernacular is exactly Makasa. McPollocks was a good approximation of

Mporokoso, the Zambian vernaculars interchanging the Ls and the Rs.[24]

Not much is known about John Makasa after his escapades in colonial Balovale, but Bill Mporokoso went on to serve as Chingola's district officer in the dying days of the colonial regime. He then served as district commissioner of Lusaka before being appointed Zambia's deputy high commissioner to London. Upon his return from London, Mporokoso served as general manager of the country's largest bakery chain.

Systemic abuse

Undermining black confidence was the inevitable consequence of the ethos of colonialism. In many ways, the humiliation inflicted on the individuals mentioned above is insignificant compared to the systemic damage done to the general population. It was virtually impossible to avoid systemic racial abuse, which was present in virtually all aspects of life, including housing where even educational and financial success failed to guarantee respectable and fair treatment.

Henry Shikopa and Nackson Longwe could not, for example, be housed in accommodation befitting their status as managers. They were expressly forbidden from acquiring housing in the low-density area of Chingola, which was considered a 'white' space. Henry Shikopa's problem was solved by housing him in the caretaker's unit in the company's office complex, even though the council lease regulating the property expressly provided that the unit had to be occupied by a European. But this provision was ignored and unlikely to be enforced because the unit was in the industrial part of town. Emboldened by the success of the Shikopa solution, the company rented a similar unit from a building contractor nearby for Nackson Longwe.

The daily humiliations took their toll, but the educated and remarkably disciplined victims took it in their stride even as they lamented its existence. The words of Tom Mtine, the first black mayor of Ndola, entrepreneur and one-time chairman of Zambia's largest privately-owned company, are probably representative of the attitudes of

---

[24] Sardanis, Andrew. Africa Another Side of the Coin, New York, I.B. Tauris, 2003 pages 34-35

the black elite of the 1950s and 60s. Commenting on the life of his late friend and business colleague, Robinson Puta, Mtine said:

> We were of course hurt by racism from time to time. This led to impatience on our part when we encountered racial discrimination. I recall once telling a white reporter that I had run into discrimination. I continued, "It does not worry me. When a person is stupid, and people who try and discriminate are stupid, he is stupid irrespective of race.[25]

Interestingly, some fifty years after Tom Mtine made this observation, research conducted by psychologists at Brock University, Ontario, found that children with low levels of intelligence are more likely to hold prejudiced attitudes as adults. Mtine may not have had this evidence at the time, but he observed human behaviour and drew conclusions based on his experience. In the context of Northern Rhodesia, it also has to be said he was more fortunate than most of his compatriots, who rarely had opportunities to engage colonial authority figures rationally on the evils of racism. Most black urbanites of the time were confined to their designated areas, internalising racism and slowly giving in to the outrageous proposition that they might actually be less than the white settlers. Not surprisingly, the general population often responded to oppression en masse when colonial injustices became unbearable or when outlets of political expression were abruptly shut.

Caught in the crossfire

In May 1960, any political group wishing to hold a public meeting required a permit from the colonial administration issued under the Public Order Ordinance. Ironically, this law purported to criminalise incitement of enmity between one or more sections of the community. But like its successor, today's Public Order Act, the law was used as a tool to divide the population and oppress groupings with political views that differed from the ruling elite's views.

On May 7, 1960, the United National Independence Party leadership in Ndola applied for a permit to hold a public meeting. At the time, Ndola was home to some of UNIP's most militant members. The meeting request was itself quite reasonable given that no UNIP meeting had taken place on the Copperbelt in two months. Political meetings

---

[25] Mtine, Thomas, Recollections, www.chekwe.com

acted as a safety valve for the oppressed majority who enjoyed the hopeful message of the future delivered by their leaders at these gatherings. These meetings were also a distraction from the daily humiliations of colonial racism.

Foolishly, the colonial provincial administration declined to issue a permit. However, the local UNIP leadership, which included diehard black nationalists such as Andrew Mutemba, Axon Jasper Soko, Dingiswayo Banda, Davies Mwaba, Levi Mbulo, Sefelino Mulenga, and Nephas Tembo, did not want to disappoint their followers by calling off the meeting. Thus, they decided to proceed without the permit. The UNIP youth wing did a good job of advertising the rally, which was scheduled to take place at ten in the morning on May 8, 1960 in Ndola's Chifubu township. Approximately 500 people showed up, but within minutes, members of the Northern Rhodesia Police Mobile Unit in troop carriers swooped on the meeting and dispersed the crowd with tear gas, truncheons, and batons. Dingiswayo Banda, who had just started speaking, responded to the police action by inviting the 'brave' to stay and face the prospect of imprisonment and telling the 'cowards' to leave.

About 300 participants were rounded up and arrested, but the rest escaped, apparently unnoticed by the police. Among the escapees was a group that went on a rampage, reaching the Ndola-Mufulira road where they stopped cars and trucks and incited black drivers and passengers to join them in the protest. They also randomly stoned motor vehicles. One of the cars stoned was a Morris Traveller driven by 39-year-old Lillian Margaret Burton, with her two daughters—Debbie (aged nine) and Rosemary (aged ten)—and the family dog as passengers. Mrs Burton and her children were on their way home from the Sunday service at the Ndola Anglican Cathedral. The car was pelted with stones as it passed the Chifubu turnoff and stopped about 300 metres further on in the direction of Mufulira. There, it was subjected to further stoning and attacked with sticks. The windscreen and windows were then broken, and one or more of the thugs poured petrol in the car, on the driver's side. Someone then threw a lit match inside the car, which quickly burst into flames. Debbie and Rosemary managed to get out of the car relatively quickly. Their mother took a little longer as she had difficulty opening her door, which was later found to have been locked from the inside. When she got out, her clothes and hair were on fire. The dog died in the blaze.

Mrs Burton hung on to life for almost a week before dying of severe burns in the European wing of the Ndola Hospital. Before her death, a group of African sympathisers sent flowers to her and the children. Of the 70 or so people who participated in stoning and torching Mrs Burton's car, four were later identified by their party colleagues and arrested. John Chanda, 26, Robin Kamima, 20, Edward Creta Ngebe, 27, and James Paikani Phiri, 20, subsequently became the defendants in Northern Rhodesia's longest and most expensive criminal trial. By all accounts, Mrs Burton was a woman of Christian faith who believed in forgiveness and love. She had no political affiliation, but those who knew her have confirmed that she tended to be empathetic to African demands for freedom and fairness. Indeed, there is evidence from the ensuing trial of her assailants that she had said, while on fire at the scene of the crime, that she had always been on the side of the Africans. Mrs Burton never had an opportunity to publicly express these sentiments, but her husband, Robert, a civil engineer, confirmed what many have said about his wife. He issued the following statement at the time of her death:

> My wife died with no malice, with no anti-African feeling. It was not her nature to hate. I feel no hate either. I am a simple man. No one had heard of me a week ago and perhaps no one will remember me in a few weeks' time. But this dreadful thing must never be forgotten. It must not be used for political purposes to stir up racial hatred, but it must be remembered as a lesson and the authority must see that it never happens again.

Initially, Mr Burton's plea fell on deaf ears as his wife's murder was used for political purposes to stir up racial hatred. White settlers called for the arming of their population against the black majority. A 1000-strong angry crowd of white settlers in Mufulira demanded the resignation of Sir Evelyn Hone, the territory's levelheaded governor. On the other side of the racial divide, violence spread from Ndola to other towns on the Copperbelt. In Luanshya, a crowd stoned and smashed windows of a store belonging to Justin Simukonda, a black member of the Federation of Rhodesia and Nyasaland Parliament.

The African political leadership generally responded appropriately to Mrs Burton's murder. Harry Mwaanga Nkumbula, the African National Congress leader, called it 'evil' to attack individuals, 'especially harmless women and children.' Kenneth Kaunda, the UNIP president, was in London where he addressed a crowded press conference. Asked if he disassociated himself from the killing, he said he had no evidence of who was responsible for the attack, but he deeply regretted it. He reportedly came across as sincere when he said this.

However, the regret expressed by Kaunda did not stop the colonial authorities from banning UNIP on the Copperbelt. UNIP remained a legal organisation in Lusaka where its acting president, Simon Mwansa Kapwepwe, received a cable from Kaunda instructing him to ask the people to remain calm. To carry out this instruction, Kapwepwe applied for a permit to hold a rally. His application was denied and the country remained tense. But there was relative calm after the assailants' trial ended with a guilty verdict. The assailants were given something Lilian Burton never experienced: a fair trial and an opportunity to state their case. They were represented by some of Northern Rhodesia's best legal minds, including Brian Gardner, who later became deputy chief justice of Zambia. After their appeals to the Federal Supreme Court (sitting at Lusaka) failed, all accused persons were hanged in Livingstone Prison on November 22, 1961.

While some radicals in the nationalist movement chose to see the criminals as political martyrs, many (possibly a majority) black Northern Rhodesians were disgusted and saddened by the savage killing of Mrs Burton. When the Voice of UNIP described the killers as 'heroes and freedom fighters', the larger circulation newspaper, the African Mail responded with: 'Don't talk such rubbish. The Burton killers aren't heroes.'

The African Mail spoke for many as evidenced by the fact that Africans from different parts of the Copperbelt attended Mrs Burton's funeral. According to Jethro Mukenge Mutti's account in the yet-to-be-published Mayibuye Zambia, some of those people walked from different towns just to pay their respects.

The words of Nephas Tembo, who served as UNIP provincial treasurer at the time of the incident, and who had given shelter to Ngebe while he was on the run from police, are instructive. After toying with the idea that the Burton murderers should have been treated as prisoners of war, he goes on to write:

While UNIP set October 1960 as target for freedom, it came four years later. If there are going to be any honours, my considered view is that

Mrs Burton should head the list because it was her blood and that of her assailants which helped make Zambia free.[26]

While we may lament that Lilian Burton has not been suitably honoured and celebrated in Zambia, there is some comfort to be derived from the fact that no monuments honor her assailants either.

For this part of the book, I often relied on conversations with my late journalist friend, Marta T Paynter, who fondly referred to me as 'My son for me', a play on the Bemba language translation for 'My son'. Marta covered the Lilian Burton trial for the Northern News. Toward the end of her life, Marta sent me material on this sad episode of Zambia's history and her papers on the Dag Hammarskjold death, which she also covered. I am indebted to Marta, one of the best journalists Zambia has produced.

Internalisation of colonial racism

While some rural dwellers may have escaped the harshest aspects of racial prejudice, it was the overriding theme in politics and popular culture in urban centres. For example, in virtually all commercial advertisements, the best-looking individuals had pink complexions rather than brown ones, although dark-skinned people featured in advertisements meant exclusively for black audiences. Jesus Christ was always portrayed as a pink-skinned person, usually with blonde hair, even in black churches. (This image remains unchallenged even after the 2015 discovery by British forensic scientists, based on archaeological skulls and drawings, that Jesus looked more like a black Ethiopian than a white European).

The lopsided educational system also ensured the best professionals would be white. The impact of racism thus went beyond the humiliations inflicted on dark-skinned persons in their individual capacities; it was systemic and resulted in significant numbers of the oppressed majority internalising the racist messages that they were constantly bombarded with. Many indigenous people, especially the susceptible, adopted the white colonial mentality that led to them hating their 'kind' and, by implication, themselves. These people concluded that the best way to maintain a distance between themselves and the rest of the colonised was

---

[26] Tembo, Nephas. The Lilian Burton Killing, Lusaka, Apple Books, 1986

to be a part of the white world. Being like white colonisers would give them power and free them from judgement based on stereotype.

This was possibly a motivating factor for many who applied for exemption from laws forbidding Africans to drink hard liquor without a permit. By acquiring the permit, they could demonstrate (at least in their minds) that they were a cut above the ordinary 'native'.

The desire to imitate the colonisers was sometimes taken to absurd lengths. I recall visiting a black friend who was keen to introduce me to another child. We agreed on a place and time to meet this child. My host was anxious that we not be late for the meeting because this friend did not 'make African promises' and would be on time. Another child at a boarding school near Ndola suddenly stopped his healthy practice of brushing his teeth every morning and every evening before bedtime after learning that white children did not brush their teeth regularly! Those who internalised colonial prejudice constantly sought the approval of white colonisers and even attempted to alter their physical features to look like Europeans or at least look less African. In the late 1950s and early 1960s, it became fashionable for black Northern Rhodesians to stretch their hair and bleach their faces. This resulted in women loathing the physical characteristics that distinguished them from what they perceived as the desirable race. Although facial bleaching is now done mostly by unsophisticated women, adornment of Caucasian wigs and hair straightening is a standard practice among Zambian women.

I am baffled that beautiful and often highly intelligent women would attempt to alter their hair texture and shun natural hairstyles that complement their natural beauty. Is this a form of self-mutilation? To seek answers to this puzzle, I sought the help of Professor Hlonipha Mokoena. Mokoena is a history professor at Wits Institute for Social and Economic Research of the University of the Witwatersrand. She specialises in South African intellectual history. Mokoena formerly worked in the Columbia University's anthropology department. A small part of her work analyses the issue of natural African hair. Mokoena identified two main misconceptions that lead to the rejection of natural African hair. The first is that natural hair is 'dirty'. The second concerns natural hair length; it is not long enough for those who crave European features.

Intelligent women and men who wear weaves and relax their hair but are uneasy about doing so typically explain their choice by claiming that their natural hair is 'unmanageable' or that it is 'dirty'. Evidence of this 'dirt' is often the presence of lice in some black people's hair. Mokoena rejects this claim, calling it an 'urban legend'. It certainly is a dangerous myth whose damaging purpose is to perpetuate the stereotype that only black hair attracts lice.

The science is clear, however, that all types of hair attract lice. In Australia, for example, Dr Cameron Webb of the University of Sydney-affiliated Institute of Clinical Pathology and Medical Research warned in early 2019 that as many as 700,000 of Australia's primary school pupils could have head lice. Only 3.3 percent of the Australian population was aboriginal in 2019. Assuming that percentage is proportionately represented in educational institutions, only 23,100 of the pupils affected by head lice would be aboriginal. The rest would almost all be white. Since aboriginals are underrepresented in educational institutions, the number of white children with head lice would be even higher.

All types of hair attract head lice.

Mokoena's research suggests that the 'dirty hair' myth comes from images of wild afro hair, pejoratively named 'fuzzy-wuzzy', sent home by British soldiers fighting Sudanese insurgents during the 1881-1899 Mahdist War. These misleading images assumed that the Sudanese soldiers neither 'dressed' nor washed their hair. The reality is that all African cultures have varied techniques for dressing hair, usually in response to occasion.

'The "Afro"', concludes Mokoena, 'is therefore not some kind of standard African hairstyle. It is just one of several hundred ways of growing and maintaining curly hair. So when a black person decides to "dread" or lock their hair, they neither need nor keep "dirt" in it to make it lock. Our hair (as does all hair) locks naturally when it is left uncombed...'

The misconception concerning the length of black hair comes partly from the concept of measurement. According to Professor Mokoena:

> Natural African hair is curly and so to measure it, one would have to stretch out the coils. This is why limiting the growth of the hair by the width of cornrows or length of strands doesn't make sense at all. One black person's coiffure will look very short because of 'shrinkage' and another black person's locks will look very long because of a loose coil.

In colonial times, imitating European ways went beyond hair stretching and facial bleaching. In extreme cases, some of the colonised even stereotyped those from their own racial group and did everything possible to minimise contact with them; quite a feat considering how segregated Northern Rhodesia was. As the country emerged from Northern Rhodesia and transitioned into Zambia, there was less pressure to internalise racism but the tendency did not disappear entirely. A year after independence, I recall spending a weekend with a very good friend whose parents were referred to as 'coloureds' on account of their mixed race background. In general, this variety of local people took comfort in the term 'coloured' because it provided some distance between them and their darker-skinned compatriots. However, in this particular family, only the eldest daughter appeared to have stereotyped darker members of her compatriots and gone out of her way to minimise contact with them.

My friend was quite dark-skinned for a 'coloured' and he was happy with his complexion and indigenous Zambian features, which are considered beautiful by most objective observers. My friend's elder sister clearly did not share this assessment. On the contrary, she went to absurd lengths to look 'European'. One of the more pathetic things she did was acquiring a nose clip that she thought would make her nose straighter and less flat. She was not, of course, successful in this endeavour, but she did succeed in something else that she considered exceedingly valuable: she acquired a European boyfriend who subsequently married her and took her back to England with him. The last I heard about this matter was that the cherished husband had subjected his Zambian wife to horrendous racial and other abuse, which led her to confess her naïveté and regret in a letter to a black family friend she had been encouraged by her parents to look up to as an aunt.

My friend's sister had uncritically accepted the notion that pink-skinned people are superior to brown-skinned people. I mentioned this experience to a young black Oxford student during the 2017 Oxford University Africa Society Conference. My interlocutor described the tendency as a kind of racial Stockholm syndrome where the oppressed develop admiration (and even affection) for the oppressor. The description seemed to fit the bill.

Segregation: The great perpetuator of myths

This desire to mimic Europeans would perhaps have been less intense had Northern Rhodesia not been segregated. Segregation allows myths to flourish about the 'other'. The architects of Northern Rhodesia knew that allowing the different people to live freely together would make it difficult to create myths of superiority on the part of the colonising force. Dark-skinned people growing up in diverse communities would have opportunities to outperform their white counterparts in some but not all areas.

In other words, these individuals would live a reality that constantly disproved the notion that anyone part of the human race can be inherently superior or inferior to another part. Instead, they would discover what science now tells us clearly: race is a social construct.

In an article in the August 22, 2000 edition of The New York Times, Natalie Angier, the science journalist, wrote:

> As it turns out, scientists say, the human species is so evolutionarily young, and its migratory patterns so wide, restless and rococo, that it has simply not had a chance to divide itself into separate biological groups or "races" in any but the most superficial ways.

'Race is a social concept, not a scientific one,' said Dr J. Craig Venter, head of the Celera Genomics Corporation in Rockville, Md.

'We all evolved in the last 100,000 years from the same small number of tribes that migrated out of Africa and colonized the world.'

Race as a sociological and not biological construct is easily understood by people raised as fully functioning members of diverse societies. Before Zambia attained independence, I had the dubious distinction of being the first black child to be admitted to a European primary school. In fact, there was another boy in similar circumstances. Caleb Chongo Nkonga's parents had recently arrived from England and he was admitted to a European school at about the same time. However, this was in Lusaka, not in Chingola where I was.

Caleb and I coincidentally ended up as boarders at the same high school three years later, and we reminisced about our experiences as the only black children in white primary schools. We discovered that our experiences were quite similar. Although most of our contemporaries came from what would be considered racist homes, racial prejudice was really only an issue in the very early days. My own recollection is that after a month or so, I was seen not so much as a black boy but as the boy who was good at Geography and hopeless at cricket. My reputation as a geographer came after I came top of my class in the subject in an examination that took place shortly after my arrival.

It is also interesting to examine the impact that desegregating the school system had on white pupils. For example, a white friend recalls how the first black classmate he ever had surprised everyone by coming top of the class in an examination they had all assumed him to be ill-equipped for because he had only recently joined the school and had not had time to adequately prepare for the test. My friend remembers the boy, Clement, to this day. Needless to say, this particular white friend has little patience for naked racism.

I also recall that when my family moved to Musenga Small Holdings in Chingola, a residential area with spacious lots, designated by colonial authorities as European, the lady who ran the local grocery store and filling station started a petition to get us out of the area. Coincidentally, I went to the same school as her son, Philip, with whom I forged a friendship that led to me occasionally being invited to his house. One of my more memorable visits to the house was for tea with the family to celebrate Philip's grandmother's birthday, which fell on the same day as mine. When this fact was revealed, I was teased by the family as Granny's twin brother!

In addition to revealing the absurdity of racism, experiences such as these encourage knowledge accumulation, understanding, and respect among people who perceive themselves as different from one another. This is why integration is important.

On March 3, 2014, a British newspaper, *The Independent*, reported the results of a study led by Professor Miles Hewstone of Oxford University. The study found that people who lived in ethnically diverse streets were less racially prejudiced than individuals who lived in highly segregated areas. Their increased tolerance was due directly to the experience of living in a more integrated society. Even when white people had just a little interaction with other groups living in the same ethnically diverse community, they were more tolerant because they witnessed positive interactions between different racial groups. The researchers called the effect 'passive tolerance' because merely living in a racially diverse community generates a positive effect. They likened this to the negative effect of passive smoking when non-smokers are affected by the smoke generated by smokers.

Members of the small but harmful white ghetto in Zambia that opposed independence in the first place and now dedicates themselves to condemning all things Zambian, and undermining Zambian confidence, often argue that integration is unnatural. When integration appears to succeed, it does so only because the community is populated by tolerant people predisposed to living in mixed neighbourhoods. Leaving aside the contradictory aspect of this argument, let us look at what the science actually says.

The findings of the Hewstone study that emerged from the analysis of seven previous studies on community relations carried out between 2002 and 2012 in England, Europe, the United States, and South Africa, specifically rule out this idea. According to the researchers, even the attitudes of the most prejudiced people who did not mix at all with ethnic minorities become more tolerant over time due to living in areas where others were mixing daily. In the words of Professor Hewstone:

> We have shown that positive contact between people belonging to different ethnic groups leads to more tolerant societies overall.

> Astonishingly, we don't just see reduced prejudice among people who have direct contact with ethnic minorities. It isn't even confined to those whose friends have contact with minorities. Simply living in a neighbourhood where other people are mixing with minorities is enough to reduce racial prejudice.

We can conclude that Northern Rhodesia would have been a much more tolerant and harmonious society had the authorities not imposed a system of forced segregation.

We are only Zambians

Colonial society encouraged the categorisation of people into winners and losers, depending on their racial grouping. Thus white people were winners and black people were losers. Some black people and other non-whites had the potential to be winners, but until that was demonstrated per criteria established exclusively by the white colonial society, they were losers.

The colonial narrative, which sadly continues in many quarters to this day, was that the black people of Zambia had neither history nor culture until the white colonisers arrived. The splendid organisation of states such as Kongo and Luba-Lunda was completely overlooked in this discourse. Instead, society was encouraged to look down on black people as a race entirely dependent on white largesse. Not everyone accepted this false dichotomy but enough did, and that has an ongoing impact on the confidence of the territory's inhabitants.

In his book Africa: Another Side of the Coin, Andrew Sardanis narrates how white settlers who had pre-school children would often employ their servants' children as companions for these children until they were enrolled in school. One of the terms of engagement for the black children employed as companions of the white children was that they had 'to put up with all the caprices and tantrums of their pickaninny bwanas [and donnas].' Sardanis writes that he initially felt sorry for the young servant playmates but that later in life he felt sorry for the pickaninny bwanas, who had been cast as the winners in the arrangement. The dichotomy was false because sometimes even the 'winners' found the euphoria of being 'superior' because of their skin colour ephemeral. These children had missed an opportunity to learn how to influence others and resolve differences of opinion.

I noticed this in some of the white children I went to school with. Their lack of respect for people who looked different from them was so evident that in a pre-independence address to my class, Mrs van Rooyen, our teacher, cautioned us that independence was coming and our lives would change and we would need to adjust accordingly. One of the changes she required us to make in our lives was henceforth 'to be polite to Africans'. Only years later, after I understood the pickaninny bwana mentality, did I fully appreciate Mrs van Rooyen's words.

Independence did come and our lives, especially the lives of my white coevals, did change. The first change was that there were a few more students in the school who looked like me. But this change was minor compared to the changes made to how pupils would be selected for secondary school. Before independence, the education system required African children to take the secondary school entrance examination, which consisted of mechanical and linguistic aptitude tests, known as Special Papers, and the 'certificate' examination based on the subjects taught during the final year. White children, being inherently superior to black children, at least in the eyes of the colonial authorities, were not required to take the Special Papers. It was assumed that by virtue of their skin colour, they would always be qualified to proceed to secondary school, and consequently, at the end of Grade Seven, they were simply 'promoted' to high school.

The new democratically elected government could not tolerate an education system that treated children differently based on their skin colour. So, the secondary school entrance examination was made compulsory for everyone. The white children were familiar with examinations in general but they had no experience with Special Papers. In contrast, almost all black children had siblings and cousins who had gone through the Special Papers process and were only too happy to prepare their younger relatives for the task. When the results came out, the failure rate among white children was extremely high. I recall only three entering the Chingola High School, and a handful qualifying to go to any Zambian secondary school. The rest were sent by their parents either to Southern Rhodesia or South Africa to continue their education.

In contrast, only one black child failed the entrance examination, although he passed the 'certificate' examination easily. The white children had done poorly because they came from a system that told them that they were 'winners' and had no need to take an examination done by 'losers' for years seriously.

Virtually every black child in a fee-paying school (as the 'European' schools were renamed after independence) used English as a second language or even a third language. Despite this linguistic disadvantage, they generally outperformed the English-speaking white pupils, even in the English language. These children may have come from relatively underfunded and underequipped schools before admission to fee-paying schools, but they had had the benefit of committed teachers and communities that placed a premium on education. This background, added to the excellent facilities they now enjoyed at the fee-paying schools, made success that much easier. Of course, there was also the reality of failure triggering severe consequences at home for most of us.

There has been a similar trend in England concerning non-white children. In 2003, the odds for black African pupils achieving five A*-C grades (including English and Mathematics) at the General Certificate for Secondary School level (GCSE) were only two-thirds of white British pupils' odds. Ten years later, black African pupils scored higher than the white British average.[27]

In both cases, the performance of these boys and girls contradicted the convenient stereotype of black people as dependent, unmotivated, and undisciplined. There is no basis for this stereotype. But the stereotype was important to the white settlers who constantly sought to justify their unearned privilege. While this continues to be a popular view in Zambia's white ghetto and among their intellectually superficial black Zambian epigones, it actually has no basis in science. In a society that emphasises 'winning', those structurally excluded from scoring many wins will sooner or later be labelled as having 'low self-esteem'. As British-born, Australian-based physician and stress management therapist Russ Harris has cautioned, the term 'self-esteem' in the hands of laypeople can be misleading.[28] Nonetheless, the system that allowed black Northern Rhodesians few opportunities to 'win', at least relative to the settler community, did take its toll and resulted in Zambians having less self-belief and confidence in themselves to run an independent and prosperous nation. They developed a tendency to defer to outsiders when seeking solutions to domestic challenges.

There is no shortage of stories about the frustrations of enlightened black Zambians who have contradicted foreign advisers in meetings and then been aggressively set upon by fellow Zambians who clearly thought disagreeing with foreigners, especially white ones, was heretical. Another complaint often aired relates to the preferential treatment given to white people in Zambian restaurants and hotels by black Zambians. During a Birmingham University reunion, a friend who had studied law with me told me that her daughter had visited Zambia and loved it, except for one incident. The incident involved her daughter and a few other white girls getting stranded on a road. A bus driver saw this and stopped by the girls and offered them a lift. So far, so good. But he then went on to ask all the black passengers to get out of the bus so he could transport the white girls!

The story reminded me of a childhood experience. Our neighbour had asked my mother if our family driver could give his son a lift home

---

[27] Strand, Steve, Ethnicity, deprivation and educational achievement at age 16 in England: trends over time, National Institute of Economic and Social Research & University of Oxford 2015

[28] Harris, Russ. The Confidence Gap: A Guide to Overcoming Fear and Self-Doubt, Boulder Colorado, Trumpeter Books, 2011 pages 89-99

after school. She readily agreed since the boy in question went to my school and giving him a lift would not be an imposition, especially as he and I were good friends. During the ten-mile drive, we talked the driver into a game of overtaking all the cars on the road that he could. But one motorist saw what was happening and decided to stop our vehicle to warn our driver against dangerous driving. The motorist was visibly upset and admonished our driver. When the motorist noticed my friend Robin, he added, 'And how dare you endanger the life of a white child!' The motorist, who spoke with a Rhodesian accent, was black! At least this incident happened a year after independence. The bus incident occurred in the 1990s, long after Zambia's independence. Both episodes serve to remind us how deeply racism can be internalised by its victims and cause them to act even more outrageously than the oppressor. Russ Harris will forgive us for using the term 'low self-esteem,' but it does appear to fit the Zambian situation.

The tendency to place a higher value on white people is found even at the higher echelons of society. For example, in mid-July 1990, a British nurse working in Iraq was freed from a 15-year prison sentence for helping a journalist suspected of espionage, who was subsequently hanged. Daphne Parish was 53 at the time and her release was the result of pleas by President Kaunda to Saddam Hussein, the then leader of Iraq.

Immediately after her release, Ms Parish was flown in a private jet to Lusaka where she was met by Zambian officials and Iraqi diplomats. She was then driven to State House, the President's official residence, where she spent the night. Meanwhile, back in Iraq, Deputy Foreign Minister Nizar Hamdoun confirmed that Ms Parish's release was 'in response to an overture from President Kaunda and for purely humanitarian reasons'. Mr Kaunda was the hero of the moment, earning rare praise and expressions of gratitude from Margaret Thatcher, the British Prime Minister with whom he had had public spats in the past. Certainly, Kaunda had invested a huge amount of time securing the release of the British nurse. It is unfortunate that he was not equally engaged in a similar problem closer to home.

When President Kaunda appealed for Daphne Parish's release, Webster Kayi Lumbwe, a former officer in the Zambia Security and Intelligence Services and Ministry of Foreign Affairs, was serving a twenty-year prison sentence for espionage. Lumbwe had been tried secretly for passing on classified information to America's Central

Intelligence Agency. The twenty-year sentence was the minimum sentence for the offence. When Lumbwe's appeal in 1986 failed, his family and friends intensified their efforts to persuade President Kaunda to release the cerebral former intelligence officer on humanitarian grounds. For a long time, these appeals fell on deaf ears. In the end, however, Kaunda did pardon Lumbwe and other political prisoners in the wake of an unsuccessful coup attempt, and also in response to a pointed question by the Christian newspaper, The National Mirror, which drew parallels between the Lumbwe and Parish cases.

The release of Lumbwe was well received, but in the context of the Daphne Parish affair, it raised questions about the value the head of state placed on the lives of his citizens. Kaunda invested a huge amount of time and political capital to secure the release of a white prisoner in a faraway land, but had chosen to ignore pleas for the release of one of his countrymen whose circumstances were not too different from the Briton he staked his political reputation on.

Intentionally or unintentionally, the willingness of some political leaders to place a higher value on foreigners, especially white ones, does influence the behaviour of both citizens and institutions. For this reason, some institutions have been known to reject invaluable help from professionals whose only disqualification was skin color. Professionals in the Zambian diaspora have discovered this.

Dr Misheck Mwaba, President of Bow Valley College, Albert, Canada, has an impressive academic achievement and leadership record. Before joining Bow Valley College as vice president (academics), Dr Mwaba was dean of media, trades, and technology at Niagara College, Ontario, Canada. He provided oversight to more than 40 academic programs, making up more than 33 percent of total student enrollment. Niagara College in Ontario is well known for its entrepreneurial focus. This was due partly to the leadership provided by Dr Mwaba in the establishment of the entrepreneurship hub. The hub reflects Mwaba's belief that entrepreneurial skill development must be integrated into programming and broader college experience. Furthermore, Dr Mwaba led initiatives to source funds for equipment renewal. The funds included a significant investment from the Government of Ontario to construct and equip a laboratory for electric and hybrid vehicles.

Before joining Niagara College, Dr Mwaba served as the electronics and electro-mechanical studies chair at Algonquin College, Ottawa,

Canada. While in Ottawa, he designed experimental facilities and managed research and development projects at Atomic Energy of Canada Limited. Institutions that have benefited from Dr Mwaba's teaching include the University of Zambia, Eindhoven University of Technology in the Netherlands, Carleton University in Ottawa, and the University of Ottawa.

On February 14, 2018, Misheck Mwaba brought pride to the Zambian Canadian community when he was appointed to the prestigious 15 member Natural Sciences and Engineering Research Council of Canada, whose mandate is to:

> Help make Canada a country of discoverers and innovators for the benefit of all Canadians. It invests in People, Discovery and Innovation through partnerships and programs that support post-secondary research in the natural sciences and engineering.

This appointment placed Mwaba in a position to positively influence scientific development in his homeland. Unusually, the Zambian press reported this prestigious appointment, and the Zambian High Commissioner to Ottawa sent a letter of congratulations to him. Mwaba believes Zambia would benefit greatly from collaboration between Zambians at home and those, like himself, in the diaspora. He is concerned, however, that not enough home-based Zambians are receptive to offers of help from members of the Zambian diaspora. Mwaba speaks from personal experience.

His offers to help typically end up being rejected. Although known in Canada for his intelligence and humility, his offers are often seen as patronizing and presumptuous in Zambia. Even in the rare cases where a real interest has been initially shown, there typically is no follow-up. This is how Zambia lost out on an opportunity from the Canadian International Development Research Centre and Foreign Affairs, Trade and Development Canada in 2015. IDRC and DFATD were in the process of issuing a call for proposals for projects aimed at developing, testing and applying ways to increase food security and nutrition innovations. Zambia met the criteria for eligibility. Dr Mwaba was made aware of the proposal by his former PhD supervisor from Carleton University, who wanted to know if there were individuals or organisations in Zambia that might be interested in scaling up food security and nutrition innovations in Zambia. Despite extensive enquiries and the obvious advantages that the proposal offered Zambia, the country showed no interest and Dr Mwaba had to go back to his old professor and report that Zambia appeared uninterested.

Mwaba persisted in his efforts to engage his homeland. This time he wanted to make himself available to the University of Zambia during annual vacations to the country. He approached two heads of department to see if he could be a guest lecturer when he was in the country. He committed two weeks per annum for this purpose. Alternatively, he suggested supervising one final year student project. Mwaba's offer was dismissed as a patronizing gesture. It appears however, the patronising was on the other side. For insance, Dr Mwaba was told, 'things in Zambia are done differently. So, two weeks of guest lecturing will be disruptive to the students'. He was also given a lecture on the intricacies of teaching university students and told that his students would suffer if he did not see them regularly. The politest responses he received informed him that 'things are okay,' or simply promised to get back to him.

One interlocutor revealed resentment for the diaspora when he said:

> You guys who are abroad only come to Zambia to attend funerals and all of a sudden you think you can solve all our problems

These challenges are not confined to the University of Zambia. In August 2019, Dr Mwaba had a serendipitous meeting with a delegation from the Copperbelt University at a Toronto hotel. The team was led by the vice-chancellor. The delegation was in Ontario to meet post-secondary institutions to establish partnerships with Copperbelt University. Since one of the areas of interest was aviation, Dr Mwaba became keenly interested in the mission. While at Algonquin College, Mwaba had overseen the aviation programmes. When he asked about who the delegation had met at Algonquin, the answer shocked him. The distinguished delegation from Zambia's second university had met a project officer from the International department, with no mandate to make the kinds of decisions the delegation was looking for.

The delegation had left Zambia without a proper briefing on higher education in Ontario. They were led by the vice-chancellor and should have been received and hosted by the President and CEO of Algonquin

College. Since that did not happen, Mwaba could only hope that his intervention, though late, might lead to positive results.

The exchange of emails seen by the writer clearly shows that Mwaba's offer to make connections with the right people at Algonquin College and other suitable institutions was not welcome. While the vice-chancellor responded to the Mwaba email offering help, he delegated the matter to another officer at the university. That officer never wrote back to Mwaba.

This is but one example of institutions run by black Zambians rejecting invaluable help because the person offering the help is a black Zambian. The reader will be forgiven for wondering if the treatment given to Dr Mwaba is the academic equivalent of the story concerning the bus driver who asked his black passengers to get out of the bus so he could accommodate stranded white girls!

The behaviour of the department heads who spurned Dr Mwaba's help and the bus driver does help explain why so many Zambians accept the sense of entitlement that stems from the unearned privilege enjoyed by white people in the country. There is no shortage of anecdote to illustrate the preferential treatment which white people expect and are given. It is not unusual for whites, especially those of Afrikaner extraction, perhaps reminiscing about 'the good old apartheid days' in neighbouring South Africa, to jump the queue at airports, hotels and other public places. They believe it is their right and are quite taken aback when challenged, usually by a foreign-based Zambian with an impressive education.

Washington-based Professor Kenneth Kaoma Mwenda serves as program manager and executive head of the World Bank Voice Secondment Program. He is also Extraordinary Professor of Law at the University of Pretoria. In addition, he has authored 24 books and more than 80 scholarly articles. Professor Mwenda is more than familiar with home country-diaspora relations issues. He has suggested that this phenomenon was not unique to Zambia, but common in the southern African sub-continent.

He believes that there is a pervasive view by many African professionals in the diaspora that their governments often lack a coherent and consistent policy on how to utilize skills offered by foreign-based professionals.

Many African countries consider remittances from the diaspora the only significant gain from the South-North brain drain. In so doing, they minimise the importance of skills transfer from the North to the South in growing a knowledge economy. This is obviously an area where the African diaspora can play an important role.

The situation appears different in West Africa. According to Professor Mwenda:

> Whereas some Western African countries have mastered the art of benefitting from the skills of their diaspora-based nationals, much of Southern Africa seems to lag behind. Admittedly, history could have favoured some Western African nationals given their early arrivals in Europe and North America due to political turmoil, military coups, dictatorships and unstable governments in that part of the world, especially in the 1970s and 1980s. As such, many Western African nations have learned the hard way and tend to show a more coordinated approach towards utilizing the human resources of their Diasporas. Also, they tend to have more structured and coordinated social networks to position their people in powerful corporate positions internationally. You just have to look at the staffing numbers of Africans in top positions in most international organizations.

Professor Mwenda adds that the situation is generally different in southern Africa where 'local professionals in some of these countries would rather have an average qualified white man take up a top position than a fellow national from the diaspora'.

While no institution today would officially tolerate the treatment Henry Shikopa was subjected to by Barclays Bank in Chingola, the idea of treating white people preferentially is not entirely dead. The irony is that this practice is perpetuated mostly by black Zambians who have internalised racism and come to accept some of the negative stereotypes against their own people, leading them to conclude that as Zambians they are deserving of unjust treatment. They are after all only Zambians.

They were only Europeans

Zambians are not the only people in history to be colonised. Peoples all over the world, including Europe, have at one time or another been colonised. The British themselves were colonised by the Romans, although the Scottish Highlands escaped the indignity because that part of the world was not rich in mineral or agricultural produce. Conquering the Scottish Highlands would have been more costly than profitable from the Romans' point of view. But the rest of Britain had natural resources, fertile land, and a large population from which to draw the empire's soldiers.

The Roman presence in Britain was rather longer than the British presence in Zambia, lasting from 43 AD to 410 AD. Nonetheless, the two systems are comparable because each had clearly defined groups of insiders and outsiders. The Romans were insiders responsible for all good things that happened in the colony. The British were there to serve the Romans, not to contribute to governance in any meaningful way. Indeed they were considered incapable of governing for a number of reasons, not least of which was lack of unity among the native tribes.

The Romans were credited with modernising Britain. They taught hygiene to the local population and introduced them to reliable, clean drinking water. Civilisation was further consolidated by the introduction of a clear calendar and a relatively sophisticated legal system that protected property rights. Furthermore, they introduced straight long-distance roads built to specification. All these innovations are considered Roman, yet they must have involved a huge amount of indigenous labour.

The confinement of natives to mostly manual work and their exclusion from governance structures partly explains the chaos, characterised by native tribes and foreign invaders battling for power, that followed the departure of the Romans. At the time, this was seen as evidence of the natives' inability to govern themselves.

The reality is however that the natives had not been given the necessary education to understand and manage the new system of government introduced by the Romans. The Roman model was so alien to Britons that many of them fled urban centres to live in less Romanised rural areas in times of strife.

In his historically accurate novel, *London*, Edward Rutherfurd does a splendid job charting the city's history. Some of the characters in his novel respond to the chaos that followed Roman departure by openly questioning the ability of Britons to govern themselves, suggesting that British confidence had been dented by Roman colonialism in the same way that most forms of colonialism undermine the confidence of natives obliged to live under foreign rule.

Barbary Slave Trade

Britain eventually recovered from the effects of Roman colonialism. It takes a long time for people to recover from colonialism, shed feelings of inadequacy, and gain the confidence to govern themselves appropriately. What is less publicised is that Britain was also a victim of slavery. Although trade in British slaves was not as devastating to Britain and Europe as the transatlantic slave trade was to the African continent, it was nonetheless equally tragic for the individual victims.

This particular trade in humans took place between the early 17th and the middle of the 18th centuries. During this time Europeans were enslaved by Barbary pirates from North Africa. While the number of victims was small compared to the transatlantic slave trade, it was still significant at an estimated 1.25 million. The treatment of the white slaves was not conspicuously less barbaric than the treatment meted out on their African counterparts.

Initially, this trade was conducted with merchant ships, pirates, or corsairs, along with the Barbary Coast, which encompassed the shores of modern-day Morocco, Algeria, Tunisia, and Libya, close to the slave markets.

But ships in the vicinity of these shores did not have enough people to satisfy North African demand for slaves, so raids were extended to coastal settlements in several European countries, including England and Ireland. The pirates would typically land on unguarded beaches in the night and capture their victims from nearby villages.

Thus, on 20 June 1631, the Irish village of Baltimore, in West Cork, had almost its entire population taken as slaves by North African slave traders. The attack on Baltimore is remembered for its brutal efficiency. More than 200 raiders landed on the shores of the unsuspecting village in the early hours of the fateful day, armed with muskets, iron bars and sticks of burning wood. They spread out silently and positioned themselves at the front doors of the cottages along the beach and other village residences close to the sea. They were waiting for a signal after which they unleashed horror resulting in the capture of 20 men, 33 women and 54 children. The victims were promptly loaded on the ship, which set sail for Algiers where they were placed in pens before being exhibited for sale at public auction.

The few historians who pay attention to the Barbary slave trade are unanimous that male slaves were typically used for hard labour while the previously free women were sexually exploited and forced to perform chores in the homes of the nobility. The children were often raised as Muslims, and when they came of age were drafted into the Ottoman army. The evidence from paintings depicting life in Ottoman North Africa strongly suggests that the trade beneficiaries were light brownskinned and dark brownskinned.

The intent here is not to suggest that the Barbary slave trade was in all aspects the same as the transatlantic slave trade. Rather the intent is to show that no one group of people has a monopoly on cruelty, in the hope that this will encourage better and more racially sensitive analysis of colonialism and racism.

As happened with the transatlantic slave trade, there were appeals to end the Barbary adventure, which began to decline toward the end of the 17th century as European navies intensified policing of the seas around North African waters. By the beginning of the 19th century, after the United States joined European navies in the fight against the scourge, the Barbary slave trade had all but ended. We can however be sure that had more people been captured from Europe in numbers similar to those in the transatlantic trade, Europe would have had a much harder road to travel to achieve the economic success with which it has been associated for much of the recent past.

CHAPTER THREE

Getting Zambians to Know Zambia

J ust as individuals who undergo traumatic events suffer consequences that drastically change their lives, nations can also have their lives negatively altered by traumatic events such as war, genocide, or colonialism. While individuals may find traumatic events debilitating, nations may find their progress hindered by trauma. While individuals may have problems maintaining relationships with family members and friends, states may have difficulty trusting their own population and developing healthy relations with other countries.

Trauma is not unique to individuals. Groups can also be traumatised. A recent study showed, for example, how wartime trauma has impaired empathy in mothers of small children in Southern Israel, affecting their ability to provide proper parenting.[29] Zambia's history shows how the country was traumatised by the colonial experience and how this experience has led to a lack of confidence and self-belief. There are of course individuals in Zambia who are sufficiently (mentally) liberated to have the necessary confidence to move the country forward. Unfortunately these individuals tend to have limited power and influence. An enlightened leadership would showcase the achievements of these individuals as a way of increasing collective national confidence.

This is not to suggest that this sad episode should be forgotten, but rather to say the multidimensional character of the county should be better appreciated, and colonialism put in context. Zambia must be given the opportunity to understand that there is more to the country than the traumatic legacy of colonialism. As the exceptionally talented Nigerian writer Chimamanda Ngozi Adichie would put it, Zambia has more than a single story.

No aspect of Zambian history should be forgotten. But history should not be allowed to hold the country back either. Victims of sexual abuse who succeed in overcoming their trauma do so by understanding what happened to them and changing how they think about their trauma

---

[29] Brain and Behaviour Research Foundation, www.bbrfoundation.org , July 25, 2019

and its aftermath, not by necessarily forgetting the experience. In the process, victims learn to control negative thoughts about the trauma and are thus able to move on and lead productive lives unburdened by the weight of untutored recollection of the hurt.

Zambia cannot, of course, be treated for trauma through individual counselling. The country can, however, embark on a programme of education and cultural change designed to change the Zambian mindset. With enlightened and dedicated leadership, this is far from an impossible task.

From Low Self-Esteem to Self-Acceptance

Bearing in mind Russ Harris' caution, we shall accept that Zambians, in general, have low self-esteem issues. We do not belive, however, the solution lies in the crude promotion of 'high self-esteem.' The term is understood differently by different analysts. In general, however, it is agreed that a person with high self-esteem is in the constant habit of positively evaluating themselves. It does not take too much imagination to see where this approach might lead. Might it not, for example, lead to an obsession with being right all the time? Might it also not lead to being disdainful of those who disagree with one since they cannot be right? If one is always right (which is what consistent and unwavering positive evaluation causes a person to believe) does it not follow that everyone who disagrees with one must be wrong. Indeed, it is easy to see how it can be concluded that those who disagree with an individual with high self-esteem will be seen by the individual as necessarily belonging to an inferior class of people.

This kind of attitude leads to social evils such as apartheid and colonialism, where the groups with power see absolutely no common ground with the oppressed group. Recalling the pickaninny bwana experiences of Northern Rhodesia, one can see how easily the offspring of parents who engaged their black servants' children as companions for them would have gone on to be champions of colonialism or at least black oppression.

They would have appreciated the notion that they were superior to the brown skinned children who kept them company by virtue of being pink-skinned. What else would one expect from children whose black child servants were forbidden from challenging them and engaging them as intellectual equals? This entirely unhealthy state of affairs undoubtedly led to an immediate but unsustainable increase in the self-esteem of the pickaninny bwanas.

Only those white children fortunate enough to have opportunities later in life to unlearn the prejudice imbued in them from an early age would have seen the danger of this high self-esteem borne out of myth, deception, and unearned privilege. They would have appreciated that in real life, high self-esteem rarely leads to lasting success.

An examination of successful people (except perhaps those whose success stems from inherited wealth) shows that triumph is typically preceded by a series of failures. And sometimes, success comes very late in life. Harland Sanders is an example of how long and winding the road to success can be. He is now known worldwide for his KFC fried chicken business franchise. In fact this success only came when Sanders was in his 60s. As a young man, he worked as a farm labourer and streetcar conductor before working for railway companies across the southern part of the United States. Sanders studied law by correspondence and practiced in magistrates' courts in Arkansas until a courtroom brawl with a client ended that career. Other jobs included steamboat ferry operator, life insurance salesman, and even delivering babies born to poor housewives.

While acknowledging that too many Zambians have low self-esteem and that this contributes to a collective lack of self-belief, we should also understand that conditioning Zambians (or any people) to have high self-esteem would not lead to long-lasting improvements in the national psyche. The focus should instead be on self-acceptance, self-awareness, and self-motivation.

Zambia should learn to accept itself. This means understanding both the country's pre-colonial history, its post-colonial circumstances, and its failures and successes. It also means that Zambia should be willing to get out of its comfort zone; a zone characterised by costly dependency on foreign aid and obsequious deference to foreigners. Stepping out of the comfort zone will allow Zambia to re-examine itself, take stock of its strengths and weaknesses, position itself to exploit opportunities and, equally important, manage threats to its success. When this happens, Zambia will discover the value of Zambianness.

Once outside its comfort zone, Zambia will no longer have the option of defaulting to failure in the mistaken belief that there are no serious consequences to this failure since the country can always rely on international donors to come to its aid. In this new world, Zambia will sometimes be surprised at how easily goals can be achieved. At other times, however, the country will fail. Whatever the case, Zambia will now be in the real world, controlling her own destiny and development agenda and moving forward despite setbacks.

This new world will involve optimal utilisation of Zambian talent and natural resources. And because of the ethos of the new era, out-of-the-box thinking will flourish out of sheer necessity and national pride. Pulling Zambia out of its comfort zone and weaning the country off international aid will not be easy. It will trigger anxiety in many citizens, including decisionmakers. This is entirely understandable. Sudden change always induces anxiety. But Zambia would not be the first country in the world to grasp the nettle and take charge of its destiny.

Do or Die

Singapore, founded in January 1819 by Jamaican-born Sir Thomas Stamford Raffles, is an example of a country that has travelled this road. Although inadequately educated and growing up in a highly indebted household that forced him to end schooling at the age of 14 and join the East India Company, Raffles became quite successful in later life and was knighted in 1816.

Singapore was never expected to survive on its own. When Raffles founded Singapore, it was little more than a fishing village, home to a thousand Malay fishermen and a handful of Chinese farmers. With no natural resources and its status as a transhipment port threatened by declining international trade, Singapore needed to be part of the Malayan hinterland common market. Thus on September 16, 1963, Singapore became part of the Federation of Malaysia.

However, Singapore's sense of economic security brought on by membership of the Federation of Malaysia was short-lived. In August 1965, the island city-state was forced to leave the Federation to become an independent city-state. This induced anxiety in the citizens of Singapore, including former Prime Minister Lee Kuan Yew, who wrote in his memoirs:

> We had been asked to leave Malaysia and go our own way with no signposts to our next destination. We faced tremendous odds with an improbable chance of survival... On that 9th day of August 1965, I

started out with great trepidation on a journey along an unmarked road to an unknown destination[30]

The expulsion of Singapore from the Malaysian Federation forced the city-state out of its comfort zone and unleashed a period of unprecedented ingenuity among its citizenry leading to the transformation of the island from a fishing village in the early nineteenth century to a globally admired economic model in much of the twentieth century. Singapore's gross domestic product per capita increased from USD428 in 1960 to USD95, 508 in 2019. By the end of 2018, Singapore had USD292.7 billion in official reserves, the 13th largest in the world.

Only eight countries in the world have a higher score on the United Nations Development Programme human development index which combines statistics on average and expected years of schooling and life expectancy with income levels. The Human Development Index is scaled from 0 to 100. Countries with a score of 80 or more are considered to have very high human development. Those with a score between 70 and 79 are high, countries between 55 and 69 are medium, and those under 55 are low. The 2017 HDI published in 2020 shows Singapore sitting at 93.2, higher than the United Kingdom, the United States, Canada, Denmark, and the Netherlands.

With the benefit of hindsight, we can say Singapore's founding prime minister need not have worried about his country's future. We can also use this model to design Zambia's road map to prosperity.

Singapore is a small territory today, but with a land area of 581.8 square kilometres in 1965, it was even smaller at independence. Since then, Singapore's land area has expanded to 719 square kilometres. The increase in land surface area has been due to ingenuity, not conquest or divine intervention. Singaporeans have invested in land reclamation from rivers and seas. While this has resulted in some environmental damage, the wealth generated by the country through this exercise enables Singapore to address this damage. Furthermore, most people would agree that accommodating a growing population through land reclamation is preferable to war, which is the traditional way of acquiring land.

---

[30] Lee Kuan Yew, The Singapore Story: Memoirs of Lee Kuan Yew, Singapore Press Holdings 1998

Singapore did not reclaim land for the sake of it. The country needed skilled immigrants who in turn needed land to inhabit once they got to Singapore. These circumstances encouraged Singapore to adopt a liberal immigration policy that focuses on skill and employer requirements.

As a result of its immigration policy, the small village with a thousand Malay fishermen and a handful of Chinese farmers in 1819 now has a population of 5.7 million. Moreover, the policy has clearly contributed to the boosting of employment opportunities on the island. Whereas the unemployment rate was over 14 percent in 1965, Trading Economics reports the seasonally adjusted unemployment rate was 2.3 percent at the end of 2019.

The last point to be made here is that none of this would have been achieved easily without the Corrupt Practices Investigation Bureau, which has a well-earned reputation for enforcing the Prevention of Corruption Act impartially and professionally. According to Transparency International, Singapore is the least corrupt country in Asia.

Nothing is more devastating to a country than genocide or war, and few countries fully recover from these calamities because of foreign investors' understandable reluctance to invest in countries with a recent history of genocide or war. Rwanda appears to be one of the countries fortunate enough to have attracted investment after a genocide. But this ability to attract investment and grow the economy once again was not a result of luck or divine intervention. It took discipline and planning.

Rwanda enjoyed an annual GDP growth rate of 6.5 percent from 1973 to 1980, thanks mostly to good coffee prices. This growth slowed to 2.9 percent per annum between 1980 and 1985 and came to a virtual halt from 1986 to 1990. The country was forced to turn to the International Monetary Fund who implemented a structural adjustment program in 1990. Measures implemented prior to the 1994 genocide included large currency devaluations and the removal of subsidies on consumer goods. The measures could not have come at a worse time as civil war between the official Rwandan Armed Forces and the rebel Rwandan Patriotic Front started on 1 October 1990, culminating in the genocide which resulted in the death of an estimated 900,000 Tutsis and moderate Hutus. During this period of strife, Rwanda's gross domestic product declined by more than 40 percent.

Few observers would have given Rwanda much chance of recovery but in 1995, a 9 percent increase in real GDP was recorded. The new

Rwandan leadership welcomed this development which gave them breathing space as they planned the new economy. One of the lessons learned from the genocide was that Rwanda could not place its security in the hands of foreigners. After all, the international community did nothing to stop the slaughter.

Thus the new government established a programme designed to guarantee peace and governmental legitimacy. The new Rwanda aggressively supressed ethnic particularism and moved toward a merit-based society. Institutions were strengthened and, where necessary, created for the purpose of combating corruption.

The results were quite spectacular. Average GDP growth was 8.8 percent between 2000 and 2014. GDP per capita increased from USD500 in 1994 to USD2,090 in 2017. Concerning industrial output, Rwanda had an average annual increase of nine percent between 2007 and 2017. Only ten other countries in the world performed better.

In 2015, Rwanda surprised the world by being named the globe's seventh most efficient country by the World Economic Forum. The 2014-2015 edition of the Global Competitive Report placed Rwanda 7th for the efficiency of its public management. The country beat Switzerland (9th) and Luxemburg (10th). Rwanda was particularly praised for minimising waste in government expenditure.

The head of the Rwandan Governance Board truly spoke for his proud nation when he told Xinhua news agency:

> We are not surprised by this ranking because it just expresses the reality of what happens in our country. In Rwanda, there is a clear process for management and accountability reporting, particularly in the use of public resources...Rwandans have access to critical information about the government action, the decisions of the administration and the way it establishes its priorities and makes its choices.

Rwanda minimises waste in government expenditure by taking the anti-corruption fight seriously. Post-genocide Rwanda has strengthened oversight institutions and coordinated the fight against corruption. The result has been to reduce global concerns about corruption in the country and make Rwanda more attractive to investors. In 2019, Rwanda was ranked 51st among 180 countries on the Corruption Perceptions Index published by Transparency International. A year earlier, Rwanda was ranked 48. Despite this slight drop, the East African country remains the least corrupt in its region and the third least corrupt on the continent. Rwanda is more transparent than Argentina, Bulgaria, Croatia, Cuba, Greece, Hungary, Mauritius, Slovakia, and Zambia.

There are lessons here for Zambia, whose fight against corruption is erratic and selective. Rwanda's fight against corruption is attributable to strong institutions able and willing to enforce laws without fear or favour, in addition to political will and public anti-corruption education campaigns.

With respect to levelling the playing field so that connections with government officials do not necessarily result in favouritism, Rwanda has introduced an online procurement system for public tenders. This, together with the use of ICT in services such as recruitment, has significantly reduced corrupt practices that almost always arise from interactions between government officials and the public.

Ethnic particularism encourages corruption as government officials seek out persons ethnically affiliated to them for favourable treatment. Rwanda has been aggressive in promoting a One Rwanda policy. Thus, the old colonial-style identity card that showed the holder's ethnicity has been replaced by one that only stipulates Rwandan nationality. This policy, which is reminiscent of Singapore's constitutionally mandated multiracialism, has aided fair treatment for all Rwandese by their government.

Rwanda can now claim a culture of transparency and accountability, making corruption a risky and costly adventure. Every official knows that there are grave consequences for being corrupt. The 2018/2019 report from the Ombudsman's office reports an 80 percent conviction rate in the 45 cases of corruption examined.

Lee Kuan Yew's Singapore and Paul Kagame's Rwanda have been criticised by some observers for running authoritarian regimes. The argument goes further to claim that had these countries been fuller democracies, economic progress would have been much slower. The implication of the argument is that economic prosperity is easier to deliver in countries that are not fully democratic.

It is certainly true that the United Kingdom experienced phenomenal economic growth in the late 18th century when only one-fifth of the men had the right to vote and no women could vote at all. Evidence of authoritarianism is abundant during the early years of other prosperous countries such as the United States and the East Asian Tigers.

Authoritarianism is not, however, a prerequisite for prosperity. Indeed it can hinder progress as North Korea never fails to demonstrate. Democracy, on the other hand, is more likely than not to promote prosperity. Consider the case of Botswana.

When Botswana became independent in 1966, there was widespread concern about the new nation's ability to fend for itself. The country was one of the poorest on earth with a GDP per capita of only USD60. Many considered the country 'dead on arrival'.

From its inception, however, the Botswana government has been democratic, championing human rights (including gender rights) and promoting social welfare. From independence to the 1990s, Botswana recorded the highest economic growth rate in the world. Botswana's GDP per capita in 2018 stood at USD18,616, higher than Albania, Bosnia & Herzegovina, Brazil, Cambodia, China, Colombia, and Kosovo.

Botswana has far less rain than Zambia and what Zambians call drought conditions tend to be the norm in Botswana. Like Zambia, Botswana was also threatened by apartheid South Africa from inception until 1994, when democracy was finally introduced in its large neighbouring country.

The impact of both bad weather and negative geopolitics was mitigated in Botswana by good leadership. The country's founding president promoted ethnic harmony along Singaporean lines. He was equally aggressive in implementing policies that enhanced economic growth, respected long-term planning, and promoted order and stability. Furthermore, he guarded against corruption at a time when few understood the negative impact of corruption on economic and social development. President Sir Seretse Khama united Botswana's ethnic and cultural groups by identifying common cultural practices and explaining the structures of the new government as no more than a modernisation of the practices they were already familiar with. This made it easier for the Batswana to understand and indigenise democracy.

Khama's policies, which were followed by his successors, are largely responsible for Botswana's astonishing growth from being one of the world's poorest nations to being a stable middle-income democracy. The country moved rapidly from being a largely agrarian society to an export economy built around beef, copper, diamonds, and tourism. These gains were consolidated when the Botswana Development Corporation was established in 1970 to attract foreign investment in tourism, manufacturing and agriculture.

In 2017, only 38 countries in the world had a larger balance of payments current account surplus than Botswana whose surplus was greater than those of Bermuda, Brunei, Cuba, Malta, and Portugal. Because of a sustained period of balance of payments surpluses and prudent investment guidelines, Botswana has accumulated significant reserves relative to the country's total import of goods and services.

In April 2008, Botswana's foreign exchange reserves reached an all-time high of USD10.3 billion. From late 2008, reserves started to decline on account of outflows and asset revaluations arising from the global economic recession. This trend has, however, been reversed in recent years.

As of April 2015, the reserves stood at USD7.2 billion. With a drop in reserves to USD6.5 billion, the import cover was also reduced to 9.8 months in November 2019. While this figure may appear low to the Botswana government, most economists consider a six-month import cover in reserves healthy. In any event, based on past performance, there is reason to believe that Botswana's reserves will go up again.

By way of comparison, Zambia's foreign exchange reserves decreased to USD1.352 billion in November 2019 from USD1.407 billion in October 2019, representing about eight weeks of import cover. In reality Zambia's foreign exchange reserves are illusory because with the external public debt standing at a minimum of USD11.1 billion, representing 54 percent of GDP, the country must spend USD1.5 billion in external debt servicing in 2020. That represents over 110 percent of current international reserves. According to The Economist, only 29 countries globally, led by Mongolia, have a higher debt burden than Zambia.

In contrast, in 2020, Botswana had an external public debt of USD2.5 billion, representing 35 percent of GDP, making it one of the least indebted countries in the world. Debt is fuelled in part by corruption, such as bribery to win a contract. The construction industry is particularly noted for this vice. While estimates of the value of losses through corruption vary, the World Economic Forum puts the figure at between 10 and 30 percent. This figure does not include losses arising through mismanagement and inefficiency. This means that when a government with corrupt officials requires USD1 million to construct a kilometre of paved road, that government could be forced to borrow as much as $1.3 million for every kilometre of road it needs to build, the extra USD300,000 going into bribes.

Botswana's low debt may be explained in part by the relative transparency of the country. Transparency International's Corruption Perception Index of 2019 ranks Botswana as the 34th most transparent country of 180 jurisdictions surveyed. That ranking may not be as good as Singapore's but it is much better than Zambia's ranking of 113th.

Singapore, Rwanda, and Botswana do not have any conspicuous natural advantages over Zambia to explain their superior economic and social performances. There is nothing that has been achieved in any one of these three countries that Zambia cannot achieve.

Indeed, Zambia can be even more successful, being better endowed with natural resources than these countries, in addition to having peaceable people. The people of Zambia need to have more self-belief and a greater commitment at the individual level to national wellbeing. All three countries referenced above took concrete steps to enhance national unity and to encourage nationals to think of themselves as nationals first, and not as members of any of the constituent ethnicities. They also made conscious efforts to develop viable domestic economies driven by the private sector, with nationals playing a key role. They further invested in institutions designed to eliminate corruption.

CHAPTER FOUR

Rediscovering Africa

While it is understandable that persons born outside the continent and possessing limited education will readily fall into the trap of believing the (mostly) negative narrative about Africa, it is unfathomable that many Zambians, who ought to know better, enthusiastically cheer on as this narrative is told. Even a casual glance at social media postings reveals an unhealthy enthusiasm for negative propaganda about the African continent by Zambians and other Africans. I have often read the most mystifying nonsense about Africa and Zambia subscribed to by even otherwise sophisticated Zambians. One sometimes gets the impression that these supporters of the foreign-inspired narrative about their region desire nothing less than general continental failure, which would fulfil the dreams of ill-intentioned propagators of the narrative.

It also has to be said that not all Africans are epigones of international afro sceptics. Indeed, most educated Nigerians show a willingness to challenge the narrative. The Ethiopian and Ghanaian intelligentsia can also be placed in this category. For example, in his book *A New Narrative for Africa: Voice and Agency*, Abiodum Alao, professor of African Studies at King's College, London calls for a fresh narrative about the continent which reflects the multi-disciplinary dimensions of Africa's journey from pre-colonial sovereignty to post-colonial independence.

Another book, Challenging Perceptions of Africa in Schools, edited by Barbara O'Toole, Ebun Joseph, and David Nyaluke, challenges the way children are taught about the African continent in the Global North, with specific reference to the Republic of Ireland. The book examines in detail the widespread negative imagery and messages about African people and African countries and the impact this has on the attitudes and perceptions of children and young people. It further explores how the kind of stereotyping addressed in this book can be challenged in classrooms through an educational approach grounded in empathy, interdependence, and social justice.

The imagery complained of is unfortunately sometimes perpetuated by Africans themselves. An example of this is a social media post published on Facebook on 23 February 2019, during national elections in Nigeria. The post claimed President Muhammadu Buhari, through sheer incompetence, had voted for his main opposition, the People's Democratic Party. The post, complete with a photograph showing President Buhari raising a ballot with an ink mark next to the PDP logo, was shared more than 6,800 times, attracting more than 1,000 comments and 2,700 reactions.

The photograph turned out to be a doctored version of a picture of Buhari voting during Nigeria's 2015 elections. Those Nigerians who protested the post were well within their rights to do so. At least they read the post with scepticism, while Zambian social media commentators, almost without exception, took the post at face value and reshared it.

While the target of this particular denigration was Nigeria, such posts generally aim to ridicule the entire African continent. Sadly, only countries such as Ethiopia and Nigeria seem consistent in challenging the narrative, although more and more Africans will do so in the future, given the growing confidence among youth on the continent.

As Richard Follett and Tosin Adebisi of Sussex University have pointed out, legacies of colonialism, bad governance, weak institutions and poverty continue to haunt many African nations. There is a new generation of young Africans however, which is using social media and gaining a global perspective that was simply not available to previous generations. This generation is self-aware and self-accepting. This may well be the generation that succeeds in changing the negative narrative about the African continent.

Until then, we can expect more stories such as the one I received from a number of Zambians, following the postponement of the 2019 Nigerian presidential election for a week. The story was that pre-marked ballot papers had been found bearing the date of the original elections. The transmitters of the story exploited the opportunity to enthusiastically spread negative information about an African country.

On this occasion, 'proof' of African electoral dishonesty consisted of a photograph showing a man standing outside a bus with a huge pile of papers.

The caption: 'A J5 Bus full of thumb printed ballot papers was intercepted by the Nigerian Police in Bida, Niger State yesterday,' seemed conclusive.

The problem is, as Africa Check, the independent, non-partisan organisation which assesses claims made in the public arena using journalistic skills and evidence drawn from the latest online tools reported, the caption relied upon by the naysayers had a different preface in different posts, depending on which side the Facebook user supported. Some claimed that all the ballot papers had been thumb printed for Buhari, while others were adamant that the ballot papers had been thumb printed for Atiku, Buhari's rival.

After examining the evidence, Africa Check found that the photo could not be of ballots seized by police on the day of the postponed 2019 election because it was at least four years old. It turned out the photo was first published on the internet in February 2015, when Nigeria held its previous election.

Nonetheless, the post made the rounds on social media without anyone asking the value of premarked ballot papers when only duly-stamped ballot papers signed by the presiding officer on the day of the election are recognised under Nigerian law. It is also telling that there was no mention that in Nigeria printing an unauthorised ballot paper is a criminal offence that carries a fine of NGN50,000,000, the equivalent of USD200,000 at the time of the story.

Another question which any intelligent observer of elections would have asked is: If it is so easy for the government to rig an election, why did the previous government allow itself to lose an election it badly wanted to win in 2015?

Electoral fraud does happen, but it is not a uniquely African vice. Indeed African democracies generally have more transparent electoral systems than say the United States. It is impossible, for example, to imagine the head of the Independent Electoral Commission in Botswana contesting an election without resigning from his job. And yet, that is what happened in Georgia when Brian Kemp, the self-styled Trump conservative, refused to step aside as Georgia's secretary of state when he ran for state governor against Stacy Abrams. As secretary of state, he oversaw the elections in the state.

The obvious conflict of interest prompted former President Jimmy Carter to opine that Kemp's candidature ran 'counter to the most fundamental principle of democratic elections—that the electoral process be managed by an independent and impartial election authority.'

At about the same time social media activists were accusing Nigeria of electoral malpractice, a North Carolina Republican political operative at the centre of an absentee ballot fraud scheme that led to the state ordering a rerun of a congressional election, was arrested and charged with obstruction of justice.

Leslie McCrae Dowless was charged with three felony counts of obstruction of justice, two counts of conspiring to commit obstruction of justice and two counts of unlawful possession of absentee ballots. Allegations that operatives working for Dowless illegally collected and filled absentee ballots on behalf of Republican candidate Mark Harris' campaign emerged shortly after the November 2018 election.

Social media critics of Nigerian electoral practices made no reference to this real case of malpractice. In a world where too many people treat Africa as a single entity, false accusations against one country have the effect of defaming the entire continent.

In many interactions with Zambian leaders, only a handful recognise this danger. One of these leaders is Dr Inonge Mbikusita-Lewanika. The former Zambian ambassador to the United States is a graduate of New York University, where she obtained a doctorate in elementary education. Dr Mbikusita-Lewanika believes, rightly, that relations between African countries and the rest of the world would improve vastly if the continent's diversity is better appreciated. Appreciation of this diversity would certainly benefit Zambia. She therefore places a duty on all Zambians to take the opportunity to educate the world about this diversity.

Understanding that Africa is a large and diverse continent would minimise the unfair treatment African countries frequently receive. When there is a problem in any of the 55 nations on the continent, that problem is almost always seen as a problem from Africa, rather than a Somali or Eastern Congolese problem, for example. I recall a conversation I had with a young Canadian woman interested in travelling to some African countries as a tourist. When she visited a travel agent for advice about where she might go, the agent told her she would need rape insurance to visit Africa! This would be the equivalent of warning someone in the 1970s not to visit Bavaria because there was a civil war ('the troubles') in Northern Ireland.

It is this kind of injurious ignorance that makes it necessary to explain that Africa is a huge continent of 55 countries, over 100 jurisdictions, and more than 1500 languages, and a similar number of cultures. In terms of land mass, it is larger than the United States, Europe, and China combined. The continent has a population of 1.2 billion people, and by 2050 that population is expected to double to 2.4 billion.

Africans are more diverse genetically than the inhabitants of the rest of the world combined, according to an authoritative report published in April 2009 in the journal Science Express. In reaching this conclusion, researchers sampled the bloodlines of more than 100 distinct populations.

It surely is an inevitable logical deduction that people as diverse as Africans cannot all be the same, as they are frequently portrayed. It is, therefore, nonsensical to predict behaviour based on being African.

Yet, that is what frequently happens.

Africa and COVID-19

At the time of writing this, a pandemic is ravaging the world. The death toll of the coronavirus disease is extremely high, particularly in the United States. This has led to legitimate fears about global health.

Assessment of the global pandemic on the African continent is quite revealing.

The head of a respected American think tank, speaking on a US television network toward the end of April 2020, bemoaned the lack of preparedness and facilities to fight the pandemic 'in Africa'. He was reflecting what has almost become conventional wisdom that the African continent cannot handle the pandemic. Certainly, some countries on this vast and diverse continent did struggle in 2020 to provide services to all who needed them as a result of the disease. Liberia is a case in point. The assistant secretary-general of the country's National Health Workers

Union said publicly that the country was far from prepared for the pandemic.

It is unhelpful, however, to assume, as the head of the think tank seemed to, that Africans have no choice but to wait for foreign aid to address this unique health challenge. Given the continent's complexities, it is prudent to listen to experts with experience managing health crises in African countries. Casual commentary by generalists is not particularly useful in this regard.

One expert who believes that (at least some) African countries have much to offer in the fight against COVID-19 is Dr Mary Stephen of the World Health Organisation. Dr Stephen noted that African countries previously hit by deadly Ebola outbreaks were using lessons learned from that experience to fight the coronavirus pandemic. These countries know how to rapidly track down, screen and quarantine potential patients. Indeed, the ability to track down potential patients is not limited to countries with vast Ebola experience. In April 2020, an undocumented immigrant in Zambia, a country with virtually no Ebola experience, escaped from quarantine in Lusaka, fearing that her status might be discovered. She was tracked down, in a different city, within hours.

This should not be surprising as Zambia designed a programme to fight COVID-19 through active case finding, tracing, and lockdown. The country ensured that every hospital and health centre had anti-body testing kits through cooperation between the cashstrapped government and the private sector. In addition, the country had two polymerase chain reaction centres. Furthermore, one of the country's new hospitals was designated a specialised COVID-19 hospital to stop the disease's spread.

The private sector also converted a warehouse into a field hospital. At the time of writing, the field hospital is less than half full. This is splendid organisation and places Dr Stephen's point that no country can experience something as devastating as Ebola without learning from the experience, in context. Zambia did not have a serious outbreak of Ebola but it did have an AIDS epidemic. This experience left behind the capacity on which the country built to prepare itself for future crises.

The coronavirus pandemic has also aided innovation in some African countries. On 13 April 2020, the Cornell Alliance for Science reported that Ugandan researchers had developed an inexpensive COVID-19 test kit that, according to Makerere vice chancellor Professor Barnabas Nawangwe, can deliver results within five minutes.

At about the same time, Al Jazeera reported that a lab in Senegal had produced a one-dollar testing kit that boosted the authorities' ambition to test everyone. The bigger worry in the country was the shortage of ventilators; there were only 50 for a population of 16 million when coronavirus was recognised as a pandemic. But that too was addressed as Senegalese engineers found a way to manufacture ventilators using a 3D printing machine. At USD60 each, most, if not all, hospitals in the country were henceforth able to afford new ventilators.

It is little wonder that at the time of writing, Senegal had the third-largest number of COVID-19 recoveries in the world, ahead of France and the United States. In addition to increased opportunities for testing, Senegal and some other countries in Africa took screening seriously even before COVID-19 being designated a pandemic. For example, as far back as December 2019, countries such as South Africa and Zambia were screening international passengers for abnormally high temperatures and isolating those in that state.

While the American think tank head made no mention of these proactive steps, he was categorical that measures such as 'social distancing' were 'nonstarters' in countries such as Egypt and Nigeria. Cairo and Lagos are certainly crowded cities, but many parts of the African continent are not. The more important point is that just because a place is crowded is no reason to give up on implementing measures designed to minimise the spread of infection through human contact.

In South Africa, for example, 30,000 community health workers were recruited to screen, test, and trace people with COVID-19. According to The Economist, many of these recruits were already working in projects to prevent HIV or trace the contacts of people infected with tuberculosis.

In densely populated townships where social isolation was not feasible, when a COVID-19 positive result was identified, the screening teams helped the resident with medical care and, if necessary, quarantine. Neighbours would, in these circumstances, also be screened and potentially tested.

In implementing these systems, South Africans understood that the country could not avoid an escalation in the number of cases. But the aim was to maximise preparedness for escalation by expanding the healthcare infrastructure before that escalation took place.

In Nigeria, a mobile app that proved effective in preventing the spread of Ebola was updated for COVID-19. The app connects health workers and potentially infected people. It also monitors potential patients' symptoms, and triggers ambulance services to move them into quarantine.

Dr Stephen praised African countries for sharing best practices with one another. Perhaps the best evidence that continental cooperation worked during the COVID-19 crisis is in the data. On 1 May 2020, there were 3,334,416 COVID-19 cases worldwide. The number of people killed by the virus stood at 237,942, with recoveries at 864,237. With a population of 1.2 billion people, the African continent had 38,825 cases, 1,634 deaths, and 12,543 recoveries. By contrast, the United States, with a third of the African population, had 1.13 million cases, 65,253 deaths and 137,000 recoveries.

It is not axiomatic that the entire African continent will be 'devastated' by COVID-19 or any other virus. Certainly, there will be loss of life and some countries will be crippled by a catastrophe of this nature. The impact of any pandemic will, however, be different in disparate countries and regions. If we are going to find real solutions to any health crisis, we must recognise the diversity of need and circumstance on the continent as Dr Mbikusita-Lewanika urged.

Misunderstanding a Diverse and Rich Continent

Lumping all countries and cultures into one convenient label called 'Africa' serves the interests of those who wish to perpetuate the image of the continent as an uncultured backward entity with absolutely no capacity for technological or any other form of advancement. The continent is depicted as a place of constant conflict and a total stranger to peace. This generalised depiction also makes it difficult for those with a more realistic understanding of the continent to respond because of the usual challenges of responding to generalisations and stereotypes. How, for example, would Botswana and Mauritius respond to claims of

African economic incompetence? The historically well-managed countries would point to their phenomenal growth since independence and their rapid transformation from low-income to middle-income countries. But that response would do nothing to silence the accuser, who would simply point out that he was referring to 'the rest of Africa'.

To understand today's Africa, we need to go back in time, as this book attempted in the first chapter. The purpose of history is to explain that the continent has an impressive past and is far from uncultured. It is all too convenient for beneficiaries of historical African oppression to call for 'moving on'. The continent must certainly move on and not allow its countries to be eternally handicapped by slavery and colonial history. But this cannot happen without understanding the past and the present. It is important to know, for example, why the instinct of so many in Europe and North American is to look down on darkskinned Africans.

From the beginning of trans-Atlantic slavery to today, North Americans and Europeans have perceived Africans largely through the prism of racism. This racism was necessary to justify slavery and the harsh treatment of officially emancipated black people. The continuation of slavery would have been that much harder had all participants accepted the humanity of the Africans who were sold as chattel.

Criminologists will agree that every offender seeks justification for his actions. A criminal might, for example, justify murder on the basis that the person slain did not deserve to live. A burglar may justify his theft on the basis that the person whose house was burgled had himself stolen his wealth and deserved to be deprived of it.

I once heard a member of the Zambian white ghetto suggest that Africans were enslaved because they must somehow have been inferior to the enslavers. The logic of this argument can have deleterious effects, especially in the context of crimes such as sexual assault, because it gives credence to the argument that victims always deserve what they get. Let us imagine a situation where a highly cerebral professor of mathematics is raped by a muscular, morally deficient man of limited intelligence. Would it not be absurd to suppose in this case that the professor, by virtue of being savagely attacked by her assailant, was somehow inferior to the assailant?

Would it not be equally absurd to suggest that the inhabitants of the Irish village of Baltimore who were taken as slaves on 20 June 1631 by North African slave traders were necessarily inferior to their captors? And yet, this is the conclusion we must draw in both examples based on the theory advanced by the white ghetto dweller referenced above.

This is the kind of reasoning that fathered race theories about Africans. The theories made slavery and racism more palatable to the beneficiaries of these practices, and succeeded in indoctrinating the victims into believing that it was their fault that they were abused, in much the same way that victims of sexual abuse tend to blame themselves for the abuse inflicted on them.

The casual manner in which these theories emerged and took root is well described by David Olusoga, Professor of Public History at Manchester University:

> The book that, arguably, did the most to disseminate racial ideas about Africans was written by a man who never set foot on African soil. Edward Long was a slave owner and the son of a slave owner, his family having been in Jamaica since the middle of the 17th century. His ideas about black people and Africa were widely accepted as being rigorous and scientific, although Long had no scientific training. The book that made him famous, his History of Jamaica (1774), was not a history book but rather a strange hybrid; part travel guide, part discussion of British colonial rule and economics in the Caribbean, and part political score-settling. But it is also the classic text of 18th-century European pseudo-scientific racism.[31]

Long was successful in conveying the idea that Africans were irredeemably inferior and might not even be human. These ideas gave comfort to beneficiaries of slavery, who might otherwise have balked at the idea of trading in humanity. Long's ideas were later to justify colonialism whose perpetrators were happy to assume that African peoples would live in a state of lawlessness and brutality without subjugation by a 'superior' power, on account of their lack of education and culture. Thus, Long set the stage for the colonial racism described in this book and the suppression of the kind of history discussed in

---

[31] Olusoga, David, The Roots of European Racism Lie in the Slave Trade, Colonialism and Edward Long, The Guardian, 8 September, 2015

Chapter One. The Kongo and Luba/Lunda peoples were not unique among Africans in creating viable civilisations as will be demonstrated shortly.

Resilient Africans

Edward Long's unscientific theories about Africans persisted even in the face of extraordinary achievements by enslaved Africans and their descendants. The prejudiced mind does not easily allow new ideas to enter it. For this reason, the achievements of African Americans in the post-slavery world rarely influence the narrative.

Not many groups of people in the world would rise from bondage and racism as experienced by African-Americans and make the contributions African-Americans have actually made to global civilisation. Slaves were not encouraged to study, and there were often severe penalties for attempting to do so. This is the environment in which Phillis Wheatley, the first African-American to publish an anthology, educated herself.

The challenges faced by intellectually curious African-Americans of the time are well articulated by Heather Andrea Williams in her book, Self-Taught. The work was approvingly reviewed in 2005 by the Harvard Educational Review. The following excerpt is from that review:

> In Self-Taught: African American Education in Slavery and Freedom, Heather Andrea Williams meticulously chronicles African Americans' quest for education. Focused specifically on the struggle that began in the antebellum period and continued through Reconstruction, Williams's analysis is punctuated with rich anecdotes of ordinary African Americans' personal and collective fight for education.

> Most White Southern slaveholders were adamantly opposed to the education of their slaves because they feared an educated slave population would threaten their authority. Williams documents a series of statutes that criminalized any person who taught slaves or supported their efforts to teach themselves. One statute in particular, passed in North Carolina in 1830, articulated that "any free person, who shall hereafter teach, or attempt to teach, any slave within this State to read or write, the use of figures excepted, or shall give or sell to such slave

or slaves any books or pamphlets, shall be liable to indictment in any court of record in this State." The statute was enacted because of a fear that if slaves became literate they would also become critical of their slave status and eventually rebel.

Slaves who attempted to educate themselves, if caught, suffered physical and psychological consequences. Nonetheless, even under the strict limitations of slavery, slaves still developed ingenious strategies to become literate. Williams tells the story of slaves who received their instruction in "pit schools," so named as such because they were "pit[s] in the ground way out in the woods away from the master's surveillance." She also writes about slaves who "hid spelling books under their hats to be ready whenever they could entreat or bribe a literate person to teach them." During the Civil War — a time when the fate of the institution of slavery was yet undetermined — African Americans' desire to learn continued to burn. Williams tells of some Black soldiers studying their lessons during their lunch breaks and grasping at every opportunity to advance their education. She found that "during the transition from slavery to freedom, many African Americans simultaneously attempted to satisfy material needs with intellectual longing." She presents detailed evidence of African Americans simultaneously clamouring for their education and their freedom.

Upon emancipation, White southerners' fear of an educated Black population did not dissipate; they used violence and arson to prevent attempts to educate the freed slaves. Yet, in spite of the danger and meagre resources, many Black freed slaves constructed and operated their own schools. Williams discusses how students would ask for longer class days and shorter vacations in order to maximize their instructional time. They would walk miles from their homes to the nearest school, some "barefoot, wearing torn, ragged clothing." Parents who could not attend schools themselves encouraged their children to learn as much as possible. These independent African American schools, Williams argues, served as "the central point of an educational sphere, as students as taught became teachers at home."

Given this history, it is remarkable that slaves and their offspring acquired enough education to make groundbreaking inventions. These inventions are too numerous to recognise here. A handful of examples will suffice for our purposes.

A Boston-based slave known only as **Onesimus**, and described as 'a pretty intelligent fellow' by his owner, the Puritan Minister Cotton Mather, proposed inoculation against smallpox in North America in 1721. Onesimus recalled a procedure from his homeland that involved rubbing pus from an infected person into an open wound on the arm.

Of the 242 people subsequently inoculated in Boston, 236 did not catch the disease; a 97.5 percent success rate.

Thomas L. Jennings was an African-American tradesman and abolitionist in New York City where he operated and owned a tailoring business. In 1821, he was granted a patent for his method of dry cleaning.

Henry Blair invented the corn planter. He was not a slave at the time of this invention and was operating his own business. At best, Blair was crudely educated and signed his patent document with an X, indicating that he was illiterate.

Sarah Boone was a North Carolina-born African-American inventor who obtained a United States patent for significant improvements to the ironing board. Because of these positive changes, Boone's wooden ironing board improved the quality of ironing sleeves and the bodies of women's garments.

Canadian-born Elijah McCoy is perhaps the best known of all of North America's black inventors. His inventions improved industrial lubrication and had 57 registered patents in the United States. One of the patents was for inventing an automatic lubricator for oiling the steam engines of locomotives and ships.

Lewis Howard Latimer is less well known than Thomas Edison, although his contribution to science is no less significant. Latimer invented the carbon filament for the light bulb, which was more durable than Edison's paper alternative. Latimer is also believed to have invented the telephone while working as Alexander Bell's assistant. There is no concrete proof that Bell is undeserving of recognition as the inventor of the phone, but the failure to recognise Latimer's contribution is disconcerting. It reminds one of the relationship between Christiaan Barnard and Hamilton Maki with respect to their collaboration on the first heart transplant famously performed at Groote Schuur Hospital in 1967.

Maki received no immediate recognition for his contribution to the medical breakthrough, although Barnard described him as having incredible dexterity and finesse. Barnard also regretted that his unacknowledged collaborator never had the opportunity to get a formal education. It was only after the end of apartheid that Maki was recognised and given an honourary master of science degree in medicine.

Sarah E. Goode was an entrepreneur and inventor. She is remembered as the first African-American woman to be granted a patent by the U.S. Patent and Trademark Office, for inventing a folding cabinet bed in 1885.

Granville Woods was the inventor of electrical apparatus that support the telephone, street cars etc. He registered 60 patents.

John Standard is considered the inventor of the modern fridge because he patented improvements to the refrigerator and oil stove.

George Washington Carver was a horticulturist who invented products from peanuts, sweet potatoes, and gasoline from soybeans. In his late 20s Carver obtained a high-school education in Kansas while working as a farmhand. His bachelor's degree in agricultural science was obtained in 1894, followed by a Master of Science degree two years later, from Iowa State Agricultural College (later Iowa State University). He had a close relationship with Henry Ford, the automobile manufacturer.

Percy Julian was an African American research chemist and pioneer in the chemical synthesis of medicinal drugs such as cortisone, steroids, and birth control pills. He attended the University of Vienna from 1929 to 1931.

Otis Boykin was an African American inventor and engineer. His inventions include improved electrical resistors used in computing, missile guidance, and pacemakers. In 1959, he patented a wire precision resistor that allowed specific amounts of electrical currents to flow for a particular purpose. This was followed by another invention: a new resistor that withstood shifts in temperature and air pressure. As a result of this invention, many electronic devices could now be made cheaply and more reliably than before.

Lonnie George Johnson is an aerospace engineer and entrepreneur. He invented the Linex robot when he was still a teenager and demonstrated it at the Alabama Science fair in 1968. He was the only black exhibitor. He won first prize.

Johnson is now better known for inventing the Super Soaker water gun, which he licensed in 1989 to Larami Corporation. Within the first two years on the market, the Super Soaker generated over USD200 million in retail sales and became the number one selling toy in the United States. By 2016, the sales figure reached USD1 billion. He was more fortunate than Onesimus, who never got a cent for introducing North Americans to the smallpox vaccine.

University of Karaouine

Pre-colonial Organisation

There is something ironic about associating pre-colonial Africa with lack of culture and education given that the oldest existing and continually operating educational institution in the world is on the continent. The University of Karueein (also written Al-Karaouine) was founded in 859 AD by a woman called Fatima al-Fihri in Fez, Morocco. Karueein established a reputation as a global centre for the advancement of science and technology and continued in this manner until 1963 when it was incorporated into Morocco's modern state university system.

To be sure, Europe did establish an excellent university—University of Bologna, Italy—but that came 229 years after the founding of Karueein. Bologna is Europe's oldest university.

Better known than Karueein is Timbukutu (or Timbuktu), which many historians say is the oldest university in the world. This does not appear to be accurate, however. The claim arises from the fact that the affiliated University of Sankore has its roots in the Sankore Mosque founded in 989 AD by Al-Qadi Aqib ibn Mahmud ibn Umar, the Supreme Judge of Timbuktu. By the 12th century, the City of Timbuktu was thriving and attracted many learned people who prioritised the creation of learning centres. This is how the city earned its reputation as the global centre of learning.

University of Timbuktu

The University of Timbuktu was not an integral part of the University of Sankore. But even if we assume a necessary link between the two, Karueein would still have more legitimacy in its claim to being the oldest university in the world because Sankore was founded 130 years after Karueein.

Nonetheless, Timbuktu is noteworthy for its contributions to learning and civilisation. Thabo Mbeki, a former South African president, initiated the South Africa-Mali Project to preserve the Timbuktu manuscripts because of his belief that the history of Timbuktu is essential for any understanding of the continent's past and can play a critical role in the renaissance of the continent.

This is the same thinking that led to UNESCO granting world heritage site status to Timbuktu to recognize its importance to world history.

The sophistication of 12th century Timbuktu is remarkable. The university awarded degrees of learning called primary, secondary and superior. These degrees would be equivalent to a bachelor, master and PhD today. The superior degree took a decade to complete and consisted of highly specialized learning under supervision from distinguished professors. In addition, the university hosted the Circle of Knowledge that served as a specialized club of scholars and professors. Most of the teaching was religious in nature, but literature, mathematics, and science were also taught.

One manuscript preserved under the South Africa-Mali Project speaks about scientific methods of child delivery. The manuscript was written in the 13th century. Social scientists are not unanimous about what constitutes a comprehensive list of the key elements of civilisation, but they agree that these elements must include organised government, population centres, religion, communication and infrastructure.

Pre-colonial Mali may well have been the contemporary paragon of education and civilisation. In 1550, Joannes Leo Africanus, a Muslim-born diplomat who later converted to Catholicism and served Pope Leo X, described Timbukutu as a place with many judges, doctors and clerics, all receiving good salaries from King Askia Mohammed of the State of Songhay. Leo said the king had great respect for educated people, which made the trade in books very profitable.

Leo did not exaggerate the value placed on books and learning in ancient Mali. Despite the destruction of thousands of documents during the insurgency in 2013, 700,000 manuscripts on subjects such as mathematics, chemistry, physics, optics, astronomy, medicine, history, geography, and many others have survived from the medieval era, both in public libraries and in private collections. These manuscripts are now being digitalised.

Impressive as it was, Mali was not the only pre-colonial empire on the African continent to easily satisfy the core elements of civilisation.

Ethiopia is one of the world's oldest countries, having been founded by Menelik 1 in the 10th century BC. The country's first capital was Axum (aka Aksum), in Ethiopia's northern part. Aksum developed a distinct architecture that involved constructing colossal stone obelisks, some of which exceeded a hundred feet in height. The Kingdom of Aksum was also one of the first Christian countries in the world, having officially adopted Christianity as the state religion in the fourth century. Indeed, the Ethiopian Orthodox Church (called Tewahedo in Amharic) is one of the oldest organized Christian bodies in the world. This early connection to Christianity has given credence to Axum's claims that it is the resting place of the Ark of the Covenant.

As the Roman Empire rose and fell, Aksum thrived but few think of it in the same way as they do the Roman Empire. This is surprising given that Aksum was a trading giant endowed with gold and ivory in great demand in ancient Europe and the Far East by the second and third centuries.

Communication and the spread of Christianity was made easier by the development of Ge'ez, one of the first written scripts to come out of Africa. The earliest known inscriptions in the Ge'ez script go back to 5 BC. Initially, Ge'ez represented only consonants, with vowel indication starting to appear only in the fourth century AD during the reign of King Ezana.

The declaration of Christianity as a state religion led to a political and military alliance with the Byzantines. The relationship was so close that the Byzantine Emperor often referred to the King of Aksum as 'brother,' suggesting that the Eastern Roman Empire saw Aksum as an equal, at least in the conduct of foreign affairs.

There is another town that lies 543.4 kilometres south of Axum, with impressive Christian credentials. In the 12th century, Emperor Gebre Mesqal Lalibela, a Christian king, responded to the 1187 capture of Jerusalem by the Muslim forces of Salah al-Din by ordering the construction of a second Jerusalem on Ethiopian soil. The result of this vision was an impressive piece of architecture connecting 11 churches, each carved from a single piece of rock to symbolize spirituality and humility. The churches were carved into the rose-gold mountain rocks. Bet Giorgis, separate from the other churches, perhaps attracts more attention than the other holy structures, being built in the shape of a perfectly symmetrical crucifix that stands 15 metres high. As the name suggests, this church is dedicated to St George, Ethiopia's patron saint. It is not unusual for visitors to Lalibela to believe the legend that this feat of engineering and architecture was accomplished with the aid of angels from above.

Lalibela

Lalibela continues to be an active centre of Christian activity, attracting multitudes of monks, nuns, and worshippers, in addition to local and foreign tourists. Pilgrims to Lalibela are typically wrapped in white clothing.

Ethiopia is fortunate not to have been formally colonised and to have living monuments of greatness such as Lalibela and the Obelisk of Axum. The country's history is well preserved in human memory and in texts aided by an alphabet first used 3000 years ago.

It is not for want of interest on the part of European powers that Ethiopia escaped colonialism. The death of Emperor Yohannes IV on 10 March 1889 was followed by disorder in the realm because of fighting among potential successors to the throne. Yohannes was a skilled emperor who allowed regional governors a measure of autonomy. His death, however, left no obvious constitutional successor. Prior to the commencement of the fight for succession, the Italians had supported Sahle Mariam of Shewa, who ruled central Ethiopia. That support included modern weaponry and funds, which helped the ambitious Mariam to consolidate his power by incorporating smaller Ethiopian kingdoms under his rule and, after Yohannes IV's death, to secure his claim to the title of emperor, taking the name Menilek II.

Menelik II joined Italy to sign the Treaty of Wichale on 2 May 1889, which included Italy's promise to provide a much-needed loan to Ethiopia in exchange for the grant of the northern Ethiopian territories today known as Eritrea and Tigray. Article XVII of the treaty was vague in defining the relationship between Ethiopia and Italy with respect to the conduct of foreign relations. Menelik understood the article to allow Ethiopia to use the Italian government in dealings with foreign powers. The Italian Prime Minister, Francesco Crispi had a different interpretation, however. He understood the article to mean that Ethiopia had to utilize the Italian government and that Ethiopia was in effect an Italian protectorate.

The different interpretations of the article triggered a dispute that led to Menelik first repudiating the offending article in September 1890 and the entire treaty three years later. Menelik knew that this was a risky move in light of the presence of Italian troops in now colonised Eritrea. So, he began preparing for a possible attack by Italy. That attack took place in 1895.

Menelik's forces, which numbered more than 100,000, were well armed with modern weaponry. But Menelik shrewdly understated his own military strength through leaked reports which falsely suggested that he not only had a limited number of troops, but that these troops were demoralised and discontented.

The emperor's plan to goad the Italians into a premature attack on Ethiopia from Eritrea worked.

Gen. Oreste Baratieri, the Eritrean-based Italian commander, advanced on Adwa with 14,500 men believing they were more than enough to overcome the reportedly small and demoralised Ethiopian army. Little did he know he was about to provoke a more disciplined army of 100,000 Ethiopians. The disorganised Italian columns found the terrain difficult to navigate and their inadequate supplies did not help with morale. After a sound routing on March 1, the Italians retreated through difficult terrain, suffering 6000 deaths and surrendering some 4000 prisoners to the Ethiopians. Thus, 69 percent of Italy's soldiers were either killed or captured. The Ethiopians also suffered casualties. 5,000 of their troops were killed, while another 8,000 were wounded in the Battle of Adwa. This, however, was only 13 percent of all Ethiopian forces.

Following Ethiopia's victory at Adwa, the Treaty of Wichale was formally abrogated and the Treaty of Addis Ababa signed in October 1896. Peace was restored. Italy was the big loser. In addition to losing its claim as protector of Ethiopia, the Italian colony of Eritrea was reduced in size to 200,000 square kilometres by a September 1900 treaty of peace.

The Benin Empire may not have had Ethiopia's military prowess or Mali's prestigious universities but excelled in engineering and town and country planning. Benin was founded in the 11th century. Benin City should be famous for its walls, but it sadly is not despite the best efforts of authors such as the London-based science writer Fred Pearce. Benin City walls should at the very least be as well-known as the Great Wall of China, which has an estimated length of 21,196 kilometres. Writing in the New Scientist in 2016, Fred Pearce, estimates that Benin City's walls were at one point 'four times longer than the Great Wall of China, and consumed a hundred times more material than the Great Pyramid of Cheops'.

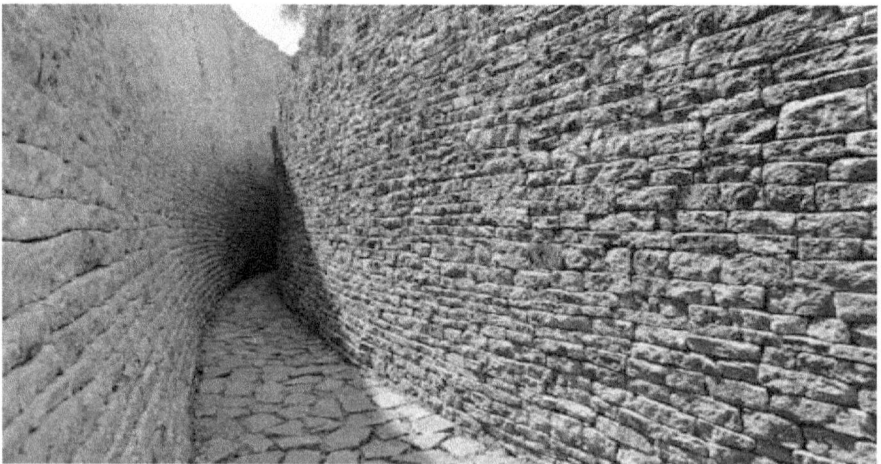

Great Wall of Benin

This account is echoed by Kylie Kiunguyu:

The astounding city was a series of earthworks made up of banks and ditches, called 'Iya' in the Edo language, in the area around present-day Benin City. They consist of 15 kilometres of city Iya and an estimated 16,000 kilometres in the rural area around Benin. The walls stood for over 400 years, protecting the inhabitants of the kingdom, as well as the traditions and civilisation of the Edo people.[32]

Benin City was also one of the first cities in the world to have organised street lighting, consisting of tall metal lamps placed around the city. The empire used its abundant palm oil to fuel the wicks of the lamps, which were routinely lit at sundown.

The first arrival of the Portuguese in Benin is recorded as 1485, the same year that another Portuguese crew landed in Kongo. As with Kongo, the Portuguese were amazed by Benin's splendour. Particular attention was paid to the way the kingdom was designed, being made up of hundreds of interlocked cities and villages. The Portuguese of the time considered Benin City to be one of the best planned cities in the world.

The observation from Portuguese ship Captain Lourenco Pinto in 1691 is worth noting:

> Great Benin, where the king resides, is larger than Lisbon; all the streets run straight and as far as the eye can see. The houses are large, especially that of the king, which is richly decorated and has fine columns. The city is wealthy and industrious. It is so well governed that theft is unknown and the people live in such security that they have no doors to their houses.[33]

The careful rules of symmetry with which Benin City was planned provoked much interest in the kingdom's planning. As Ron Eglash, the ethnomathematics expert who authored African Fractals explained, Benin City and its surrounding villages were purposely laid out to form perfect fractals, with similar shapes repeated in the rooms of each house, and the house itself, and the clusters of houses in the village in mathematically predictable patterns.

---

[32] Kylie Kiunguyu, This is Africa. African Marvels: The Walls of Benin, March 13, 2019
[33] ibid

The order of the city did also appear to affect the behaviour of the citizens as the following text from Olfert Dapper, a Dutch writer, indicates:

> Benin City is at least four miles wide. The city has wide, straight roads, lined by houses. The houses are large and handsome with walls made from clay. The people are very friendly and there seems to be no stealing.[34]

Eredo may not be as well-known as Benin, but it also holds spectacular evidence that speak to Nigeria's glorious past.

I visited Eredo in November 2016. I was in Lagos on business but made a mental note to visit the remains of this ancient civilisation in my spare time. Eredo's existence had been brought to the attention of today's world by an Anglo-Nigerian team led by archaeologist Patrick Darling.

The first disappointment I had in my search for Eredo was how few people in Lagos knew about this monument of ancient civilisation. Eventually, an enterprising friend of a colleague discovered it was less than two hours drive from Lagos.

Navigating the heavy traffic as we exited Lagos proved to be the hardest part of the journey and Eredo itself was not difficult to find as it is quite close to the main road from Lagos. When we got out of the car, we only had to walk about 90 metres to reach the huge excavation, with ramparts between 12 and 21 metres now covered mostly by thick forest which was unable, however, to shut out the stubborn rays that gave us light as we walked in history.

My second and last disappointment was the lack of attention paid to the unassuming town that hosts Eredo. Despite this lack of attention from the government, the town's inhabitants are enthusiastic about their heritage and willing to share what they know about it. I still have vivid memories of the local historian going through brisk digging motions to demonstrate how the 100-mile long ramparts were built for the queen who ruled ancient Eredo a thousand years ago. Sungbo, the queen, was

---

[34] The Kingdom of Benin, bbc.co.uk/bitesize/topics/zpvckqt/articles/z3n7mp3

wealthy but childless and wanted to secure her legacy by leaving behind a great monument.

Dr Darling's team estimated that the Eredo was probably constructed over three centuries, and its purpose was to serve as a spiritual barrier, not just a physical one. Whatever its purpose, the Eredo has been described as one of the largest monuments in sub-Saharan Africa.

The local historian was correct in estimating that Sungbo's Eredo was built a thousand years ago. Carbon analysis of parts of the rampart showed that it dates from the 10th century and suggested that a highly organized kingdom existed in the rain forest, indicating that this kingdom was strong in architecture, construction and governance.

The Wagadou Empire, also known as Ancient Ghana, exhibited all elements critical to a civilisation. It had thriving urban centres, a monetary system consistent with its status as a major trading centre, political organisation, and culture. The empire is believed to have existed from around 750 to 1235 AD, covering the land mass today known as Mauritania, Senegal and Mali. Ancient Ghana was in fact the first of three great West African empires, the other two being Mali and Songhai. It was known for its wealth and extravagance as evidenced by such practices as placing gold collars on dogs and allowing horses to sleep on custom-made carpets.

The rulers of Ancient Ghana are considered by many historians to have been the wealthiest in the entire world. The proviso here is that Mansa Musa, who became ruler of the Mali Empire in 1312, taking the throne after his predecessor, Abu-Bakr II, was lost at sea during an expedition, remains the wealthiest man ever to have lived. Historians now know that Mansa Musa's wealth was the equivalent of $400 billion in 2019 when adjusted for inflation.[35] But the rulers of Ancient Ghana never lived long enough to see the ascendency of Mansa Musa to the Malian throne, at a time when European nations were struggling for survival as a result of raging civil wars and poverty.

Ancient Ghana had a sophisticated commodity monetary system under which gold served as the unit of value and was physically used as

---

[35] Trtworld.com/Africa/not-jeff-bezos-or-bill-gates-mali-s-mnsa-musa-was-the-richest-man-ever-31658

money. Gold was thus the primary source of wealth for the empire. But iron was also an important source of wealth and used in the manufacture of tools and weapons. This strong metal contributed greatly to the empire's infrastructure and commercial prowess. But it was gold that gave Ancient Ghana global clout.

So abundant was the metal that even livestock and fabrics were traded to the empire in exchange for gold. The main means of transportation to aid international trade was the camel which easily traversed the Sahara Desert, connecting Ancient Ghana to the Near East, North Africa, and Europe. A well-planned government structure with many layers contributed to the perception of Ancient Ghana as a stable, permanent powerhouse with which to do business.

Although the empire was ruled by one king known as the Ghana, which means 'warrior king' in the Soninke language of the Mande ethnic group, the empire was in fact quite decentralised. In reality, it was a federal government system with many officials with authority to make decisions in their areas of jurisdiction. The national army remained loyal to the king for many reasons, including the practice of giving land to those who had satisfactorily performed military service for their country.

This multi-layered government structure allowed the king's edicts and other information from the government to be widely disseminated throughout the empire.

The Kingdom of Malindi had less land than the Wagadou Empire but was nonetheless influential. Ancient Malindi is believed to have been the first Swahili civilisation to come in contact with the Chinese.

Basil Davidson introduces his readers to Malindi with the following words:

> A giraffe arriving at the Chinese court in 1415, together with ambassadors from the East African city state of 'Malin', was understandably received with some attention. The emperor himself agreed to welcome it with stately ceremonial. Accompanied by a 'celestial horse', which was probably a zebra, and a 'celestial stag', which was possibly an oryx, this unlikely beast from the uttermost ends of the western sea was felt to be a singular though not surprising token of worldwide respect. Besides, its safe arrival was something of a triumph.

Its arduous journey had taken it across the Indian Ocean to [Sri Lanka] or southern India and thence, by trans-shipment, onward to China.

This giraffe in any case deserves a place in history, for the ceremonial obligation to accompany ambassadors from distant countries home was among the reasons why the renowned Admiral Cheng-Ho sailed for 'Malin' in 1417, and thus made China's first attested landfall on Africa.[36]

Forty-five years after Davidson penned these words, a joint team of Kenyan and Chinese archaeologists found a small pitted brass coin with a square hole in the centre minted in 15th century China. This important discovery was made in a Kenyan village called Mambrui, north of Malindi. With the help of the team leader, Professor Qin Dashu of Peking University's archaeology department, the inscription, Yongle Tongbao, on the coin was translated. It represented the name of the reign which had minted the coin between 1403 and 1424. The coin was issued by Emperor Yongle, who ruled China at that time, during the Ming Dynasty. Thanks to the inscription of the emperor's name on the coin, dating was relatively easy.

Emperor Yongle is known for commencing construction of China's Forbidden City and his interest in political and trade missions to the lands surrounding the Indian Ocean. He sent Admiral Zheng He, also known as Cheng Ho, to explore foreign shores.

In an October 2010 interview with the BBC, Professor Qin averred that coins such as the one found in the Kenyan village 'were carried only by envoys of the emperor, Chengzu'. He further opined that this particular coin was probably given as a gift from the emperor.

Great Zimbabwe was similar to Malindi in that it too was a city-state. But Zimbabwe had a more visible lasting legacy in the form of an architectural wonder presenting as a stone fortress with gigantic walls.

---

[36] Davidson, Basil, *Which Way Africa? The search for a New Society*, Middlesex, England, Penguin Books Ltd. 1967, page 33.

Great Zimbabwe

One of the first Europeans to visit Great Zimbabwe was a Portuguese sea captain, Viçente Pegado, who encountered the site in 1531. This is how he described the city-state:

> Among the goldmines of the inland plains between the Limpopo and Zambezi rivers [is a] fortress built of stones of marvellous size, and there appears to be no mortar joining them ... This edifice is almost surrounded by hills, upon which are others resembling it in the fashioning of stone and the absence of mortar, and one of them is a tower more than 12 fathoms high.

The construction of Great Zimbabwe began in the 11th century and the city-state was continuously occupied from that time until the middle of the 15th century. The site is dominated by a circular structure known as the elliptical building, whose construction required 18,200 cubic feet of stonework mostly in the form of naturally formed granite rocks. Great Zimbabwe is a confluence of outstanding architecture and natural beauty. The fact that the site's complex drainage system still works, being able to funnel water outside the houses and enclosures down into the valleys, speaks to the excellence of the design and construction of this ancient civilisation.

At its peak, the capital of the Kingdom of Zimbabwe, which spanned 722 hectares, had an estimated population of 18,000 people. Historians believe that only 200 to 300 members of the elite classes actually lived inside its massive stone buildings, watched over at night by guards standing on the walls, while the majority lived some distance away.

European visitors to Great Zimbabwe after Captain Pegado interpreted what they saw in a manner consistent with Edward Long's view of Africans. They struggled with the idea that darkskinned people could have built such a magnificent kingdom. Thus the common view in the 19th century was that Great Zimbabwe was an African replica of the Queen of Sheba's palace in Jerusalem built by non-Africans. The idea was promoted by Karl Mauch, a German explorer who visited the site in 1871 and was quick to dismiss the idea that indigenous Africans could have built such a sophisticated network of monuments.

In August 1978, Peter Storr Garlake, the Zimbabwean-raised archaeologist, told the BBC that theories about Great Zimbabwe's alien origins were plainly wrong. Carbon dating clearly shows Great Zimbabwe was completed in the 12th century, long after the birth of Christ and far removed from the time of King Solomon and the Queen of Sheba.

At the time of its construction, the Shona people were already settled in the area. This, together with the fact that similar (though less imposing buildings) can be found in the surrounding areas, led Garlake to conclude that Great Zimbabwe was indeed built by the ancestors of the current Shona people.

The modern-day archaeological consensus that Great Zimbabwe was built by the Karanga people of the Shona nation seems logical and obvious now, but this was not always the case. From the 1890s until 1905, the need to justify the colonisation of Southern Rhodesia superseded the need to respect archaeological and scientific evidence. For example, the principal authority of the theory that Great Zimbabwe was built by aliens, Richard Hall, was neither a scientist nor an archaeologist. He was a former solicitor and journalist.

Despite evidence after 1905 when David Randall MacIver, an actual archaeologist, showed that the artefacts found at Great Zimbabwe were consistent with other African products from the region, the white supremacist Rhodesian government of Ian Smith continued, after the declaration of unilateral independence from Britain in 1965, to deny the Shona origins of Great Zimbabwe, and in the absence of a viable theory resorted to obfuscation designed solely to take credit away from the indigenous people. Even the fact that Zimbabwe was a Shona word which roughly translates as 'big stone houses' or 'venerated stones', did nothing to persuade the settler government of Rhodesia to connect Great Zimbabwe to the Shona people.

Thus, in 1970, Ian Smith's minister of internal affairs ordered the Historical Monuments Commission to prepare a new guidebook to Great Zimbabwe that was inconclusive about its origins. This incensed Peter Garlake, who had served as senior inspector of monuments since 1964, so much that he resigned in protest and left the country.[37]

Five years after his resignation, Mozambique became independent and Garlake was invited to the newly independent state to investigate the remains of a twelfth-century civilisation. This work added to the stock of knowledge about Great Zimbabwe so that we now understand that the kingdom's wealth did not just come from gold, but also from trade in cattle whose beef was consumed almost exclusively by the Great Zimbabwe elite.

Mapungubwe, an Iron Age site discovered in 1932 but hidden from public attention until recently, also had an elite who lived separately from the common citizenry. This civilisation was located in an area of open savannah at the confluence of the Limpopo and Shashe Rivers, abutting the northern border of South Africa and the borders of Zimbabwe and Botswana.

Archaeologists believe that Mapungubwe transferred its class-based social organisation to Great Zimbabwe, with new research suggesting that a Mapungubwe dynasty introduced class structures to Great Zimbabwe.[38] This is consistent with the view that Mapungubwe is probably the earliest known site in southern Africa to host a class-based society.

Mapungubwe is almost certainly the father of Great Zimbabwe. It represents what Professor Thomas Huffman of the University of the Witwatersrand calls 'the most complex society in southern Africa and is the root of the origins of Zimbabwean culture...' The word Mapungubwe translates to either 'stone monuments' in reference to the

---

[37] BBC World Service, 04 August 1978
[38] https://www.sciencedirect.com/science/article/abs/pii/S0278416508000585

site's large stone houses and walls, or 'hill of the jackal'. The most likely meaning is the former, as the ending 'bwe' in Shona and most Bantu languages denotes stone.

This remarkable civilisation traded with China and India, and had a thriving domestic economy based on agriculture and mining. At its height, Mapungubwe had a population of about 5,000.

Mapungubwe and Great Zimbabwe have more than a common ancestry. As symbols of precolonial African civilisation, both kingdoms posed a huge threat to colonial adventurers and rulers whose authority rested on the comfortable assumption that Africans were uncivilised and incapable of ruling themselves.

Since Mapungubwe was less conspicuous than Great Zimbabwe, there was less need to invent theories about who had built it. The easier solution was to simply hide its existence. This is precisely what the South African government of the day did when the site was discovered in 1932. The government did, however, allow the University of Pretoria to excavate the site. The findings from these excavations contradicted the black inferiority promoted by the white South African government. The white population had to be 'protected' from findings such as this:

> People were prosperous, and kept domesticated cattle, sheep, goats and dogs. The charred remains of storage huts have also been found, showing that millet, sorghum and cotton were cultivated.
>
> Findings in the area are typical of the Iron Age. Smiths created objects of iron, copper and gold for practical and decorative purposes – both for local use and for trade. Pottery, wood, ivory, bone, ostrich eggshells, and the shells of snails and freshwater mussels, indicate that many other materials were used and traded with cultures as far away as East Africa, Persia, Egypt, India and China.[39]

In recent times this great civilisation has been represented by a little rhinoceros, made of gold foil and tacked with minute pins around a wooden core, made in the thirteenth century. The rare and unique gold rhino figurine now forms part of the University of Pretoria's Mapungubwe archaeological collection, dating from AD 1000 to AD 1300.

---

[39] https://showme.co.za/pretoria/tourism/mapungubwe-collection-university-of-pretoria/

In designating Mapungubwe as a World Heritage site in July 2003, UNESCO described Mapungubwe as the centre of the largest kingdom in southern Africa that thrived as a sophisticated trading centre from around 1220 to 1300.

The empires and kingdoms referenced in this section were not the only centres of African civilisation. The reader will perhaps notice that popular African empires such as Egypt were not included. The dual intent is to show that Egypt was not the only notable African empire, and debunk the baseless claim that colonial rule 'civilised' the African continent.

Far from civilising the continent, colonial rule was adept at undermining the old order, and suppressing evidence of pre-colonial African civilisation, as the cases of Great Zimbabwe and Mapungubwe so clearly demonstrate.

CHAPTER FIVE

Defying the Colonial Stereotype

The posture of colonial officialdom was often different from the approach of other non-governmental colonial actors such as philanthropic individuals and institutions who made genuine efforts to make post-colonial African life bearable. The Catholic Church was particularly active in educating young Africans, but other churches contributed too. As Brendan Carmody pointed out, Christian missions were virtually the only providers of secular schooling in any form in Zambia until 1924.[40]

The first mission in northern Zambia was established at Mambwe in 1891 by the White Fathers who also set up a school attended mostly by local children and freed indentured labourers. Mambwe was not terribly successful because of lack of support from Chitimukulu, the regional king. The traditional Chitemene system of agriculture, which required villages to relocate to new areas from time to time to allow restoration of old farmland, did not help either. Despite these challenges, the missionaries were determined to educate the local population, resorting at one point to paying small sums of money to school attendees. They also trained catechists who learnt to read and studied Latin. These catechists were typically sent to other parts of the territory to spread the gospel.

The missionaries at Mambwe also appear to have been gender-sensitive. For example, they encouraged girls to attend school, persuading them that education would make them better housewives and mothers.

Despite these efforts, Mambwe was not a great success. That honour must go to Kayambi, the missionary opened by the White Fathers in 1895. This is recorded as the first European settlement in what was known as Bembaland. This mission was directed by the charismatic Father Joseph Dupont, a physician who later became a bishop. Dupont

---

[40] Carmody, Brendan, Catholic Schools in Zambia : 1891 – 1924 , History of Education , XXVIII (1999)

was diplomatic in his dealings with the Bemba aristocracy and soon won their confidence. Having persuaded the kingdom that he posed no threat, Dupont was able to focus on building the mission school which grew from 57 boys in 1896 to a regular attendance of between 150 and 200 in subsequent years. Many graduates from this school were selected to evangelize in neighbouring villages.

Another early centre of learning in Zambia is Canisius School located at Chikuni Mission near the southern Zambian town of Monze. The Christian mission with which Canisius is associated was founded by Father Joseph Moreau, a French Jesuit, with the help of Father Jules Torrend, in July 1905. Like Joseph Dupont, Moreau had a high level of emotional intelligence, allowing him to befriend and positively work with local people and their leaders. Two years before establishing the Chikuni mission, Moreau persuaded Chief Monze to give him some young men to help develop the centre. Moreau arranged for these young men to be trained in farming in Southern Rhodesia (now Zimbabwe). In turn, the young men taught Moreau how to speak Tonga, one of Zambia's main languages. Thanks to this partnership, Moreau, who had a French farming background, was able to set up a farm to sustain the Jesuits and the local population. The introduction of more efficient farming methods, such as ox-ploughs, guaranteed the farm's success, allowing Moreau to focus on evangelization and education and allowing Torrend to develop his unique linguistic skills. Ensuring that the community had a reliable source of food before venturing into evangelisation and education is consistent with Moreau's philosophy that 'the hungry stomach has no ears'. There was certainly enough evidence to show that teaching the gospel to a hungry audience was next to impossible.

Some accounts record that in 1910, Moreau and other Jesuits were expelled from the country, to be replaced later by Polish Jesuits. This version of history has not been verified by this author. Indeed it is a puzzling account. It is true that the republican government in Portugal expelled all Jesuits from the home country and the colonies. Thus, about forty Jesuits in Portuguese Mozambique were reassigned outside the country. A small group made up mostly of Polish priests crossed the Luangwa River and set up a mission in 1912 at Katondwe and later in 1914 at Chingombe.

The edict from Lisbon would have had no binding effect on the British-governed Northern Rhodesia where Chikuni was located. Indeed, the Jesuits expelled from the Portuguese territory of Mozambique took refuge in Northern Rhodesia.

Therefore, if Father Moreau was expelled from Northern Rhodesia, this would have been done independently of the edict in Lisbon. It is also noteworthy that Moreau did return to die at Chikuni in 1949, the year that the secondary school was founded at the mission.

One year before the establishment of Chikuni Mission, another centre, 1,460 kilometres away, was founded. This time, the Livingstonia Mission took initiative, which, according to Arie Nicolaas Ipenburg, stressed the education of Africans in practical skills and qualities that were consonant with the Calvinistic ethic.[41] Thus, Lubwa Mission used a slightly different model of evangelization from the rival Roman-Catholic White Fathers' mission.

To reach the Bemba and to pre-empt the expansion of the White Fathers in North-Eastern Rhodesia and Nyasaland, James Henderson, the Scottish-born educational missionary who helped pioneer Christian work in Zambia, suggested increasing the use of indigenous teachers and evangelists as a way of occupying the area in a non-threatening way. In this way, future European missionaries would be seen as temporary supporters of the work done by African evangelists and teachers. Henderson was also keen to see Lubwa included in the missionary sphere of influence of his beloved Livingstonia Mission, where he had served after his studies at Edinburgh University in 1895.

In August 1904, a group of 24 trainee teachers on vacation from studies at Khondowe institution in Malawi and one evangelist were sent into Bemba-Bisaland. One of the trainee teachers was named David Kaunda. The group also included two Bemba Christians who, a few years earlier, had been rescued from a slave caravan near Mwenzo. The would-be slaves had been sent as orphans to Khondowe, where they received teacher training.

The group of young trainee teachers subsequently produced a report on Christian prospects in Bembaland. The report concluded that the

---

[41] Ipenburg, Arie Nicolaas, The Development of Lubwa Mission, Chinsali, Zambia 1904-1967, Ph.D. thesis, University of London, School of Oriental and African Studies, May 1991.

Bemba people were ready to receive Christ as their Saviour. Based on this report, the Livingstonia Mission Committee approved the opening of a mission station in Chinsali District to be established close to the Lufu tributary of the Chambeshi River.

To manage the new mission at Lubwa, and in accordance with James Henderson's policy of giving more responsibility to indigenous teachers and evangelists, it was suggested that Julizya Kaunda, baptised as David, be sent to the area along with his wife Helen Jengwera Nyirenda, to open a school and start the mission work. With a Standard Six certificate to his name, the 27-year-old David Julizya Kaunda was considered well qualified for this role. It was a bonus that David's wife, Helen, was also a teacher. Another key player in starting the school was Hezekiah Nkonjela, a freed Bemba slave.

Lubwa and Chikuni missions are good examples of institutions that defied the colonial stereotype. Schools at both centres produced leaders who made huge contributions to colonial and post-colonial Zambia. Matthias Mainza Chona, for example, attended Chikuni before completing his secondary education at Munali Secondary School and proceeding to England for further education. Upon successful completion of his studies at Gray's Inn in London, Mainza Chona became the first black barrister in Northern Rhodesia. He was also a towering figure in the struggle for Zambian independence. When independence finally came, Maiza Chona was named Minister of Justice. He went on to serve in different capacities, including as vice resident and prime minister.

Mainza's younger brother, Mark, was less politically ambitious, preferring instead roles that allowed him to use his troubleshooting skills. By attending both Chikuni and Munali, Mark followed in his elder brother's footsteps. But unlike Mainza, Mark attended Salisbury University in neighbouring Southern Rhodesia where he read History and Economics. A year after graduating from Salisbury, he was sent to England for an administrative course at Gonville and Caius College, Cambridge University.

Mark served splendidly in several technocratic roles in the Zambian government, including senior principal adviser to the president and as a permanent secretary in the ministry of foreign affairs.

Another pair of brothers to benefit from Chikuni are Clement and Luke Mwananshiku. Clement served as a cabinet minister in Kenneth Kaunda's government, as head of commerce and health ministries. His brother Luke served as governor of the Bank of Zambia before becoming finance minister. Later, Luke served as a director of the IMF in Washington D.C.

Lubwa Mission has a claim which no other centre can make: it provided the environment in which Zambia's first president, Kenneth David Kaunda grew up and received the bulk of his formal education. Indeed, Kaunda's philosophy had its genesis in his experiences at Lubwa.

The emphasis on the education of Africans in practical skills and in particular qualities which were consistent with the Calvinistic ethic, as explained by Ipenburg, seems to have had positive results. Lubwa graduates disproportionately participated in the independence movement, offering an intellectual basis for the independence campaign. They also played crucial roles in post-independence Zambia.

For example, Simon Kapwepwe, Zambia's first foreign minister, was a Lubwa graduate and mission teacher. He later served as vice president. Kapasa Robert Makasa, who served as minister of Northern Province, High Commissioner to Kenya, and member of the Central Committee of UNIP during the one-party years, was also a Lubwa graduate.

Other famous Lubwa alumni include Robinson Chisanga Puta Chekwe, who served as vice president of the African National Congress under Harry Nkumbula, member of the African Representative Council, founding president of the Northern Rhodesia Traders Association, director of Rhodesia Railways, founding chairman and chief executive officer of Zambia Railways, and chief executive officer of his family business.

Malama John Sokoni, who served in the pre-independence African Representative Council and later as a diplomat and politician in independent Zambia, was a Lubwa graduate, as were Hayden Dingiswayo Banda and Wesley Nyirenda, who were both prominent in the first Zambian government.

On the education front, Lameck Goma, the first indigenous vice-chancellor of the University of Zambia, was a Lubwa graduate. So was the respected Exeter University-trained educationist, Patrick Chella, who served as the first secretary-general of the Kenneth Kaunda Foundation, a state-supported publishing house.

With respect to its contribution to national leadership, Lubwa did live up to the expectations of the Livingstonia Mission, which had hoped to create in Northern Rhodesia a centre similar, if not identical, to the Overtoun Institution at Khondowe in Nyasaland (now Malawi).

The history of Chipembi Mission is not dissimilar to that of Lubwa Mission. Like Lubwa, Chipembi is home to a school founded by Scottish missionaries. Chipembi is, however, two decades younger than Lubwa, having been founded in 1926. It was the first girls' boarding school in Zambia with prominent alumni like Lombe Chibesakunda, Inonge Mbikusita-Lewanika and Flavia Musonda Musakanya.

Ms Chibesakunda has an impressive résumé. She was the first indigenous Zambian woman to qualify as a barrister, called to the Bar at Gray's Inn in 1969. She then served as a state advocate for six years before trying her hand at private practice for a year. She went back to the public sector in 1973 to serve as solicitor-general, deputy minister of legal affairs, and Member of Parliament for the Lusaka constituency of Matero. In addition to these accomplishments, she served as ambassador to Japan and high commissioner to the United Kingdom.

Her foray into the judiciary started with an appointment as chair of the Industrial Relations Court, and by meritorious progression, she became a Supreme Court judge. It was from the ranks of the Supreme Court that President Michael Chilufya Sata selected her for the position of chief justice.

Dr Inonge Mbikusita-Lewanika served as Zambian ambassador to the United States. She is a graduate of New York University, where she obtained a doctorate in elementary education. After she departed from the government, she continued to support citizens through many community-based life-enhancing initiatives.

Flavia Musonda Musakanya was a fascinating woman who never went to university but in business easily functioned at the level of an MBA holder. She and her husband established a group of companies whose assets included Honda Zambia Ltd and other agriculture, distribution, and electrical engineering businesses. Within a decade of starting the family business, Mrs Musakanya's business acumen was severely tested. Her husband Valentine, who served as chairman and

CEO of the family business, was detained as a political prisoner. Mrs Musakanya was left with running the business and the responsibilities of looking after the family, some of whom were at school abroad.

She proved to be a versatile multitasker who succeeded in strengthening the business balance sheet. She continued to run the business after her husband's release from prison and raised her profile as a philanthropist. She donated a large piece of land to the Catholic Church to construct a boys' school, among many charitable deeds.

Lombe Chibesakunda, Inonge Mbikusita-Lewanika, and Flavia Musonda Musakanya are just a few examples of women who benefited from a Christian education at Chipembi. While it is true that Christianity was frequently used by imperial powers to justify their colonial actions and undermine traditional belief systems, it would not be fair to equate the work of Christian missionaries to the deeds of the official agents of colonialism. For example, while colonialists aimed to keep the education of indigenous people at a minimum, Christian missionaries expanded educational opportunities.

The mission schools named here are not, by any stretch, the only educational institutions established by Christian missionaries. Other schools include Malole, which produced, among other alumni, Emmanuel Kasonde. Kasonde served as permanent secretary in the Zambian ministry of finance before becoming a successful entrepreneur. He returned to public life as minister of finance later in his life.

The distinguished civil servant Peter Chilufya Kasolo is another alumnus. Kasolo received his entire primary school in Catholic Church mission schools. He later went to Munali before taking his teacher training course at Chalimbana Training Centre.

His career before Zambian independence includes service as headmaster at two schools and the manager of schools for 14 White Father mission schools in Chinsali and Isoka districts. It speaks to the quality of Kasolo's early education that after 33 years of faithful and unbroken public service, he had no difficulty adjusting to life in the private sector, where he served as area manager for a large Zambian-owned company.

With respect to girls' education at a time when gender sensitivity was largely an alien concept, Mabel Shaw stands out as a figure to be respected. Born into a non-Christian lower middle class family in

Wolverhampton in 1888, Mabel Shaw left home to live with her Christian grandmother at the age of five. It is here that she was introduced to practical Christianity.

Shaw founded the London Missionary Society's Girls' Boarding School in Mbeleshi (also written as Mbereshi), Northern Rhodesia, serving as head teacher from 1915 to 1940. Mbereshi's guiding philosophy that Christian evangelisation could not succeed without education, served as a model for other mission schools. Among many accomplishments, Mbereshi produced Northern Rhodesia's first indigenous nurse: Lucy Chisha Kanondo.

Therefore, we can conclude with a fair amount of confidence that although Christian missionaries are associated with colonialism, on balance, they did more good than harm.

CHAPTER SIX

Being Zambian

Z ambians need to be more comfortable with their Zambianness. This cannot happen, however, unless the good people of the country accept themselves fully and understand that they can achieve anything humanly possible. To get to this state, Zambians need to understand both their past and their current circumstances. The history they learn must include the colonial era but must not be exclusively dominated by it.

The colonial era must be better understood to counter the false narrative that colonialism was in all respects a good thing for the territory. Unfortunately, this narrative is now reinforced by a romanticised and skewed recollection of colonialism as an era of disease control, good diet, and education.

Concerning disease and colonialism, the following extract from a paper by Ada McVean, science communicator at the University of McGill's Office of Science and Society, is instructive:

Once colonies in North America and the Caribbean were established, many of Europe's poor emigrated there, bringing malaria with them. The agricultural practices used in the U.S. to grow cotton and rice, combined with the overcrowding and horrid conditions that slaves faced resulted in epidemics of malaria that ravaged the Southern U.S.

Colonialism's effects on malaria were not restricted to its spread, however. Even in areas where malaria was already present, colonial influence often worsened conditions and caused epidemics.

In the southern African country of Swaziland, malaria was common but nonfatal before colonial intervention. This was due to the immunity that can be acquired with repeated exposure. When colonists arrived, however, they removed Swazi inhabitants from their homelands, forcing them to move into lowlands with larger mosquito populations.[42]

As for food, the staple introduced by the Europeans was not an improvement on the traditional diet. Maize was introduced to the region in the 1600s, but it did not become a southern African staple until the 1900s. Prior to that, the dominant staples in Zambia were cassava, millet and sorghum; all more nutritious than maize.

Cassava is a calorie-rich vegetable with key vitamins and minerals, in addition to abundant carbohydrates. It is an especially good source of vitamin C, thiamine, riboflavin, and niacin. The plant's leaves are delicious and contain up to 25 percent protein.

Millet is similarly rich in nutrients being a great source of protein, dietary fibre, several B vitamins and numerous dietary minerals, especially manganese. Millet aids digestion, is known to mitigate diarrhoea, and supports healthy gut flora to prevent peptic ulcers and reduce the risk of colon cancer. Furthermore, catechins, compounds with anti-oxidant properties which boost liver and kidney function, are also present in millet.

Sorghum is rich in nutrients, having vitamins and minerals such as B vitamins, magnesium, potassium, phosphorus, iron, and zinc. It is also an excellent source of fibre, antioxidants, and protein.

By any measure cassava, millet and sorghum are healthier staples than maize. While in its original form, maize contains nutrients such as vitamin A, vitamin C, iron, and fibre, most of the goodness is lost when it is processed into a meal. Moreover, millet, sorghum, cassava, and even sweet potatoes are less susceptible to drought than maize. Therefore, it makes sense to substitute nutritious food based on these crops for less nutritious maize-based meals. A dietary change is urgent in light of the finding by the UN-linked ReliefWeb that about 40 percent of Zambian children under five years are stunted because they do not eat well.

As for claims that colonialism brought high quality education, health care, and great infrastructure development, these must be challenged because they ignore the exclusion of the majority of the population from enjoying these benefits.

---

[42] www.mcgill.ca/oss

Furthermore, while the indigenous population contributed hugely to the building of colonial Northern Rhodesia, this contribution was systematically minimised by promoting a false narrative depicting 'natives' as lazy and feckless. The reality is that the black population earned whatever benefits they received from colonialism. The benefits were not given to them on a plate.

The Work Ethic

While there is abundant evidence of industriousness in the Zambian population prior to the advent of the one-party state, and during the precolonial period, that fact is less self-evident today. It was industry and discipline that made the Kongo state work. Equally, discipline and hard work are evident in any analysis of the Luba/Lunda Empire. This work ethic continued well into the colonial era.

In a 1958 report,[43] Audrey Richards disputed the widely held view among colonial Europeans that African cultivators were lazy and feckless. This claim was not supported by her research and lived experiences, despite its notoriety in post-slavery discourse.

Richards analysed the traditional chitemene system of agriculture practised by the Bemba people. In essence, the system was the burning of circular piles of branches to form a weed-free ash-bed with a high potash content. The ash-bed helps the seed to germinate healthily. Richards rejected the often-repeated claim of colonial officials that the chitemene system was damaging to the environment because it resulted in trees being reduced to mere stumps. This did not happen in the Bemba system, as it is the branches, not the trunks, that were cut.

Concerning how the men did their work, this is what Richards said:

> The pollarding of trees is men's work and to the Bemba is an exciting and daring occupation to which important ritual was attached. It is one of those forms of traditional cultivation which the Bemba found it impossible to abandon at the command of the Government, partly because they had no other system of agriculture which was as efficient, and partly because the tree cutting was a matter of prestige. Men vied

---

[43] Richards, Audrey I, A Changing Pattern of Agriculture in East Africa: The Bemba of Northern Rhodesia, The Mrs Will Gordon Lecture, September 1958

with each other in their skill in reaching to the top of trees. It was a point of honour to leave no tree unpollarded, even though it meant slashing at the top-most branch and slithering down the trunk as it crashed to the ground, and even though injuries and deaths occurred each year.

Their tree cutting was a source of pride and associated with rituals in which their chiefs played an important part.

By no stretch of the imagination can the men described by Richards be characterised as lazy and feckless or as lacking a sense of responsibility. Furthermore, this dedication to duty was not confined to the Bemba people. As seen in the preceding chapter, two years before establishing the Chikuni Mission, Moreau persuaded Chief Monze to give him some young men to help develop the mission. Moreau arranged for these young men to be trained as farmers in Southern Rhodesia. Moreau would not have invested in these young men had they not been disciplined and hard working. Indeed, Moreau's investment paid off handsomely as the farm they established produced enough food for the community.

At a time when there is concern that the traditional value of industriousness is waning, Zambia remains an exceptionally enterprising country. The 2020 edition of The Economist's Pocket World in Figures named Zambia 'the most entrepreneurial country on earth'.

Since accusations of laziness and fecklessness are often levelled at all Africans, the reader may also recall Portuguese ship Captain Lourenco Pinto's description of Benin City in 1691 as a 'wealthy and industrious' city.

Industry is a traditional Zambian value, and with the right leadership, it can once again be placed at the core of national behaviour.

Responsibility for Self and Others

The culture of self-improvement is similar to the value of industry because it too was perhaps more evident in the past than it is today. As Andrew Sardanis observed, in the 1950s, most of the indigenous Zambians employed by the mining companies had no formal skills to speak of, except for a few drivers and clerks, on account of the severity of racial discrimination in skilled trades training. Despite this, Zambian workers learned skilled trades through experience and performed well in jobs they were not qualified to do officially. In so doing, the Zambian workers were motivated by a sense of responsibility for themselves and others. They were not going to run away from this responsibility.

The traditional saying *Kinyema maulu, muchima wikiyuka* means more than the literal translation, 'when someone runs away, he himself knows what he runs from', suggests. This wise saying places a duty on citizens to be responsible for their actions and accept the consequences. It is understood that a person who has no sense of self-worth cannot have the sense of responsibility called for by traditional Zambian society. For this reason, an indentured labourer or slave cannot have an independent sense of gratitude or responsibility as the saying *Uushitasha mwana wa musha* suggests.

The erosion of self-confidence in individuals has been quite noticeable over the past quarter of a century. In some cases, this has led to self-rejection. During a visit to a rural area near the city of Ndola, I noticed a young woman with a baby on her back. That sight is not uncommon. Many women carry their babies on the back in Zambia. It is a tested way of keeping babies comfortable and safe while allowing mothers to walk in relative freedom. This particular young mother, however, had a blonde wig on her head which, to some, made her look bizarre.

We cannot draw sweeping conclusions from this woman's wig. It is possible she was wearing it simply as a fashion statement. It is also possible that she was indoctrinated into believing that Caucasian hair was more desirable than her own natural hair. Either way, women should not be slaves to beauty standards as a tool to hide what they think are deficiencies. They should do what they are comfortable with even as they celebrate their uniqueness. Reasons for preferring non-natural hair are as complex as the factors that drove Rachel Dolezal, a white American woman to represent herself as black for years. At one point Dolezal (who changed her name to Nkechi Diallo) headed a local chapter of the NAACP in Washington state.

Professor Hlonipha Mokoena of the Wits Institute for Social and Economic Research, University of the Witwatersrand, may help us understand some of these complexities.

There is a certain curiosity about what Mokoena insists we should call 'black hair'. She recalls her hair attracting attention when she was at school, with fellow students wanting to touch her mane. Mokoena avers that this fascination with the texture of black hair is not new. 'In slave societies, white women would often hack off the hair of their enslaved female servants because it supposedly "confused white men"'.

According to Mokoena, black hair is seductive. This may explain, in part, why Lupita Nyong'o, who wears her hair natural and chemical-free, has become a household symbol of beauty. Her confidence also contributes to this.

Therefore, it is ironic that some Zambian women prefer straight blonde wigs to their natural hair. It is possible these women are victims of historic propaganda and conform to an entirely false standard of beauty. They should not be slaves to false beauty standards but should instead celebrate their natural beauty, however they choose to express it. Successful and sophisticated African women such as Lupita Nyong'o do this and are infinitely more confident and happier than black women who do not.

A culture of self-improvement can only succeed when people are comfortable in their skins and value their intellects and physical appearances. Equally, people will be responsible to themselves only if the self, in all its complexity, is worth being responsible to. The self must be loved and accepted.

Lack of education contributes to unhealthy diffidence. A step in addressing this would be the promotion of community learning centres that focus on adult education. They will teach literacy, numeracy, and civic responsibility.

Most Zambians born before or shortly after independence will recall advertisements by the Central African Correspondence College placed in the main newspapers, which urged education by correspondence. At least in the urban areas of the Copperbelt, virtually every literate person was aware of these advertisements, and a considerable number of readers used the correspondence college to improve their academic and professional qualifications.

Parents and all who stood in loco parentis to children took every opportunity to encourage younger people to get an education. I recall a teacher who was related to my father being quite excited upon discovering that I would do Latin in high school. He immediately gave me a standing invitation to his home for Latin lessons. I did not visit him as often as he would have liked because I also had an aunt in the vicinity who was a nurse and had been required to take a Latin course as a nursing student in Southern Rhodesia. She was only too keen to pass on all the Latin she had picked up as a student to me.

When night schools became more accessible, many, including my mother, took advantage of this opportunity. I recall my mother driving ten miles on school nights to the Northern Technical College in Chingola to complete her high school education, before finally leaving for England to study accounting for business. My father had no university education at all, save for a very short stint at Cambridge to do a course in trade unionism, but he enjoyed reading books on commerce and economics. Many years later, his Keynesian arguments were helpful in my economics classes.

This was an age that emphasised personal responsibility because people understood that progress could not be made without it. There was a feeling that with determination and appropriate strategy, anything could be achieved. This may explain why individuals with only a modest formal education had the confidence to challenge the then mighty British Empire's representatives and succeed.

Things are different today. While technology has increased opportunities for online learning, it has also contributed to the culture of instant gratification. But technology alone is not responsible for this culture of entitlement. The absence of consistently ethical, responsible and visionary leadership at virtually all levels of society is also responsible. There are certainly fewer role models like my would-be Latin tutor keen to help younger people progress. There are even fewer equivalents of Godwin Mbikusita-Lewanika, who took several younger men under his wings and arranged scholarships for them to study in India. The scholarships were financed by the Indian Overseas Scholarship Programme initiated by Jawaharlal Nehru, India's first prime minister. One of the beneficiaries of Mbikusita-Lewanika's efforts and foresight was Simon Mwansa Kapwepwe, who later served as vice president of the republic.

Being patient and understanding that rewards should go to those who play by the rules was once a cardinal feature of Zambian culture, which was suspicious of sudden wealth. It is from this culture that sayings such as *tafimbwa lubilo* and *Kushembo fumu ni mombocima* come. Mbikusita-Lewanika understood this.

He was also motivated by a sense of family. Over the years, he had come to consider younger colleagues such as Kapwepwe his kin. The Zambian family is defined very broadly. Membership of the family entails both privileges and responsibilities. Mbikusita-Lewanika would have seen it as his responsibility to aid younger people who looked up to him and revered him as an elder brother.

This is an area of culture that the Zambian population continues to be interested in preserving. Unfortunately, the economic circumstances are such that few can devote the time and resources to supporting less fortunate family members. Whereas prior to the late 1980s there were virtually no destitute children in Zambia, today, Mission Direct, the United Kingdom-based Christian charity that supports some of the world's poorest people, estimates that there are in Lusaka alone around 1000 children living on the streets. Ninety percent of these children are HIV positive and many of them are addicted to a jet fuel-based substance that they sniff in an attempt to mitigate their misery.[44]

The very term 'street children' is offensive in Zambian culture which places the responsibility of raising children on the entire community. The streets did not give birth to these children. They were born to Zambians or foreigners based in Zambia and are deserving of care by Zambia. Unfortunately, the Zambian community is not living up to its historic and traditional responsibility of raising children.

The appalling circumstances that these children find themselves in must be addressed urgently by building an economy that will produce enough to guarantee food, clothing and shelter for these young people.

Respect for elders

Denying street children the opportunity to live in family environments and attend school also deprives them of education in etiquette. The abandoned children have little time for anything other than basic issues

---

[44] Mission Direct, Six children reintegrated from the streets in Zambia, 6th December 2019

of survival. They certainly have no time to learn the value of respect for self, others, and, especially, elders in any systematic way.

There are very good reasons for respecting elders. They are the principal custodians of Zambian history. Although Mbemba Nzinga did turn the Kikongo language into a written one in the 16th century, reading and writing was not widespread in cultures with origins in medieval Kongo, until relatively recently. Nonetheless, the accuracy of oral history is remarkable.

It is consistent with written texts dating back to the establishment of the Kongo state. For this, we owe a debt of gratitude to the elders who have diligently passed on their people's history to younger generations.

In addition to history, elders also teach etiquette, especially those aspects children would find awkward discussing with their parents. This is the forte of grandparents. In Zambian culture, as in many other cultures, the relationship between grandparent and grandchild is very close and encourages unrestrained inquiry by the grandchild. The grandchild quickly learns not only that grandpa or grandma is more likely to grant fastidious requests more readily than mum and dad, but that grandparents can be relied upon to resolve difficult problems in confidence. For this reason, children are more likely to open up to their grandparents and share life's challenges with them.

This is perhaps one reason why sexual abuse of children was so rare in traditional Zambian society. If a child had confidants in the form of grandparents, that in itself would have discouraged prospective community predators. Children rarely found themselves in vulnerable positions. There was always a loving grandparent nearby. Another reason is that in Luba/Lunda jurisprudence, as inherited from the Kongo state, every adult was potentially liable for any harm befalling any child of the community. For example, parents going away without making adequate arrangements for the care of their children while abroad would be liable for harm suffered by the children during their absence; but so would the neighbours, whether or not they had been informed about the parents' absence.

The duty to care for all children and not just one's biological offspring encouraged adults to take an interest in all children of the community. As a result, they were especially alert to harm that these children may suffer.

Although less evident now in urban areas, the concept of universal adult liability for the welfare of children is still understood and considered a Zambian value.

The traditional Zambian approach to grandparent-grandchild relationships is supported by scientific evidence. A study by Boston College researchers found that emotionally close ties between grandparents and adult grandchildren reduced depressive symptoms in both groups. The study, published online in 2014 in The Gerontologist, included 374 grandparents and 356 adult grandchildren. The researchers looked at data collected over a 19-year period and found that intergenerational bonds between grandparents and grandchildren come with distinctive benefits.

And it is not just the grandchildren who benefit. Grandparents also benefit as their grandchildren act as conduits to new ideas and ways of thinking. In addition, grandchildren benefit from their grandparents' life experiences and history passed on from earlier generations.

A study by Professor Ann Buchanan from the Department of Social Policy and Intervention, Oxford University, found that a high level of grandparental involvement increases the well-being of children. A study of more than 1,500 participants showed that children whose upbringing involved a high level of grandparental care had fewer emotional and behavioural problems.

So, in Zambia, elders should be respected not just for the sake of it but also because in addition to being great teachers of etiquette and history, they play a critical role in maintaining the emotional balance of children. Respect for elders is surely a Zambian value worth preserving and strengthening.

A diplomatic people

Vernon Johnson Mwaanga, who served as foreign affairs minister in both the second and third republics, once had a notice in his office that read, 'A diplomat is someone who tells you to go to hell in such a way that you look forward to the trip'. VJ, as the veteran foreign affairs minister is known, must have taken these words to heart. There is virtually no public record of him using intemperate language.

On one occasion, after being detained without trial by Kenneth Kaunda, prisoner and jailer met, and the jailer was anxious to know whether VJ was bitter about his imprisonment. VJ's reported reply was, 'Not at all Your Excellency. But I am not amused either.'

Cultured Zambians would rather describe a dullard as '*si wochenjera*', which translates to, 'he is not clever', rather than, 'he is stupid'. Strangers to traditional Zambian culture are sometimes impatient with what appears to them to be undue attention to ceremony and circumlocutory speech. The avoidance of direct and offensive language has historically helped to maintain the peace. It certainly helps people from different backgrounds to get on better by encouraging more attentive listening.

Sadly, in recent years, abusive language has become more evident in public discourse, thanks to the ascendency to power of persons largely unqualified to govern a country as complex as Zambia. This breed of politicians believe that abuse is a suitable substitute for analysis. A casual glance at the daily newspapers will prove this point. For example, the Zambia Daily Mail reported on 2 December 2017 that the Zambia Centre for Interparty Dialogue was concerned about what the organisation called 'politics of insults and character assassination'. In the considered view of ZCID, this deterred good people, especially women, from entering the political arena. ZCID executive director, Monica Kanjimana, said:

> The current environment is not favourable for women because of the insults which have dominated our political arena. As ZCID, we want to see issue based politics.

Exactly 21 months later, Elias Chipimo, the politician consistently admired for his diplomacy and focus on issues, graciously stepped down as party leader of the National Restoration Party. The mudslinging continued unabated.

Diplomacy and measured public speech can be dominant features of the Zambian value system once again, but only if both rulers and the led are suitably educated on their benefits.

A peaceable people

Every government since independence has claimed credit for the country's peace. But, this peace has more to do with the citizens themselves than any particular regime.

Despite speaking many languages and dialects, the people of Zambia have a collective common history going back 130 years. That history has, in turn, provided opportunities for a common Zambian culture to emerge. Until independence, this new culture was most evident in the Copperbelt Province, which acted as a melting pot for job-seeking Zambians from all parts of the country.

The Copperbelt even accommodated foreigners whose native-born children were considered local denizens. The Copperbelt developed a common language and adapted it to suit local conditions. Thus emerged what is sometimes referred to as Town Bemba, a language not unlike Lamba, the indigenous tongue of the land. The ease with which the diverse citizens of the Copperbelt Province intermarried helped consolidate their new common identity.

Intermarriages on the Copperbelt watered down ethnic cleavages within the province. This, together with the Lamba tradition of dispute resolution by respectful dialogue rather than violence, has contributed to the peace that many politicians have claimed credit for.

Similar developments have taken place in Lusaka where the dominant language is Nyanja. Livingstone also has a measure of integration, with both Tonga and Lozi being spoken in a manner that does not necessarily reflect ethnicity.

Juliette Crespin-Boucaud, a PhD student at the Paris School of Economics, has researched interethnic marriages and, in December 2019, provided the first quantitative evidence on interethnic and interfaith marriages in sub-Saharan Africa.

According to this research, the lowest ratio of interethnic marriages can be found in Kenya. It is not surprising that the highest is in Zambia. With respect to interfaith marriages, the lowest ratios were observed in Guinea and the highest in Gambia, Niger and Zambia. Thus, for both interethnic marriages and interfaith unions, Zambia is on the right side of the balance sheet. In other words, ethnic and religious cleavages are less likely to be a source of turbulence in Zambia than in other countries.

Despite this reality, the assumption is often made that Zambia as an African country is necessarily less peaceable than high-income countries such as the United States and the United Kingdom. It is assumptions such as this one that informed the travel agent's advice referenced earlier that the would-be tourist to an African country should take out rape insurance.

Let's look at objective criteria and see how Zambia fares as a country of peace as compared to more established democracies and other countries.

Each year, the Institute for Economics and Peace releases the Global Peace Index (GPI), which analyses data from 163 independent nations and territories worldwide. The index uses 23 indicators to determine which nations are the most dangerous, as well as which are the most peaceful. The indicators are split across categories such as militarisation, safety and security; domestic conflict; and international conflict.

The 2020 GPI showed Zambia fell from 41st in 2017, when it was tied with the United Kingdom, to 44th. The most peaceful country in the world for the tenth year running is Iceland. The second most peaceful country is New Zealand. In Africa, Mauritius, Botswana, and Malawi sat at 23rd, 29th, and 39th, respectively. In Europe, The United Kingdom is at 42nd. France and Bosnia i Herzegovina are 59th, and 78th, respectively. In the Americas, The United States is at 122nd, while Argentina is at 72nd. Globally, the least peaceful countries are Afghanistan and Syria at 157th and 156th, respectively.

Zambia can easily improve its performance on this index with appropriate leadership and a shift to a more orderly culture. A peaceable people are more likely to establish institutions supportive of democratic development than a people prone to violence. Institutions alone are, however, not enough. The leadership must have a sense of responsibility and a sense of fairness, in addition to being diplomatic. Combining this leadership and appropriate institutions can again place respect and peace at the core of cherished traditional Zambian values.

CHAPTER SEVEN

Building a Culture of Success

There is a relationship between culture, defined as a society's beliefs and value systems, and economic performance. For example, a culture that encourages social cohesion through good leadership is more likely to be economically successful than one that does not.

Good leadership will be respectful of citizens, enforce laws fairly without fear or favour, promote good work ethic, productivity, peaceful and diplomatic discourse, selflessness, and personal responsibility.

When fully operationalized, the culture promoted by good leadership will increase individuals' beliefs that their country values them and that they are full members of society. Beyond salutary feelings of belonging, inclusion increases the likelihood of individuals investing meaningfully in their society. Thus inclusion generates greater social cohesion and encourages investment in social capital defined by the OECD as 'networks together with shared norms, values and understandings that facilitate co-operation within or among groups'. In this sense, Godwin Mbikusita-Lewanika was very much a pioneer of social capital in Zambia.

Social capital is more than an informal norm promoting co-operation between individuals. It also has significant economic consequences as it reduces transaction costs and promotes the kind of associational life necessary for an efficient government and democracy. While only imperfectly evident today, social capital is supported by Zambian tradition, shared historical experiences, and other cultural norms.

Zambians must learn to think of their country as an entity that will last for a very long time as a self-perpetuating force for good. Many Zambians had business opportunities thrust upon them at independence but declined to make the necessary investments, adopting a 'wait and see' approach.

These Zambians followed the lead of the white ghetto whose fervent wish at the time of independence was the swift and total failure of the new nation. Today, these Zambians are elderly and full of regret that they never made the investments when they had the opportunity to do so. 'If only we had been more optimistic', they rue. This cycle should not be repeated as failure to exploit a commercial opportunity today results in a lost job opportunity for another citizen tomorrow.

There is heavy lifting to be done in the creation of a new culture of performance. Once Zambia demonstrates to itself that it has a culture that encourages enterprise and economic growth, and produces positive results on a consistent basis, the culture thus created will become self-sustaining. Nationals will take pride in their country's achievements and probably internalise this 'new' culture of success and instinctively work to maintain it. For a change Zambians would be internalising something positive.

Creating (or recreating) a self-sustaining culture of success may not be as difficult as is often assumed because Zambia has exhibited many of the elements necessary to do this in the past. These elements include authentic leadership, commitment to democracy, self-acceptance on the part of the population, and commitment to education and innovation.

Authentic Leadership

Since national culture is typically established at the top, especially in young nations, Zambia must not accept anything less than credible leaders, accountable to the nation, and who lead by example.

The country's Zambezian ancestors had an unwritten constitution that obliged their 'king of kings' to govern fairly. The king's authority rested on election, and he could be deposed in the event of abuse of authority or failure to use power wisely. Thus, the constitution placed an obligation on the king to consult the people or their representatives on key issues. Regrettably, no modern Zambian constitution has created institutions to genuinely consult the people's representatives on key issues.

Instead, all Zambian constitutions have been based on a fusion of the American and British governance models without regard to the suitability of the hybrid constitution to Zambia's culture, history, and needs. As a result, the hybrid constitutions have undermined democracy and eradicated it completely during the one-party dictatorship. But even after the return of democracy, the Zambian constitution, which requires the executive branch to also be a part of the legislative branch, has weakened executive oversight by making it easy for the executive branch to neutralise the legislative branch. This is done by co-opting into government as many legislature members as possible, and then subjecting them to the doctrine of collective responsibility, thereby rendering them incapable of criticising the government, even when the criticism is legitimate.

Each constitution has prioritised the interests of the ruling elite over the public interest. No Zambian leader can be credible unless that leader is elected democratically according to a constitution that reflects Zambian values and is itself credible in the eyes of the citizenry. It follows that crafting a non-partisan constitution that creates strong institutions designed to safeguard the public interest is a pre-condition in the country's endeavour to establish authentic leadership.

Once Zambia has a good constitution which guarantees strong and politically independent institutions such as an effective judiciary, a free press, independent prosecutorial agencies, an independent electoral commission, a non-partisan police service, and a non-partisan civil service, then the opportunity will be created to encourage the emergence of authentic leaders.

Citizens are more likely to respect and support leaders elected through credible constitutions than leaders elected based on flawed constitutions. Similarly, potentially authentic leaders are less likely to contest flawed elections. Thus, the absence of participation in elections by bright and principled leaders such as Elias Chipimo inevitably leads to politics being dominated by the mediocre.

What qualities should Zambian leaders have?

Integrity

To start with, leaders must be upright, having strong moral principles. This is generally referred to as integrity. Leadership comes with many temptations and a leader without integrity will soon succumb to these temptations and create a culture of corruption. Unfortunately, there is evidence of this culture in Zambia.

In May 2012, a Lusaka magistrate's court sentenced a former minister of labour, Austin Liato, to two years in prison with hard labour. Mr Liato had concealed the equivalent of USD394,000 under a layer of concrete at his farm outside Lusaka. The prosecution was successful in proving that the money had been obtained illegally. Mr Liato appealed the verdict and was allowed out on bail pending the appeal. On June 2, 2015, the Supreme Court confirmed the conviction and ordered that Mr Liato's farm and the $394,000 cash be forfeited to the State.

In August 2015, Mr Liato was released from prison after receiving a pardon from President Edgar Lungu on compassionate grounds. Liato had spent one month in hospital. The pardon did not sit well with Transparency International Zambia which feared that pardoning convicted politicians sent the wrong message: that crime and corruption would be tolerated as long as the perpetrators were friends of the government. This concern was shared by National Restoration Party president Elias Chipimo who accused President Lungu of abusing the law.

Liato was not a uniquely bad person and in his role as minister for labour had performed reasonably well, although he tended to sometimes unduly interfere with the operations of private companies. His resume is not unimpressive. Trained as an accountant, Liato served as president of the Zambia Electricity and Allied Workers Union and served as vice president of the Zambia Congress of Trade Unions.

Liato is, however, an example of a politician with an integrity deficit. In 2003, he defected to the ruling Movement for Multi-Party Democracy from the opposition United Party for National Development, and was re-elected in a by-election. In January 2005, President Levy Mwanawasa appointed him Minister for Copperbelt Province, but the appointment was cancelled after it became known that Liato was facing a judicial enquiry.

The ease with which Liato jumped political ship suggests an absence of ideological commitment and possibly an opportunistic character. His ability to illegally accumulate such a vast sum of money at a time when the World Bank estimated the moderate poverty rates in urban and rural areas at 35 percent and 74 percent, respectively, suggests callousness and unbridled greed. But it is also reasonable to argue that Liato may well have avoided this avaricious behaviour had there not already been a culture of corruption in Zambia. This culture made it easy for Liato to succumb to the temptations associated with political power.

Vision

A leader's ability to lay out future plans with inventiveness, imagination, and intelligence is generally referred to as vision. Thus, a leader without a clear idea of how the future should look and who, for that reason, cannot set out concrete steps to translate that vision into reality, is not a good leader.

Zambia's campaigners for independence such as Kenneth Kaunda, Simon Kapwepwe, Mainza Chona and many others were visionary leaders who had an understandable vision of an independent Northern Rhodesia that captured the population's imagination. Frederick Chiluba had a clear idea of what the post-one-party state should look like: freedom of speech, freedom to form and belong to political parties, freedom to transfer money out of the country. The concrete steps taken to implement this vision included ending the state media monopoly, removing restrictions on political activity, and removing foreign exchange restrictions.

Visionary leaders are not necessarily free from controversy as the examples of Lee Kuan Yew and Paul Kagame show. Both leaders transformed hugely disadvantaged societies into examples of good economic management. But both leaders are also criticised for their alleged mistreatment of political opponents. So, while visionary leaders may not guarantee universal satisfaction with their rule, they typically have a bottom line that allows the nation to set standards and make concrete plans.

A country without visionary leadership soon begins to look like a rudderless ship with no particular destination. That ship would be vulnerable to piracy. In states' case, the chief pirate is corruption, which benefits from an absence of standards and a national bottom line.

When Edgar Lungu, as candidate for the ruling Patriotic Front party, declared in 2014 that his vision did not go beyond that of the late president he was seeking to replace, he greatly harmed his credibility as a leader. The clear message to the public was that Mr Lungu had no vision at all. Thus, the public was genuinely fearful that he was about to turn their country into a rudderless vessel. It has not helped that efforts to explain the president's vision deficit was left to surrogates.

Vice President Inonge Wina explained, while on a visit to India, that Lungu's vision was 'to further improve nutritional levels which is in conformity with India's Prime Minister Narendra Modi's vision of ending poverty by empowering rural communities.' The vice president's explanation highlighted the two challenges President Lungu had in articulating his vision.

In the first place, the vision is more convincing from the leader than surrogates. The second challenge is that once again Mr Lungu's vision was attached to another person's worldview, this time the leader of a foreign country.

Ability to Delegate

A good leader must be able to prioritise to establish which high-value activities to focus on. Focus on these high-value activities will be impossible unless the leader knows how to delegate. Furthermore, a failure to delegate will deny the leader time for strategic thinking.

Delegation must not happen in a vacuum. The persons to whom the leader delegates must be given training concerning the work they are expected to do and be held accountable. In response to confusion arising from contradictory statements by ministers in the new MMD government in 1991/1992, President Chiluba decided to add the title of chief government spokesperson to the role of minister of information. While this move did reduce contradictions, it did not eliminate them. More importantly, it did not address the root cause of the contradictions and confusions, which was an absence of an accountability framework for each cabinet minister.

Delegation of responsibilities in the new Zambia must therefore include mandate letters that outline the government's expectations from each cabinet minister and against which ministers' performance can be measured. Identifying a ministry's priorities in a mandate letter will help concentrate the minister's mind and encourage her to focus. The head of government to whom ministers are accountable should then have the discipline to allow the ministers to do their job even as he makes himself available as a coach to be consulted by any minister needing help or a sounding board.

Under no circumstances should the president, as head of government, get involved in the ministry's day-to-day business. Doing so makes it difficult for the minister to do her job and makes it unfair for that minister to account for errors the president contributed to by getting unduly involved in the minister's work.

The absence of an accountability framework is probably responsible for the embarrassing public dispute that the ministers of health and local government found themselves in in early May 2020.

Local Government Minister Charles Banda had advised the Lusaka City Council that it could continue charging churches and other places of worship ZMW100 (USD5) for issuance of certificates to congregate. This advice reversed the directive issued by Health Minister Dr Chitalu Chilufya, banning fees for the issuance of certificates to congregate.

Dr Chilufya went further and directed the Council to refund the fee to those who had already paid it. In light of the COVID-19 situation, the health minister did the right thing by advising churches wishing to congregate to seek guidance from the National Public Health Institute.

The local government minister disagreed with his counterpart, taking the position that only the ministry of local government can issue guidance to the city council. He added that the city council was permitted by law to charge fees for the issuance of certificates. The minister did appear to allow for the possibility of exemption from these fees, but took the view that such exemptions can only be approved by his ministry.

In its May 07, 2020 edition, the Lusaka Times identified this development as 'the latest in what appears to be the growing trend of officials contradicting each other on various issues affecting the nation'. The paper then cited a statement by Dr Chilufya in connection with a health worker who had died in a road accident involving a public bus in which he was a passenger. The health worker was carrying COVID-19 samples. On that occasion, the minister's statement that there was nothing unusual about health workers with samples using public transport contradicted the president, who expressed regret that a health worker on such a crucial assignment was obliged to use public transport.

The dispute between these two well-educated cabinet ministers highlights the importance of delegation and accountability frameworks. Clearly worded mandate letters may well have prevented this dispute, for each minister would have known precisely what was expected of him.

Instead, the ministers engaged in behaviour that undermined confidence and trust in the government.

Communication

The example of the two warring ministers above is also relevant to the importance of effective communication. An authentic leader must communicate to convey the vision and motivate people to attain the desired objectives. Zambia is not going to transform itself without effort. The country is going to need both leadership and an active citizenry to do so. The ability of the country's leaders to communicate effectively is critical.

Each significant change in Zambia has been preceded by clear messages communicated effectively by the leadership. Sometimes the messages have been lengthy but more typically they have been succinct, even monosyllabic. Thus Kenneth Kaunda reinforced his campaign for independence with phrases such as "an egg a day for every Zambian". The idea here was to capture a glorious and hunger free future in one simple sentence.

The execution of the campaign was also well communicated. When the British government showed hesitation in agreeing to the breakup of the disliked Federation of Rhodesia and Nyasaland, the United National Independence Party embarked on a campaign they called Cha-Cha-Cha. This was a term that applied to different things. It could refer to a novel dance, tandem bicycles, public buses with automatic doors in Elizabethville, or chaos. Whatever the context, this term signified revolution.

So, when UNIP's 'war cabinet' (as the committee given the task of overseeing the campaign was called) resolved to make the country ungovernable as a way of applying pressure on the British government, the leader of the 'war cabinet', Lewis Mutale Changufu, named the campaign Cha-Cha-Cha. Changufu had received extensive training in security matters in the United States and must have been aware of the importance of appropriately naming the campaign of civil disobedience.

Although the committee's work involved a certain amount of violence, such as destruction of bridges and blocking roads, the territory's generally peaceable people went along because the campaign's objective had been well communicated to them.

When the Movement for Multi-Party Democracy campaigned for a return to democracy, they articulated their cause well and captured their mission in the slogan, the hour has come. The people understood it was time to overthrow the dictatorship. People dreamt about a free press, free flow of capital, government accountability etc.

Enthusiasm was not dampened even when Frederick Chiluba, the head of the movement, warned that restructuring the Zambian economy would result in short-term pain. The people were ready to sacrifice because the need to do so had been effectively communicated to them.

The MMD did win power, governing for twenty years, before losing to someone whose message resonated more with the people. The MMD lost to the Michael Chilufya Sata-led Patriotic Front, who promised the people freedom from foreign influence, especially the Chinese, and a closing of the ever-widening gap between the haves and the have nots.

Sata, during his campaign, called the Chinese businessmen in Zambia 'infestors', calling into question their legitimacy as investors and highlighting their notoriously poor labour relations. Sata rode into victory on the wave of the popularity of his slogan, 'more money on your pockets', and the term 'infestors,' which resonated deeply with the people.

In a country where 66 percent of the population lived below the poverty line, Sata's campaign platform resonated, especially when he made the wild claim that he could provide housing for everyone 'within 90 days'. Once in government, however, all this proved difficult to implement, as Sata fell seriously ill, eventually dying after serving for only three years. The point here is that Sata communicated his message effectively to get elected. He connected with communities that felt left out of Zambia's prosperity.

Sata's party continued in power, but far from expelling the Chinese, the PF government became very dependent on them. Far from lowering taxes, the PF introduced new taxes, at one point contemplating a tax on boreholes for those who provide their own water supply because they cannot rely on local government water systems.

While communication devoid of principle may succeed in the short term, positive long-term results are more likely to be achieved with honest and sincere discourse. In this endeavour, the leader must find their own voice and not be seduced by popular jingos. Nor should the leader invest in emulating someone else. The leader must be authentic, allowing followers to easily discern who and where the leader comes from. Without this, the leader will struggle to convey their value system.

Oratory is a huge advantage for a leader, but it is not necessary for effective communication. Zambia's first president was a gifted orator during the campaign for independence, but his record in government indicates a failure to clearly explain the economic challenges that characterised his rule from the 1970s until he was ousted from power. The second president was equally gifted as an orator while campaigning for the return of democracy. While in office however the management of his alleged desire to alter the constitution and run for a third term, left much to be desired.

In contrast, Anderson Kambela Mazoka was not an orator. He was, however, an effective communicator. The American-educated mechanical engineer thought with clarity and expressed his ideas plainly. He was good at assessing an audience and quickly determining the best way to communicate with them. He knew the value of sharing information with different audiences. This quality helped him found the United Party for National Development as president and quickly spread the new party's footprint across the country.

Mazoka had another vital quality for a modern leader: he knew how to handle the rapid flows of information within his new party, the country, and the broader international community. At any one given time, Mazoka had a good idea of the concerns of critical stakeholders.

Three years after its inception, UPND participated in its first national election and lost by two percentage points. Most who follow Zambian politics would agree that had Mazoka lived, he would have won the 2006 election and assumed the presidency.

Visibility is also a form of communication. An effective leader is adept at being seen regularly without being overexposed. Even in this social media age, the leader needs to appear in person for as many meetings as possible. This is why good political leaders are keen to hold frequent press conferences to brief the nation on relevant issues.

In this regard, the presidency of Michael Chilufya Sata is instructive. Sata had a reputation as an action leader. After all, he was the man who, as mayor, expanded Lusaka's infrastructure despite severe financial constraints. He kept his city clean and left its finances in the healthiest state they had been in a long time. This resulted from Sata providing disciplined leadership to the city council and establishing several revenue-generating ventures, which helped the local authority eliminate its historic deficit.

As minister of health, Sata regularly toured hospitals and often fired underperforming nurses on the spot. His visible leadership led to a marked improvement in the delivery of health services. As president, however, Sata was not as visible. This appears to have been a result of illness rather than choice. Whatever the reason, the absence of leadership led to unnecessary unrest and disregard of the law, as the following example illustrates.

On Saturday April 14, 2014, the UPND leader, Hakainde Hichilema, narrowly escaped physical violence by armed PF cadres opposed to his being interviewed by a radio station in Ndola. The PF thugs, dressed in blue aprons and armed with pistols, machetes, and other objects, blocked the entrance of the commercial building where the radio station was housed, with the stated intention of assaulting Mr. Hichilema. Realising that the PF cadres, reinforced by political thugs from the neighbouring town of Kitwe, intended to violently disrupt Hichilema's programme and even destroy the station's building, the radio station's staff called the police.

The cadres were clearly indifferent to Hichilema's constitutional right to seek support for his political platform. They did not believe Hichilema had a right to campaign in 'their' territory. One of them was quoted by The Post newspaper on April 14 as saying he wanted to burn Mr Hichilema alive with a tyre.

The violence perpetrated by the political hooligans was serious, resulting in injury to UPND supporters and damage to a car parked near the station. Mr. Hichilema himself was able to escape, shaken but physically unharmed.

This behaviour should be condemned by everyone, especially by democratically elected leaders. Violence and democracy are incompatible. Sadly, there was no response from the head of state. The only voice from the ruling party to offer anything resembling condemnation of the savagery came from Mr. Wynter Kabimba, the party's secretary-general. Kabimba, however, qualified his response, saying, 'if indeed those who wanted to attack Hichilema were members of the PF,' they should heed Kabimba's message about discipline within and outside the party.

Mr. Kabimba must have been the only person aware of the incident who did not know who the perpetrators were. Kabimba nevertheless added that PF members should accept that Zambia was a democracy and competitive politics required tolerance.

Mr. Hichilema was in Ndola to explain to the people of the Copperbelt Province what programmes his party would adopt in the event they come to power. The appropriate response for the ruling party would have been to state their own position in an appropriate forum, not to threaten violence against a legitimate political opponent.

But these threats took place because restless young members of the PF saw an absence of leadership committed to managing democratic order. It would have been helpful for President Sata, who was well known for never bearing a grudge, to be visible during these times.

Good communicators are also good listeners. Leaders who listen actively gain a clear understanding of the viewpoints of other people. These wise leaders learn from what is said and what is not said. They also create opportunities to expand their own knowledge base. A leader who does not listen soon becomes intellectually stale and resorts to recycling old discredited ideas. This state of affairs typically ends in humiliation for the leader.

Listening also fosters trust as people being listened to feel respected and become respectful of the leader. Overall, an open environment in which ideas are exchanged freely develops. The leadership of the Second Republic provides an example of the dangers of not listening. While there were many specific complaints about this sad chapter of Zambian history, the main grievance was that the 'general' atmosphere was such that people were not permitted to voice their concerns, however legitimate. Indeed, airing concerns of a political nature was viewed as an act of provocation, with dire consequences.

The leadership did not listen enough to the people who, in turn, felt disrespected. When the people finally had an opportunity to render judgment through the ballot box, the result was shocking and devastating for the government.

Diplomacy

Traditional Zambia places a duty on leaders to be diplomatic. Therefore, it is disappointing that contemporary political discourse has become so disagreeable and verbally violent as to discourage good people from public participation in civic affairs.

Monica Kanjimana's observation that 'the current environment is not favourable for women because of the insults which have dominated our political arena', is real. On October 03, 2017, the Speaker of the National Assembly suspended Mr Bowman Lusambo for 30 days for assaulting a fellow member in parliament. Another parliamentarian was suspended for seven days for 'pouring water on and hurling unprintable insults' at a fellow member. Like Mr Lusambo, Ms Jean Kapata, the other parliamentarian suspended from the House, was a government minister.

These were not the only leaders to behave inappropriately in public. But their misbehaviour is noteworthy because as government ministers, many, including children, looked up to them to set examples of appropriate behaviour. Those children may now believe that abusive language and physical violence are acceptable. This is not the standard the country should be setting for future leaders. Furthermore, the fact that these two parliamentarians suffered no sanctions in their capacity as government members gave credence to the view that the current political leadership in Zambia is a complete stranger to political decorum.

The acceptance of abusive and violent behaviour in politics is not unique to Zambia. On December 11, 2013, the BBC reported that a session of the Georgian parliament had descended into a brawl over a 'gesture' allegedly made by one member. The row between Soso Jachvliani of the ruling Georgian Dream coalition, and the United National Movement's Giorgi Baramidze led to a fistfight on the floor of the House involving several members.

A similar brawl took place on January 20, 2015 in Nepal's parliament in Kathmandu when opposition MPs tried to block the government from pushing through a draft of a new constitution. According to the BBC, the opposition MPs attacked the parliamentary speaker and broke chairs in protest against plans by the ruling coalition. Several security guards were injured during the struggle.

While these examples may be worse than what Zambia has ever experienced, that does not mitigate the harm done to Zambian etiquette and traditions. Furthermore, there is evidence suggesting that political misbehaviour by adults does affect the behaviour of younger people. For example, consider what two young people said after the 2016 United States presidential campaign, which gave centre stage to Donald J. Trump, one of the most morally unrestrained bullies in American politics.

Writing in the March 19, 2018 edition of Teen Vogue, Samantha Black and Sayre Burwell had this to say:

> Since the 2016 election, we have noticed a huge increase in bullying from both politicians and young people. According to a post-election survey conducted by the Human Rights Campaign, 70 percent of young people ages 13 to 18 reported seeing bullying during or after the presidential campaign. Of those, 79 percent said that they witnessed bullying behaviours more frequently since the onset of the presidential campaign.

Zambian children, like many children, will imitate their parents' behaviours and attitudes. It is for this reason that many parents actively instruct their children in social etiquette and morality. The influence of politicians can therefore be mitigated by active parenting. That, however, is not as comforting as it sounds because the reality in present-day Zambia is that many children are growing up in parentless 'households', according to Mission Direct. The duty of politicians to behave more responsibly as role models for young people becomes even more pressing when we recall Mission Direct's estimate that around 1000 children are living on the streets in Lusaka alone.

Gratitude

Among the many values all children should receive from their leaders and parents is the value of gratitude. The Zambian saying, *uushitasha mwana wa musha*, is pregnant with meaning. While its literal meaning translates roughly as 'The ungrateful one is the child of a slave', the saying crystallizes a comprehensive guide for leaders on the value of gratitude.

For example, leaders are expected to cultivate gratitude as a way of engaging the communities they lead. Traditional Zambia understood that gratitude encourages positive interaction between the leaders and the led.

When a leader expresses gratitude for good work done by a colleague or any stakeholder, that colleague or stakeholder is immediately motivated to focus on their successes and work harder in the belief that their work matters. An obsession with the success or failures of competitors will also wane, if not completely disappear, because the person to whom gratitude has been expressed now has a standard to follow and adhere to. Meeting or bettering that standard becomes the focus of attention. Since gratitude is contagious, the recipients of gratitude also endeavour to motivate others around them.

During the one-party state, the government claimed control of everything, but the reality was that it could not. The consequence of this was that events took place for which the government took credit even though it was not responsible for these events. The authors of these events were invisible and could not therefore be thanked in person. This phenomenon partly gave rise to a culture that reserved all gratitude for the leadership, especially the president.

Recognition of good deeds is critical to the management of the citizenry. Gratitude towards citizens serves as a constant reminder that citizen participation is vital to realizing national goals. Conversely, an absence of gratitude toward the citizenry has the effect of unduly expanding the leader's ego at the expense of achieving the national goals.

There is a gratitude dividend for enlightened leaders who take every opportunity to thank colleagues and citizens. People tend to gravitate toward leaders who are thankful and optimistic. Anderson Mazoka, for example, always thanked people who helped him and his political party. While he was critical of the way Zambia was run at the time, he was always optimistic about the country's future. This aspect of his leadership style made him an extremely attractive public figure with whom many wanted to be associated.

I remember meeting Mazoka serendipitously at Lusaka International Airport. It so happened that we were both travelling to London on the same plane. When he saw me, he exclaimed, 'Ah, I am so glad to see you. I have an assignment for you.' His party was in the process of writing its constitution and Mazoka wanted my input. He gave me the draft and, in typical Mazoka fashion, added, 'You have all night to do this.' In fact, it took me about two hours to go through the draft and make my suggestions. When I handed the draft back to him the next morning, he was profuse in his praise for the help I had rendered. The praise was out of proportion to the work I had actually done, but that is to be expected from real leaders.

I was not the only person Mazoka asked to look at the draft constitution. Later, he sought the opinion of a fine Zambian lawyer based in England, Chaloka Beyani, who concurred with my suggested changes. Several months later, when I saw Chaloka, he told me that Mazoka had expressed gratitude for my contribution. In truth, I did not do that much, but it was not in Mazoka's nature to miss an opportunity to say 'thank you'.

On another occasion, Mazoka was visiting Toronto and took the opportunity to call and see if we could meet. Although my family residence was in Ottawa, I worked mostly in Toronto, so we had a condo in the city. I would typically go to Ottawa on Friday afternoon and return on Monday. Mazoka proposed we meet for supper with some friends of his who had worked for the Bata Shoe Company in Canada. After dinner, we bid farewell to his friends and returned to his hotel. Mazoka was so engaging and solicitous of good ideas that it was after 1 am when eventually I bid him good night to take a cab back to my residence.

Learning Agility

Mazoka's ability to seek help when he either did not know what to do or needed a fresh look at a proposal is consistent with the leadership characteristic experts refer to as 'learning agility'. This is another indispensable attribute in an authentic leader. Leaders who are incapable of seeking help will inevitably fail, taking the people they are meant to be leading down with them. A leader must be willing to learn from others as well as his own experiences. The stock of new knowledge equips the leader with the tools to successfully address unusual situations.

Lee Kuan Yew, Seretse Khama, and Paul Kagame are examples of leaders with learning agility. The success of their countries is attributable, at least in part, to this leadership trait. In today's dynamic world, countries must constantly look for what may work and what may not work. Strategies that worked in the past do not guarantee future success. In the case of Zambia, the assumption that earnings from the export of copper will always come to the rescue actually undermines progress by encouraging complacency. Innovation is much harder to achieve when there is a source of easy income. Zambia has the human resources both within and without the country to diversify the economy to the point where copper earnings are turned into no more than icing on the cake.

The best-performing countries have (or were founded by) leaders who thrive on change and can make sense of uncertainty. Lee Kuan Yew, Sir Seretse Khama, and Sir Seewoosagur Ramgoolam inherited countries considered by experts to be incapable of surviving on their own. Paul Kagame achieved power in Rwanda after a genocide that many believed the country could never recover from. All four countries are infinitely better off now than they were at inception. Singapore and Rwanda are leaders in innovation, Botswana is known for good governance and economic management, and Mauritius has the highest per capita income in its region.

Innovation

Leadership with learning agility leads to innovation. Singapore, for example, continues to benefit from the learning agility of Lee Kuan Yew and the leaders who followed him. So it is not surprising that the Global Innovation Index 2019 ranked Singapore as fifth—first in Asia—for innovation performance out of 127 countries worldwide.

Less well-known globally in the area of innovation is Rwanda. It may be helpful to focus on how Rwanda has been innovative in managing the COVID-19 crisis. As of 28th August 2020, the country had lost 15 lives to the pandemic. Belgium, the former colonial power which has a similar population as Rwanda, had 9,884 deaths. The reason for this massive difference is that Rwanda is a leading innovator.

Let's examine Rwanda's innovative response to the COVID-19 public health crisis.

Rwanda took the coronavirus disease seriously as soon as it was known and launched a campaign to educate the population about the importance of preventive measures such as physical distancing, washing hands, and wearing masks. In short order, this became a way of life in the country.

After these basics had been understood, several innovations were initiated to minimise disruption in national life and the lives of individuals. The purpose of the measures taken was to ensure a rapid return to normalcy.

In March 2020, ECOMEM, a Rwandan company founded by Paulin Murego, started distributing mobile sink-like facilities that allowed people to properly their wash hands with soap, pushing water up with a foot, without the hand coming in contact with any surface that may be hosting the virus. These contraptions can be found almost everywhere in Kigali.

In May 2020, the Rwandan Ministry of Health introduced five public health workers: Akazuba, Ikirezi, Mwiza, Ngabo, and Urumuri. They are human-sized robots programmed to perform temperature screening, take vitals, and deliver video messages. They can also detect people not wearing masks and instruct them to do so. Urumuri was deployed to the Kigali International Airport, where she performs mass screenings. She can screen 150 people per minute and report any abnormalities to officers on duty.

In August 2020, the Rwanda Biomedical Centre launched and placed locally manufactured spraying booths at the entrance of schools and other public institutions. The spraying booths were equipped with motion sensors and spray a 360-degree mist of foggy hydrogen peroxide in an automated response to human movement. The machine, which can sterilise 1000 people a day, has a 90 percent disinfection effect. Some versions can also measure temperature, and depending on the model, collect other information.

An important component of the fight against COVID-19 is political leadership. There have been jurisdictions where the professionals have done their best to manage the pandemic only to be undermined by harmful statements and a lack of positive leadership from the politicians. Rwanda cannot be accused of this.

All levels of leadership have cooperated to mitigate the impact of the disease. As a result, the residents of Kigali are now accustomed to the sight of drones hovering over their city, loudly relaying COVID-19 related information and reminding the public to observe precautionary measures such as frequent handwashing and social distancing. The drones are deployed by the Rwanda National Police, mainly in high-risk and densely populated areas.

On April 24, 2020, Zambian President Edgar Lungu directed churches to reopen despite concerns about COVID-19. Many churches immediately countered this directive by advising their congregants that they would not be reopening. The state took note but in so doing revealed that little planning had gone into the president's initial directive. Reverend Godfridah Sumaili, the minister responsible for religious affairs, issued a statement that promised further guidelines. In a well-organised governance structure, these guidelines would have accompanied the president's directive.

While the president did make the reopening of the churches conditional on adhering to preventative measures such as social distancing and mask wearing, he also acknowledged that his government was 'still determining the extent of the disease through escalated testing and screening to assess when we shall reopen our economy fully.'

The urgency of reopening churches when other areas of the economy were required to remain closed was never full explained.

In contrast, the reopening of churches in Rwanda in August 2020 was preceded by well-publicised guidelines concerning social distancing and other measures. Worshippers who showed up for service after the stipulated numbers of occupants had been reached, were turned back. In response to this challenge, Rock Software Solutions Ltd built a mobile app that allowed worshippers to reserve seats in advance.

Empathy and Influence

Traditional Zambian leadership values emphasise empathy and influence because a leader cannot be effective without a complete understanding of the issues facing the population. The saying, *Mueteleli ki mutano wa sicaba* translates roughly as 'a leader is a bridge for the people'. When read together with *Kuba ni kooleka*, which roughly translates as 'to give is to retain', this saying points to a strong belief in traditional society that empathy and influence are intimately connected.

A leader who places herself in the shoes of vulnerable members of the population will find it easier to win society's confidence than one who does not. A genuinely empathetic and influential leader will be keen to protect national resources and ensure minimum waste, as Seretse Khama did in Botswana. Corruption, which eats away at the fabric of society and disproportionately harms vulnerable members of society, is therefore unacceptable to empathetic and influential leaders.

Zambia's Leadership Choice

Zambia needs to be uncompromising in choosing the best leadership, guided by today's requirements and the country's traditional values. Unless this happens, badly needed positive change will remain elusive. Through a viable constitution and public demand, Zambians ought to insist on specific values and behaviours necessary to reinforce the new culture. When this happens, the benefits of authentic leadership will be felt almost immediately.

For much of the last fifty years, Zambians have been inclined to question leaders' credibility because of the gulf between their words and their actions. For example, in the 1970s and 80s, Zambia had a motor vehicle manufacturing industry that was allowed to wind up because leaders declined to support the industry by buying its products. This happened despite Kenneth Kaunda's public declaration that 'we shall all be Fiating', referring to the Fiat car, which was locally assembled.

Far from 'Fiating', President Kaunda's government purchased brand new Mercedes Benz cars for the president, UNIP central committee members, and cabinet ministers. At one point, the leadership absurdly claimed that the posh cars had been fitted with Fiat engines when challenged about the cost of the new vehicles.

There is no shortage of examples where leaders have said one thing and proceeded to do the opposite. Because of this, it is now more difficult for political leaders to be a bridge to the Zambian people, as required by traditional leadership tenets. The tone set at the highest level of national leadership affects the behaviour of others in the nation. The result of this failure to be a bridge to the people is reduced transparency and general acceptance of corruption.

The case of the 42 firefighting trucks purchased by the Zambian government in September 2017 speaks volumes about transparency and corruption in Zambia today. The high price-USD42 million-paid for the equipment did not deter the government from defending its decision to procure the firefighting trucks. The government's basic defence was that the procurement process had been transparent and that the cost reflected the fact that the trucks had been custom-made.

A high-end fire truck can cost USD975,000. That truck, which is much larger than the conventional one, would come with the heavy-duty 107-feet long aerial ladder, rather than the standard 75-feet one. The new ladder can accommodate two fighters as it has a tip load of 500 pounds. (In the discourse, both supporters and opponents of purchasing the vehicles refer to them as firetrucks, although they can pump water, and should therefore strictly be referred to as fire engines. We shall stick to the vernacular).

None of these features were used as an excuse for the massive expenditure on the fire trucks, which appeared very ordinary indeed. Concerned citizens asked why the government spent so much money on these particular trucks when it could have bought similar trucks, with a good track record of service, for an average price of USD300,000. According to sources, the actual price indicated on importation documents was USD250,000 per truck.

The government reacted to these questions, not with answers, but with intimidation. On 29 September 2017, Lewis Mwape of the Zambia Council for Social Development, Laura Miti of the Alliance for Community Action, Sean Enoch Tembo of Patriots for Economic Progress, activists Bornwell Mwewa and Mika Mwambazi, and musician Fumba Chama, better known as Pilato, protested outside the Zambian parliament to raise awareness about the abuse of public funds as evidenced by the procurement of the 42 fire trucks.

The demonstrators were immediately arrested and charged with 'disobeying lawful orders'. After spending more than 10 hours in police custody, they were finally released on bail. The length of time it took to bring the 'suspects' to trial shows that the charges were indeed flimsy.

Fifteen months after the initial arrests, the protestors were acquitted by the Lusaka Magistrate Court. Magistrate Mwaka Mikalile found the defendants to have done nothing more than exercise their constitutional right to assemble. The magistrate went further and cautioned the police not to unlawfully interfere with that right.

The harassment of these civic minded citizens had come to the attention of the Southern Africa Litigation Centre which condemned the arrests in categorical terms. While the decision fortified Zambia's reputation as a country with a largely independent judiciary, it did nothing to enhance its democratic credentials. This kind of publicity is not helpful to a country that styles itself as a democracy.

It was now clear for all to see that the charges were, at best, flimsy. Indeed the easy acquittal of the civic leaders raised questions as to why they had been arrested in the first place. It is also reasonable to assume that the state was simply trying to find a way to silence Laura Miti and her colleagues from propagating their views. Teldah Mawarire and Laura Miti co-authored an opinion article titled: Corruption in Zambia: 42 fire trucks for $42m: The African Union is promoting an anti-corruption agenda, but is the Zambian government committed to it?

Here is an excerpt from that article as published by Al Jazeera:

There are enough cases of corruption reported in Zambia's media in the last couple of months to show that the state is not committed to anti-corruption measures.

In May 2018, it was discovered that medication and medical kits, donated by international aid agency Global Fund, worth $1m vanished from government custody. Zambia has since committed to reimbursing the Global Fund.

In June 2018, Zambia's Financial Intelligence Centre (FIC) released a report that found some cabinet members and presidential aides had siphoned billions of Zambian kwacha from government coffers through money laundering.

Instead of acting against those named in the findings, the state has chosen to go after the FIC chairperson saying the report was released in an irregular manner.

Democracy cannot flourish in the circumstances described by Mawarire and Miti. Zambians, therefore, have a responsibility, when given the opportunity to do so, to identify leaders who reflect the values described in this section and who are committed to democracy. It must be understood that an authentic democratic leader would much rather lose an election honestly than win one dishonestly.

Such a leader would be intolerant of corruption and waste. As a result of this aversion to corruption, they would ensure transparent governance, which maximises opportunity for investing in people. In the best Zambian tradition, this would be a leader capable of being a bridge to the people.

CHAPTER EIGHT

Building Institutions for a New Zambia

I f Zambia is to be an authentic and inclusive democracy, it must create institutions that reflect traditional Zambian values. The reforms leading to the creation of these institutions must result in greater and uncompromising respect for the rule of law, setting the stage for robust and sustainable economic growth, and reducing poverty through consistent provision of basic services to citizens.

Building better institutions has been a challenge for Zambia because the constitutions which would bring about these institutions have almost always been drafted by the executive branch of government motivated by, among other things, a desire to stay in power. Thus, the one-party constitution was designed mostly, if not entirely, to prolong Kenneth Kaunda's stay in power as leader of the only lawful political party in the country. The 1996 constitution, on the other hand, at least in its original intent, was designed to keep Kaunda from returning to power as head of state.

Constitutions must be drafted by men and women of goodwill keenly aware of both the country's past as well as its present circumstances. Accordingly, the people given the task of drafting a viable constitution for Zambia must look at the country's traditional values as articulated in the preceding chapter and examine the reasons for the relative success of 15th century Kongo and, subsequently, the Luba-Lunda empire.

In building credible institutions for Zambia, there should be healthy cross-pollination of ideas. That however should not be understood to mean uncritical acceptance of foreign ideas. In the past, efforts to build better institutions have failed partly because of excessive reliance on foreign concepts which do not necessarily reflect Zambian values. For example, all constitutional dispensations have used a combination of the British and American constitutions as the starting point. Zambia has thus found herself with a presidential system free from the checks and balances entrenched in the American system.

The fact that no Zambian constitution has provided a limit on the number of executive branch members who may sit in Parliament has diluted the legislature's oversight role over the presidency.

Despite this, the legislature has occasionally been able to pass good laws. But these laws are not always enforced by effective and trusted institutions. This results in waste of resources and service delivery failures in the economic arena, all of which undermine the fight against poverty.

We know that robust institutions can promote poverty reduction. Reference has already been made to Botswana, Rwanda, and Singapore as examples of countries that started life as very poor jurisdictions but succeeded in significantly raising the population's standards of living, partly because they invested in robust institutions to promote the common good. In crafting their constitutions, these countries also paid great attention to their unique circumstances and settled on constitutions that reflected both their aspirations and values.

A New Constitution for Zambia

A review of Zambia's constitutional history suggests that there are a few areas which urgently need reform. These include creating a more credible electoral commission, strengthening perceptions of judicial independence, strengthening the independence of prosecutorial agencies, and modernising the prison service.

Electoral Reform

Even before the formal conclusion of the August 2016 general election, Zambia's main opposition party alleged fraud and called for a recount of votes in Lusaka. The United Party for National Development went further and withdrew from the ballot verification process. At that point, President Edgar Lungu of the governing Patriotic Front party held a slim lead over his rival, Mr Hakainde Hichilema, with votes counted in more than 80 percent of constituencies.

The UPND accused the Electoral Commission of Zambia of bias favoring the PF, pointing to the slow publication of the results. The ECZ denied bias and said slow publication of results was caused by five different ballots taking place on Election Day. In addition to the presidential election, parliamentarians were also being elected, as were executive mayors and councillors. Furthermore, there was also a proposed constitutional amendment on the ballot.

This was not the first time that an opposition party had cried foul after losing an election. In fact, claims of electoral malpractice by the losing party have almost become a ritual in Zambian elections. The reason for this appears to be a lack of trust in the electoral commission.

Increasing the credibility of the Electoral Commission of Zambia may not guarantee unreserved acceptance of election results because there will always be politicians such as Silvio Berlusconi of Italy who lost the 2006 election and claimed, with no evidence, that there had been widespread fraud. Former American President Donald Trump's refusal to accept the results of the election he lost is an even more spectacular example of an irresponsible politician refusing to accept the clear will of the people. But a more credible ECZ would reduce the number of such claims. And when these claims arise, they would be adjudicated swiftly and be credibly dismissed or upheld.

How then does Zambia increase ECZ's credibility, an organisation which already has a good constitutional mandate under Article 229(2), and whose mission is to be 'an independent and autonomous constitutional body that delivers credible elections'. ECZ has also attracted qualified leaders since its inception in 1996 because chairpersons must be eligible for appointment to the Supreme Court. Despite the clear mandate and the high qualifications set for chairpersons, the perception that the Electoral Commission of Zambia may not be as independent as it claims has increased.

The reason for this lies in part in the way the chairperson of the commission is appointed. Section 5(1) of the Electoral Commission of Zambia Act gives the republican president the power to appoint the chairperson and four other members of the Commission. One of the four members serves as vice-chairperson and is specifically appointed for that role.

The Zambian president is not a titular head of state. He is also the country's chief executive officer and commander-in-chief of the armed forces. Furthermore, the president is the head of the political party in power. Had Zambia had a more traditional parliamentary system with an executive prime minister and a non-partisan head of state, the appointment of the chairperson of the Electoral Commission of Zambia by the president would have been less contentious.

In circumstances where the appointing authority is partisan and potentially able to derive an advantage from the appointment of the chairperson, it is reasonable to be concerned about the independence and impartiality of the appointee.

To avoid perceptions of bias on the part of the Electoral Commission of Zambia, the country's future constitution must give the powers of appointment of the head of the electoral commission to parliament. These powers can also be given to another body as long as that body is not controlled by the president. For example, the Botswana Independent Electoral Commission's chairperson and deputy chairperson are appointed 'directly by the Judicial Service Commission'. Five other members of the IEC are appointed from a list of persons recommended by the All Party Conference. As in Zambia, the chairperson and deputy chairperson must be eligible for appointment as judges on the country's highest court. The purpose of these arrangements is to ensure the commission is 'an autonomous, non-partisan body whose primary purpose is to conduct free, fair and correct elections efficiently and effectively in accordance with universally accepted electoral principles and practices'.[45]

Rwanda's National Electoral Commission consists of 12 members. The Commission's president and vice president are appointed by parliament, as are four other members. The remaining six members are permanent employees of the Commission. Article 180 of the Rwanda Constitution makes the National Electoral Commission a permanent body independent of the other branches of government.

Singapore's management of the electoral process is markedly different from that of Botswana and Rwanda. Elections in Singapore fall within the scope of the prime minister's responsibilities and are administered by the Elections Department, headed by a civil servant.

Before an election, the prime minister typically appoints a Boundaries Review Committee to review the number and boundaries of electoral constituencies. The Boundaries Review Committee is dominated by civil servants. When the review is complete, the committee submits its report to the cabinet whose decision to accept or reject it is final. Thus, parliament has no say in the adoption of the report and no opportunity

---

[45] Tsie, Balefi, Professor, The Role, Functions and Performance of Botswana's Independent Electoral Commission,
Journal of African Elections, Vol. 2 No. 1

to debate it. All the government has to do to effect the report is publish the new boundaries in the Government Gazette.

The Singaporean executive branch's apparent control of the electoral process has led to criticism of this otherwise splendidly managed state. For example, Lee Hsien Yang, the prime minister's brother, who clashed with him over a family dispute and backed the opposition PSP, was quoted in the July 09, 2020 edition of The Japan Times as follows:

> Singapore needs fairer elections before it can have truly competitive elections…One-party rule is dangerous for a nation… It leads to groupthink, to arrogance and entitled behavior. It means people's real concerns are dismissed and policies bulldozed.

This criticism is not widespread as most voters support the government and do not consider electoral reform a priority. The ruling party in Singapore has a proven track record of improving living standards and eliminating corruption, transforming Singapore from a small trading port into an economic superpower. GDP per capita has soared more than 150 times over the past fifty-five years and is now higher than that of the US, Germany, and Australia.

As long as Singapore continues to prosper, electoral reform in Singapore is not likely to be a salient issue for most citizens. Electoral reform is however an issue in Zambia where citizens increasingly associate economic prosperity with good governance.

Zambian constitutional reforms should include the fortification of ECZ as an independent and impartial body that is seen as such by all reasonable people. In addition to the Botswana and Rwanda models, Zambia can also look at Canada, where the office of Chief Electoral Officer was created in 1920 by the Dominion Elections Act.

The Chief Electoral Officer is appointed for a 10-year non-renewable term by a resolution of the House of Commons, the main parliamentary chamber. The Chief Electoral Officer, who plays a similar role to that of the ECZ chairperson, reports directly to parliament and is thus completely independent of the government of the day and all political parties. They can be removed from office only for cause by the governor-general (the titular head of state) after a joint request following a majority vote by both the House of Commons and Senate.

In the Zambian case, both the chairperson and vice-chairperson should each be appointed to a ten-year non-renewable term. That way, the chairperson cannot be influenced by anyone with a promise of term renewal. The other commissioners should be treated similarly, although their appointments should be staggered to ensure continuity and preservation of corporate memory.

The Public Order Act

The notorious Public Order Act is associated with elections. It is a law inherited from the colonial era and designed to suppress citizens' freedom of assembly. The most remarkable aspect of this law is its staying power, given the statute's clear violation of the Zambia Constitution Act which guarantees the right to freedom of assembly in Article 21. On this basis alone, the Public Order Act is surely unconstitutional and therefore invalid. The author is not alone in holding this view. In a comprehensive article published in the Lusaka Times on May 06, 2019, Professor Muna Ndulo, William Nelson Cromwell Professor of International and Comparative Law, Cornell Law School and Director of Cornell Law School's Berger International Legal Studies Program and the Institute for African Development, reached the same conclusion.

Needless to say, the constitution of any country is supreme to all other laws. Indeed, all other laws derive their legitimacy from the constitution. It follows that any law which contravenes the constitution is inherently invalid.

On this basis, on March 26, 2020, Uganda's Constitutional Court nullified parts of Uganda's Public Order Management Act of 2013. The court stated that the public order law gave the police excess powers to prohibit public gatherings and protests.

Like its Zambian counterpart, this law has been used to deny legitimate opposition parties the space they need to air their views and to seek to influence the electorate. The Ugandan court was unsettled by the appearance of the police being given de facto powers of interpreting the constitutional right of assembly. In welcoming the court's decision, Deprose Muchena, Amnesty International's Director for East and Southern Africa, said:

This law has for years been used as a tool of repression in Uganda therefore this ruling is a welcome development for the human rights to peaceful assembly and freedom of expression in the country. Under this law police have brutally dispersed spontaneous demonstrations and opposition rallies, while opposition politicians have been beaten up and arrested simply for exercising their rights

The petition leading to the Uganda Constitutional Court ruling was filed in December 2013 by human rights groups, including Human Rights Network Uganda, Development Network of Indigenous Voluntary Associations, Uganda Association of Women Lawyers, and Chapter Four. The issues of concern are remarkably similar to ongoing issues in Zambia.

Consider, for example, the following extract from the Amnesty International Report (2017/18) on Zambia:

Freedoms of Assembly and Association

The space for civil society, human rights defenders, journalists and opposition political parties was increasingly restricted. The authorities continued to use the Public Order Act to prevent political parties and civil society organizations from gathering. Section 5(4) of the Act provided that anyone intending to assemble or convene a public meeting or demonstration was required to give the police seven days' notice. However, the police interpreted the law as imposing a requirement to obtain prior authorization for any public assembly to proceed. On 24 August, police dispersed a prayer meeting convened to welcome Hakainde Hichilema's release from Mukobeko Maximum Security Prison in Kabwe city where he had been held for four months on charges of treason, which were dropped.

On 10 January, UK lawyer Oliver Holland was arrested and charged under the Public Order Act with unlawful assembly for meeting with a community in Chingola city who was challenging in court environmental pollution allegedly caused by a mining company. He was released the same day and charges against him were dropped; however, he was later charged with conduct likely to breach the peace and ordered to pay a USD5 fine.

Police frequently used unnecessary and excessive force to disperse protesters.

In April, police stopped a UPND rally in Kanyama Township in the capital, Lusaka, on "security" grounds. Although the UPND had notified the police in advance of the rally, they unlawfully dispersed the rally, shooting 20-year-old Stephen Kalipa, one of the protesters. He died later from gunshot wounds at the hospital. An investigation was opened, but no one had been arrested in connection with the incident by the end of the year. The police claimed that he died of knife stab wounds at the hands of an unidentified assailant.

On 23 June, police arrested senior UPND officials on charges of unlawful assembly alleging that they held a press briefing at the UPND's secretariat offices without obtaining prior authorization. On 29 September, police arrested six human rights defenders who gathered outside Parliament and protested peacefully against the government's purchase, at the inflated cost of USD42 million, of 42 fire engines; they were charged with refusing to obey police orders. The protesters were beaten during the protest by members of the ruling Patriotic Front.

Excessive Use of Force

On 8 April, Hakainde Hichilema and other UPND members – Lastone Mulilandumba, Muleya Haachenda, Wallace Chakwa, Pretorius Haloba and Hamusonde Hamaleka – were arrested and charged with treason and disobeying a lawful order following an earlier incident in which Hakainde Hichilema's motorcade refused to give way to President Lungu's convoy. Police raided Hakainde Hichilema's house without a warrant, using tear gas against him and his family. On 28 April, his wife, Mutinta, was threatened with arrest after she reported the police's use of excessive force. No charges had been brought against the police in connection with the incident by the end of the year. On 15 August, the Director of Public Prosecutions withdrew all charges against Hakainde Hichilema and the other UPND members.

Section 5 (4) referred to in the Amnesty International report requires any person intending to assemble or convene a public meeting, procession, or demonstration to notify the police in writing of their intent to do so 14 days before the meeting. Under the public order 'law', this notice must contain an undertaking by the persons intending to assemble or convene a public meeting, procession or demonstration that order and peace shall be maintained through the observance of six conditions that include being informed by the police that the proposed site for the meeting has not already been granted to another group; that the route and the width of the route is suitable for the holding of processions in accordance with the width and route specifications for such purposes as specified by the Minister by statutory order; that marshals of a number sufficient to monitor the public meeting, procession or demonstration are available and shall co-operate with the Police to ensure peace and stability; that the commencement, duration and destination of the public meeting, procession or demonstration shall be notified to the Police; that the public meeting, procession or demonstration shall not create a risk to security or public safety, a breach of the peace or disaffection amongst inhabitants of that neighborhood; and that the conveners of the meeting, procession or demonstration have been assured by the Police that at the time the proposed activity shall be held, it will be possible for it to be adequately policed.

The reader will notice how the requirements of section 5(4) of the Act shift the primary duty of the police from protecting citizens and helping guarantee their constitutional rights to determining who may and may not enjoy the constitutional right to assemble.

Where, for example, it is not possible for the police to adequately supervise any particular public meeting, procession or demonstration, the regulating officer of the area is effectively given the power by section 6 to postpone the meeting. In practice, determining what is 'possible' is left entirely in the hands of the police.

Any breach of this order to postpone the meeting effectively makes the meeting illegal, as was the case with the May 07, 1960, rally called by the United National Independence Party leadership in Ndola. The reader will recall that the consequences of the colonial government's unwise decision to deny UNIP a permit to hold the meeting led to the unfortunate death of an innocent woman.

In politically tense times, people need outlets to express their frustrations and anger. When these outlets are denied, violence becomes an attractive option. It is perhaps for this reason that international law, as expressed by treaties to which Zambia is a party, recognises freedom of assembly as a fundamental right in a democratic society. More importantly, the Zambian constitution is equally uncompromising in recognizing freedom of assembly as a fundamental right.

The Public Order Act needs to be repealed.

No Democracy without Opposition

The Public Order Act has survived for so long because the different constitutional dispensations offered to Zambians have not fully embraced political opposition as an essential element of democracy. This disdain for the opposition was, of course, most evident during the one-party years. The one-party state system's imposition was not driven by popular demand but was rather a crude attempt by the ruling elite to permanently silence the opposition. Not surprisingly, the one-party dictatorship encouraged the emergence of an unprincipled class of politicians whose main objective was self-aggrandizement.

It was at this time that the country also witnessed a cultural shift from relative freethought to sycophancy. In state institutions, for example, political loyalty replaced merit as the determinant for success. Furthermore, the absence of an opposition deprived the country of a government in waiting, which is essential for smooth transfers of power from one administration to another.

While reverting to democracy in 1991 was a good thing, it has to be acknowledged that Zambian democracy only accepts the opposition grudgingly.

On September 17, 2010, The Lusaka Times and other media showed a video of ruling party thugs damaging an opposition party campaign vehicle in Kasama as police officers watched. In the clip, bystanders could be heard in the background expressing their disgust at police inaction. This was yet another example of how certain elements of the national police service had begun to see themselves as an extension of the ruling party and to view the opposition as illegitimate.

The propagation of political violence is not one-sided. On July 11, 2020, the Diggers newspaper reported that 'two Patriotic Front cadres [had] sustained injuries' after being attacked by Mufulira UPND activists. The attacks followed efforts to prevent the UPND leader Hakainde Hichilema from participating in a radio interview. Independent sources reported that the PF cadres had gone to the radio station to stop the radio program featuring the UPND leader, but they were overpowered by a group of opposition party loyalists.

According to the Diggers report, the station's owners complained that ruling party activists had become so emboldened as to make daily checks on the radio station to determine who was being interviewed. Whether initiated by the opposition or ruling party, this behaviour is completely unacceptable in a democracy. Violence and democracy are incompatible. Why then does violence feature with such frequency in Zambian democracy today?

The answer to this question lies in the apparent failure of the ruling party to accept the legitimacy and indispensability to democracy of the opposition. It also lies in the inadequacy of the Zambian constitution. Constitutional practice in a democracy should provide clear incentives to both the opposition and the ruling party to play by the rules.

An opposition party that believes that it has a role to play in national politics and has a reasonable prospect of one day winning power legitimately will shun violence, as will a ruling party that is certain that the opposition will always play by the rules.

Air Time for the Opposition

Traditional Zambian society respected the diversity of opinion in matters of governance. Starting with the Kongo kings, all rulers understood the importance of different, even contrarian, views and felt duty-bound to expose themselves to as much public opinion as possible. Critically, they knew that few citizens would be free enough to express opposing views in the presence of the monarch. The desire to know what was going on in the kingdom led to the creation of the office of the Ing'omba.

Ing'omba was a poet in the king's employ whose duty was to gather opinion in the kingdom and report back to the king in the form of poems or songs. To ensure that Ing'omba was not restrained in what he reported back, the office was given absolute immunity from prosecution for the reports sent to the king, whether in the form of poetry or song.

Royal advisors also took into account a diversity of views as they counselled the monarch. When dealing with monarchs unduly sensitive to criticism, the advisors would follow the lead of the Ing'omba and disguise their criticism as praise. The king would know the issue of concern, but untutored onlookers would take the 'praise' at face value.

In a modern democracy, there must be a free market of ideas, expressed respectfully, as dictated by Zambian culture. This free market of ideas should not be just for the benefit of the executive branch of government but for everyone. One way to achieve this is to mandate broadcasters to air free messages by political parties. In this new world, any political party with significant support at the previous election would be entitled to free broadcasts three months before the next general election. For example, a party receiving five percent of the national vote could be entitled to 15 minutes of air time per week for the three months preceding the next election.

The fifteen minutes would be used as a benchmark for all parties culminating in political parties that secured 30 percent of the vote or more, having a maximum of ninety minutes per week. These figures are obviously working figures to be refined when the regulations are written.

Instituting a system like this one would give credible but underfunded small parties a fighting chance to get their message across. Ideally, political advertising should be checked for accuracy by independent authorities. Certainly, foreign funding of political parties should be outlawed, with heavy penalties for those breaching this law. Without this law, Zambian sovereignty will continue to be undermined.

Beyond these minimum requirements, which would be part of the licensing requirement, broadcasters and their professional bodies should be free to make their own judgments about the amount of election-related news to be broadcast in the usual course of business.

A Seat at the Table

Zambia's current 'winner takes all' system is also inconsistent with traditional Zambian governance practices. No reasonable voice is excluded from participation in matters of state in traditional society, as evidence from 900 AD Zambezia shows. It is not possible to govern with equity when political players with significant support in the country are completely excluded from governance.

When the 2001 presidential election results were announced, Anderson Mazoka, leader of the United Party for National Development, finished second, with 27 percent of the vote. The winner, Levy Patrick Mwanawasa of the MMD, had only two percent more votes than Mazoka. Furthermore, in the national assembly elections that took place concurrently, the UPND won 49 seats, becoming the second-largest party after the MMD.

To Zambians aware of traditional political systems, there was something wrong with Mazoka and the UPND going into the political wilderness until the next election, after such an impressive performance. This sentiment was expressed by sympathizers of both the ruling party and the UPND.

Opposition parties performing as well as Mazoka's UPND did should have an opportunity to participate in the country's formal decision-making processes. Parliament is a necessary but not sufficient forum for opposition representation. Where the opposition performs as well as Mazoka's UPND did in 2001, the country would benefit from opposition representation in the executive branch too.

It is proposed that where the runner-up party in a general election comes as close to winning as Mazoka's UPND did, Zambia should allow the opposition to nominate a maximum of five candidates for inclusion in the cabinet. The portfolios to be held by the nominated persons would depend entirely on the president who would be given a list of ten potential ministers from which to choose the five 'opposition' cabinet ministers. (There may be some merit in restricting these appointments to persons who had not been candidates themselves in the election.) This need not disrupt orderly executive functioning as the 'opposition' would be as bound by the principle of collective responsibility as any other cabinet member. They would also take the same oath of allegiance.

In addition to reflecting good traditional governance values, this dispensation would give opposition parties an incentive to be loyal to the constitution and to shun undemocratic practices. It would also ensure that the best policies of the opposition are given a platform at the heart of government. Needless to say, this arrangement would also encourage continuity in the event the opposition wins the next election. This is because corporate knowledge would be shared by the ruling and the opposition parties' cabinet ministers. Most of all, this dispensation would encourage cross-party collaboration and emphasize the acceptance and indispensability of opposition parties in Zambian democracy.

Strengthening the Separation of Powers Doctrine

The current constitution would make it a little harder to implement the proposal of opposition participation in the Zambian cabinet because of the requirement that members of the cabinet should also be members of parliament. Zambia does not have a clear separation of powers between the legislative and executive branches of government. Experience shows that the integration of these two branches of government has not aided good governance and has in fact undermined democracy.

Too frequently, the government has dominated the legislative branch so much as to effectively make it a puppet of the president and his cabinet. This has undermined the legislature's ability to review, monitor, and supervise the government as it enforces laws and implements programmes.

It has become common practice for governments to appoint members of the opposition to ministerial posts as a way of weakening parliamentary oversight, although occasionally, this has been done as a way of enhancing national unity by broadening diversity in a cabinet. Whatever the motivation, the result of incorporating certain members of the opposition into a cabinet, under the current constitution is to reduce the legislature's ability to hold the government accountable.

This was one of the concerns in August 2015 when President Edgar Lungu appointed the UPND Sinazongwe Member of Parliament Richwell Siamunene as defence minister. Siamunene joined three other opposition MPs who had earlier been incorporated into the government. The appointment helped mute criticism of the government as the ambitious Siamunene, who lists 'making friends' among his hobbies, focused on supporting the government rather than checking it.

But the executive branch is also harmed by the absence of a clear separation of powers between the executive and legislative branches. Save for the eight nominated members, parliamentarians are elected by constituencies. Although there is a certain amount of political sophistication and respect for ideology in urban constituencies in the Copperbelt Province, there is a significant lack of diverse political information and sophistication in rural and semi-rural areas.

To win in these constituencies, candidates must identify strongly with the area and be well versed in local issues. Often, these issues are unique and quite different from national issues. A person elected in one of these constituencies and subsequently elevated to the cabinet will sometimes find it difficult to reconcile local interests with national interests, and when this happens, the default position is to protect local interests.

This conflict often leads to the parliamentarian seeing himself as 'his' people's champion in the cabinet. Many ethnic tensions, typically provoked by a development project getting placed in one part of the country rather than another, have their roots in this perception. A clearer separation of powers would avoid this problem by allowing the president to appoint more seasoned and visionary ministers to the cabinet, since the president would have a larger pool to choose from.

The Prison Service

There is perhaps no area of Zambian life more at odds with traditional Zambian values than the treatment of criminal offenders. The emphasis in modern Zambia has been on the punishment of criminals rather than their rehabilitation, despite a dearth of examples of imprisonment in pre-colonial Zambian history. In Lord of the Kongo, Peter Forbath, using original records from various sources, writes that the first Portuguese explorers to reach the Kongo kingdom were imprisoned in makeshift jails, suggesting that even a comparatively sophisticated kingdom such as Kongo did not have formal prisons. This aversion to imprisonment is evident in many African cultures. Writing in the January 2008 issue of the International Journal on Human Rights, Jeremy Sarkin, Professor of Law at the University of South Africa, had this to say:

> Prison is not an institution indigenous to Africa. Rather, like so many elements of African bureaucracy today, it is a holdover from colonial times, a European import designed to isolate and punish political opponents, exercise racial superiority, and administer capital and corporal punishment.

> Incarceration as punishment was unknown to Africa when the first Europeans arrived. While pretrial detention was common, wrongdoing was rectified by restitution rather than punishment.

> Local justice systems were victim- rather than perpetrator-centered with the end goal being compensation instead of incarceration. Even in centralized states that did establish prisons, the goal of incarceration remained to secure compensation for victims rather than to punish offenders. Imprisonment and capital punishment were viewed as last resorts within African justice systems, to be used only when perpetrators such as repeat offenders and witches posed discreet risks to local communities.

> While imprisonment-as-punishment did not take root in Africa until the late 1800s, there were two exceptions to this characterization. First, prisons were used in connection with the Atlantic Slave Trade. Second, Southern African nations began to rely upon imprisonment much earlier than the rest of the continent, in some cases as early as the beginning of the 19th century.

Even when the colonial powers arrived [from] Europe, they utilized imprisonment not as a means by which to punish the commission of common crimes but rather to control and exploit potentially rebellious local populations. Therefore, Africa's earliest experience with formal prisons was not with an eye toward the rehabilitation or reintegration of criminals but rather the economic, political, and social subjugation of indigenous peoples. It was in these early prisons that even minor offenders were subjected to brutal confinement and conscripted as sources of cheap labor.

Sarkin's observations are consistent with Zambian oral history. Extreme punishments in traditional Luba-Lunda society, for example, would include exile, letting the offender become *akapondo*, or amputation in the case of serious larceny.

There is evidence of the execution of offenders in Swaziland for extremely serious offences. The Nyonyane Mountain is known as Execution Rock for good reason. This magnificent peak acquired its name from ancient practices which involved criminals, especially suspected witches, being forced to walk off the edge of the mountain at spear point for their crimes.

There is not much evidence of peacetime executions in pre-colonial Zambian history, and no evidence of mass incarceration.

A Better Bail Regime

The picture is very different in modern Zambia. According to the World Prison Brief, the online database, in 2019, Zambia had a total prison population of 22,823. That represented an incarceration rate of 123 per 100,000. With the official capacity of the prison system at 8,250, the prison occupancy level was 303 percent. In comparison, the occupancy levels for Singapore, Botswana, and Rwanda were 79.2, 100.9, and 101.3, respectively. In other words, Zambian prisons are three times more crowded than the prisons in Rwanda. It is hard to find a country with more crowded prisons than Zambia.

The data show that Zambia has a large number of remand prisoners. In 2019, persons awaiting trial made up 28 percent of the prison population. This suggests that accused persons are being denied bail unduly. Furthermore, the ease with which people are remanded undermines the constitutional declaration that persons are innocent until proven guilty.

In some cases, such as treason, murder, and motor vehicle theft, the accused cannot be granted bail by law. While some sort of argument can be made for automatic denial of bail in cases of treason, there appears no rational reason why this should be extended to cases of motor vehicle theft. Until the presidency of Frederick Chiluba, persons charged with motor vehicle theft could apply for bail and have their application determined on the merits. The circumstances that led to the change in the law have more to do with animosity between private citizens and powerful state players than with legal analysis and propriety. Whatever the motivation behind the change in legislation, the new provisions have been used to harass political opponents by imprisoning them for alleged motor vehicle theft.

Michael Chilufya Sata, who later served as the fifth president of the republic, was charged with motor vehicle theft while he was an opposition leader. The charge was entirely baseless as the relatively swift acquittal suggested, but Sata was conveniently kept out of circulation for a while.

The spirit of the constitution would be better reflected if all accused persons were entitled to apply for bail. Whether or not they actually get bail would depend on how persuasively the State made the case that without imprisonment, the accused were likely to flee the jurisdiction or that they would in some demonstrable way be a danger to society.

A good example of the purpose and concept of bail comes from Rwanda. On September 17, 2020 a Rwandan court denied bail to Paul Rusesabagina, whose story inspired the film Hotel Rwanda. Despite being charged with 13 offences, including financing terrorism, complicity in murder, recruiting child soldiers, and forming a rebel group, Rusesabagina was entitled to apply for bail.

Rusesabagina asked to be released on bail because of poor health, resulting in him being taken to a hospital three times in the preceding three weeks. Rusesabagina's application was unsuccessful only because the court was persuaded by the prosecution that all detainees are offered necessary medical treatment. Flight risk was also high in this case given that Rusesabagina is a Belgian citizen and a United States permanent resident. In denying the bail application, Judge Dorothy Yankurije ruled that Rusesabagina needed to remain in detention so that he did not sabotage the investigations.

The fact that bail is open to accused persons facing grave charges such as those faced by Rusesabagina may explain why only 7.5 percent of inmates are remanded in Rwanda, significantly lower than Zambia's 28 percent.

In Singapore, bail is not granted for offences punishable by death or life imprisonment. The main reason for denying bail is that an accused person is a flight risk or, alternatively, that they have previously breached the terms of their bail. The percentage of prisoners on remand in Singaporean prisons is 9.8.

In democratic Zambia, bail applications should be determined by independent and impartial magistrates and judges. The State should not interfere in this process. The law denying bail applications in cases of motor vehicle theft clearly defies this principle and the spirit of the constitution.

Reasons for Incarceration

There are four main reasons for incarcerating offenders duly convicted by competent courts. These are to rehabilitate the offender; to punish the offender; to deter others from committing the crime for which the offender is being punished; and to protect the public from the offender.

Traditional Zambian society looked upon offenders as persons in need of rehabilitation, not necessarily as individuals in need of punishment for the sake of punishment. Consequently, rehabilitation of offenders almost always occurred outside physical confinement. The emphasis in rehabilitating the offender was on compensating the victim of the offence. This is in contrast to the reality of today's Zambian criminal justice system, which treats the victim as no more than a witness to aid the conviction and sentencing of the offender.

In the early 1980s, Mpima State Prison (used mostly to house political prisoners until the late 1970s) had a convicted prisoner known to his fellow inmates by the sobriquet of Chikanda. He was named after a popular savoury snack in Zambia made from a combination of orchid tubers, peanut flour, and peppers. The vegetarian mixture is cooked into a solid, meatloaf-like consistency.

The prisoner was given the name after being convicted for stealing a piece of chikanda at a market. He served a three-month sentence for this. The prisoner did not undergo any form of rehabilitation while in prison, spending much of his time working in the prison garden. He did, however, learn from more seasoned criminals to be more ambitious in his criminal endeavours.

The victim of his crime, a marketer, gained nothing from the incarceration of the young man. And society, far from benefitting from the incarceration, spent money on the welfare of the offender while he was incarcerated.

It is possible that this offender, having learned a few tricks while in prison, went on to commit more serious crimes. The appropriate sentence for Chikanda would have been a fine and compensation to the victim of his crime, or community service that would have obliged him to, for example, clean the premises of the victim's market stall for a given period of time. That would have been more sensible and more consistent with traditional Zambian values.

While murder, treason or rape justify punishment by imprisonment, this remedy should not be the standard response to any crime. In many instances where incarceration is ordered, society rarely benefits from the imprisonment of the criminal.

When a former minister of labour, Austin Liato, was sentenced to two years in prison for concealing the equivalent of USD394,000 of illegally obtained money under a layer of concrete at his farm outside Lusaka, the court ordered that his farm and the cash be forfeited to the State. Forfeiture of the property was a very good idea and beneficial to society. Instead of sending Liato to prison, however, there should have been a further fine imposed. That fine could have been the equivalent of the amount stolen. In other words, Liato would have been obliged to pay the state a total cash amount of USD788,000. It should, however, have been open for Liato to keep his farm, or a part of it, upon demonstrating to the court that he needs it to earn a living.

This approach would have done two things. First, the large financial penalty would have acted as a deterrent against public corruption. Second, allowing the convicted minister to keep his farm, or part of it, because it was a source of livelihood would have constituted a powerful signal that Zambia is a humane society which discouraged destitution. A person does not cease to be human just because he has been convicted of a crime. Surely, this is what being a Christian nation is about.

Imposing custodial sentences willy-nilly is not the way to deter convicted offenders from repeating the crime. In the case of Liato, for example, it is unlikely that the two-year sentence imposed on the offender, on its own, deterred either Liato or other would-be financial criminals.

A hefty fine that will likely exhaust the offender's savings, or the threat of imprisonment in the event of failing to repay the debt would have been a much more effective deterrent.

Consider this hypothetical case. Mr Keleputi has, over the years, acquired USD1 million through corrupt practices. Like all greedy persons, he does not know when to stop, so he continues. One transaction goes wrong and it is soon discovered that Mr Keleputi has illegally transferred $10,000 to a personal account. Would a two-year sentence involving the forfeiture of $10,000 really deter him? Most would answer the question in the negative.

What would deter Keleputi and others is a hefty fine determined after a pre-sentencing hearing involving a lifestyle audit. If, after these submissions, the court imposes an additional fine of, say, USD1 million, the deterrent effect would be real. For Keleputi, there would be the threat of financial ruin, even if he were allowed to keep some income-generating assets. For would-be offenders, the message would be clear: crime does not pay.

Protection of the public from criminal diversion of public resources is particularly relevant to Zambia where there has been an increase in economic crimes. These crimes do not typically involve direct physical harm to individuals, but they are deeply injurious to society. The amount of money illegally obtained by Austin Liato, for example, was enough to pay the monthly salary of 788 recently qualified nurses.

In August 2019, the Zambian ministry of health announced that the cost of constructing Bangweulu Regional Hospital would be ZMW154,174,340.72 or USD11,859,564.67. The hospital would be an ultra-modern medical facility with an 800-bed capacity which, in addition to training health professionals, would also serve as a specialist referral institution for the northern region.

Let's consider this project in the context of the fire trucks referenced earlier. The allegation that the fire trucks' cost was inflated to illegally benefit some individuals has yet to be credibly disputed by the government. Until that happens, we can assume that each fire truck should have cost around USD250,000, not USD1,000,000, for a total cost of USD10,500,000. In other words, it is possible that Zambia lost USD31,500,000 in the fire trucks transaction.

That amount of money could build another hospital identical to Bangweulu Regional Hospital, and the people of Zambia would still be left with USD7,700,000 to invest, perhaps, in upgrading hydrant systems to aid effective firefighting.

The case for buying the expensive fire trucks is further undermined by the fact that in early August 2020 one of the controversial fire trucks failed to put out what was considered by observers to be a minor fire in Lusaka. The 'state of the art' fire truck did not have enough water!

There are examples from around the world of fire trucks not having enough water to put out fires. The point here is that the extraordinarily expensive equipment bought by Zambia was not extraordinary in its performance. Furthermore, the authorities took the fire truck's failure in their stride, apparently incurious as to why such an expensive piece of equipment failed in its most basic task.

In 2018, a similar situation arose in Japan, but the matter was resolved quickly and the erring officers were punished. According to Japan Today's November 21, 2018 issue, a fire truck arrived at a burning home in the Kagoshima Prefecture of Isa City without water on the night of October 23, 2018. In this particular case, the firefighters were lucky because the blazing fire they were sent to put out was close to a lake. They drew the necessary water from that lake but that exercise delayed the hosing down procedure by five minutes.

With the fire truck arriving at the scene ten minutes after the emergency phone call was made, two-thirds of the home and warehouse had already been engulfed by flames. It took an hour and eight fire trucks to fully extinguish the fire. Fortunately, no injuries were reported.

The reason for the dangerous bungle was that the truck dispatched to the scene had undergone repairs just four days earlier and crew members forgot to load the vehicle with water upon its return to the depot.

The Isa fire department was unimpressed with the excuses and issued the following statement: 'This careless mistake is unacceptable among professionals. We promise to conduct thorough inspections and show better leadership from now on'. Furthermore, the department reprimanded five fire chiefs for neglecting their duties.

As far as is known, no one was reprimanded for the Lusaka incident and the Lusaka City Council is not on record denouncing the incident as unprofessional or unacceptable. This is not unusual in a country increasingly at ease with corrupt practices.

Since the people of Zambia collectively suffer when corrupt practices occur, proceeds of economic crime should be deposited into a fund dedicated to investing in social services such as education, health care, and food security.

The Death Penalty is Cruel

Article 15 of the Zambia Constitution Act reflects traditional Zambian peacetime values when it proscribes 'torture, or… inhuman or degrading punishment or other like treatment'. Despite this prohibition, the Zambian legal system has kept the death penalty, although actual executions are rare. We should not be in any doubt that the death penalty constitutes inhuman punishment. In November 2018, the Zambian delegation at the United Nations voted to maintain a moratorium on the death penalty. Since in previous years, the Zambians had abstained from voting, this is a hopeful sign.

Despite the death penalty being apparently permitted by the country's constitution, no Zambian leader has signed an execution warrant since 1998, earning Zambia the reputation of an 'abolitionist' country. The government itself considers the death penalty inhumane. The excuse for not abolishing it outright is that it is part of the bill of rights and can only be amended by referendum.

This view is influenced by Article 12 (1) of the Constitution which reads as follows:

> No person shall be deprived of his life intentionally except in execution
> of the sentence of a court in respect of a criminal offence under the law
> in force in Zambia of which he has been convicted.

Nowhere does the constitution say Zambia 'shall' have a death penalty, and Article 12(1) does no more than excuse the death penalty where a statute provides for this punishment. Therefore, it must follow that amending the Zambian Penal Code to remove execution as the maximum punishment for crimes such as murder and treason would be sufficient to abolish the death penalty in Zambia. Indeed, a statute passed for the specific purpose of abolishing the death penalty would appear lawful and consistent with the constitution, which lays so much emphasis on respect for human life.

The death penalty must be abolished at the earliest opportunity because apart from being a relic of colonial times when black Zambian life was undervalued, it goes against the spirit of the Zambian constitution. Furthermore, like all legal systems, the Zambian judicial order is imperfect. We must remember that a single overworked judge of the High Court can impose a death sentence.

Conscious or unconscious bias can also lead to persons being wrongfully sentenced to death. There is ample evidence of this from the United States. For example, in the 2016 case of Foster v. Chatman, the appellate court set aside a death sentence rendered by a jury from which potential black jurors had been systematically excluded.

In the United Kingdom, Mahmood Hussein Mattan, a former merchant seaman born in British Somaliland was wrongfully convicted of the murder of Lily Volpert on 6 March 1952. The prosecution relied mostly on the evidence of a single witness. Racial bias was the order of the day during the trial with Mattan's own counsel considering his client as only 'semi civilised'. Mattan was executed on September 03, 1952. His wife Laura only found out about the execution when she visited him at the prison and was presented with a notice indicating he had already been executed.

Mattan's conviction was quashed 45 years later on 24 February 1998, after the Court of Appeal, responding to a referral from the newly formed Criminal Cases Review Commission, found that Mattan had in fact been innocent of the crime for which he had lost his life. The USD1.4 million in compensation given to his widow and children was a pittance compared to the suffering his wife and children endured.

Respect for the Elderly

In the Luba-Lunda culture that helped father Zambian traditional culture, the elderly have a right to respect their seniority. This respect was relatively easy to grant in traditional society because the wisdom and experience acquired by the elderly was seen as an asset of the community. Indeed, in traditional Zambian society, boys got the bulk of their education at the *Nsaka*, where elders tutored them. Girls got their education in similar fashion but from elderly aunts and grandmothers. These girls would be considered especially fortunate to get instruction from the oldest woman in the community who would also be the most revered person. An incentive for younger people to accept the status of the elderly is the hope and expectation of respect when they themselves reach an advanced age. Respect for the elderly is so deeply ingrained in

Zambian culture that it should be reflected in the judicial and prison systems.

One of the most heart-wrenching episodes from the Kaunda era was the detention without trial of Morris Kapepa. When I met Kapepa in 1981, he was in his mid-70s and well settled at Mpima State Prison based on a detention order signed by President Kenneth Kaunda. Kapepa was accused of having links to a person considered by many to have been Zambia's most notorious dissenter, Adamson Bratson Mushala, whose rebellion lasted from 1975 to 1982.

At the time of his arrest, Kapepa was employed on a commercial farm off the Chingola-Solwezi road. He appears to have been in semi-retirement because his employers, a white Zambian family, were unwilling to let him go completely. They had found him trustworthy and reliable. So he continued to live on the farm.

One day in 1977, officers from Zambian security forces showed up at the farm as part of a campaign to seek out and arrest Mushala sympathisers. The workers were assembled and asked to provide any information they might have about the Mushala Gang. No one had any useful information to offer. The workers were then asked to produce their UNIP cards. Those who had the cards produced them. Mr Kapepa, however, was unable to do so, as he had not belonged to a political party for many years.

He did, however, remember that he had an old African National Congress card with his important papers, so he produced that. This was enough to make him a person of interest to the security forces, and Kapepa was taken away to Kamfinsa prison near Kitwe, where he was interrogated at length. The interrogators got nothing from him and decided that he was hiding important information. To make him talk, the officers resorted to an old tactic: torture. Kapepa was beaten and then suspended from a tree. At this point, a statement was written by one of the officers who told Kapepa that he could end his suffering simply by signing the statement. He was wise enough to know that he was in effect being accused of treason and that the consequences of admitting to such a crime would be dire. He declined.

At this point, Morris Kapepa was stripped naked and subjected to gruesome torture concentrated on his testicles. In fact, one of Kapepa's testicles was crushed, threatening his very life. It was clear to all that Kapepa needed urgent medical treatment but the security officers would not allow him to go to hospital until he signed the statement written for him. In the end Morris Kapepa had no choice but to sign the piece of paper. After his surgery, Kapepa was imprisoned, without trial, at Mpima State Prison in Kabwe.

Kapepa's family did not have the resources to pay him regular visits and bring him food and other necessities. His wife could not afford the bus fare from Chingola to Kabwe, so she only saw him once every six months. He kept himself busy, weaving baskets, an art that he and the other 'Mushala' detainees had mastered perfectly. Despite the suffering he endured daily, Kapepa always appeared dignified and totally without bitterness, but he often asked those who had met Kenneth Kaunda whether the president was entirely human.

The question was not provoked by anger or bitterness but by sad curiosity. Kapepa could not understand how anyone could be so callous about another's life.

His question was particularly pertinent in a society that professes to value the elderly. Kapepa had committed no crime. He was detained because the president of the day deemed him a threat to national security. How this frail septuagenarian could threaten anyone, let alone the state, is impossible to fathom.

What was clearly understandable was that prison was no place for Morris Kapepa, even with the statutory protections of political prisoners. We can only imagine what elderly persons convicted of criminal offences experience while incarcerated.

According to Ubumi Prison Initiative, an organisation dedicated to improving health and nutrition in Zambian prisons, inhumane treatment and poor prison conditions are concerning. In 2018, the Zambian Correctional Service held more than 21,000 inmates, and with only 25 health facilities throughout the prison system, most prisoners had no access to consistent health care. These are not conditions under which the elderly should spend some of the remaining years of their lives

Except for the most serious crimes, there should be no imprisonment for offenders older than 70. In general, an elderly offender should only be required to pay compensation to the victim of his crime. In appropriate cases, this should include community service. This approach would be more consistent with Zambian traditional values than the disrespect shown to Morris Kapepa when he was improperly incarcerated by the government of the day.

In Search of Judicial Independence

Most cases in Zambia are adjudicated by competent magistrates and judges with no vested interest in the outcome of the matter. Over the past decade, however, there has been concern that the Zambian judiciary has become less impartial in the adjudication of cases with a political flavour. There may be no concrete evidence for this, but that does not matter.

What matters is that there is a widespread perception that some judges are not up to the task of adjudicating a matter involving the government or the governing party, fairly. The concern prior to adjudication is that certain individuals or classes of individuals are targeted for prosecution. In cases of corruption, for example, there is a perception that it pays to belong to the ruling party, in much the same way as it paid 'to belong to UNIP' in a less democratic era.

Focus on the judiciary intensified after the 2016 election, which saw Edgar Lungu win the presidential poll by three percentage points. The opposition UPND disputed the result because of alleged collusion between the PF and the Electoral Commission of Zambia. The UPND petitioned the Constitutional Court, asking for the nullification of the result. In early September, the Constitutional Court dismissed the petition because the time allotted by the law to hear the matter had lapsed, since the case was not ready for hearing within fourteen days of filing the petition. Two judges disagreed with the other three judges who constituted the majority. The dissenting opinion was authored by Constitutional Court President Hilda Chibomba, who said the 14 days to hear a presidential petition was not workable and practical, adding that the legal provision requiring this should be revised.

The petition's outcome was disenchanting for opposition supporters, especially as the ruling could not be appealed. Whichever side observers fell on, all reasonable people rued the fact that the matter was not heard on its merits. It is possible the judges would have still dismissed the UPND petition after hearing the case on its merits. That decision, however, may not have been accepted by all because the Zambian judiciary is perceived by many as less independent than it should be. The important lesson from this case is encapsulated in Justice Chibomba's dissenting judgement. Zambia needs to have practical and transparent laws to govern election disputes. The law should not handicap the ability of judges to conduct comprehensive judicial inquiries into alleged electoral malpractice.

Appointment of Judges

Zambia cannot be a viable democracy unless the judiciary and its constituent parts are impartial and independent of external pressure, in whatever form it may come. Persons appearing before judges are entitled to have confidence that their cases will be decided fairly and in accordance with the law. In today's Zambia, this expectation is undermined by the perception that the judiciary is often subjected to improper pressure by the executive branch and individual litigants.

There are other improper influences such as media, pressure groups, and even senior judges. These senior judges may or may not act in concert with the executive branch or other influencers.

In late October 1980, several prominent Zambian citizens were detained on the order of the president on suspicion that they were plotting to overthrow the Zambian government. At a press conference held to explain the detentions, Kenneth Kaunda told the nation that the alleged coup plotters would eventually be tried. He then promised to recall the chief justice, who was at the time doing post-graduate work at London University, to deal with the suspects.

This was clearly an attempt to influence the eventual outcome of the criminal trial. There was absolutely no reason for President Kaunda to recall the chief justice, especially since the country already had an acting chief justice. Few had confidence after these remarks that the detainees would get a fair trial.

It is reasonable to infer that since Annel Silungwe had been made chief justice ahead of more qualified candidates such as Brian Gardner, Godfrey Muwo, and Bonaventure Bweupe, Kaunda felt that Annel Silungwe was beholden to him. Kaunda's behaviour was reminiscent of the relationship between the judiciary and the sovereign in England before 1701, when senior judges held office at the sovereign's pleasure.

Senior judges in Zambia are appointed by the president on the recommendation of the Judicial Service Commission, subject to ratification by the National Assembly. Under the Service Commission Act, the chairperson of the Judicial Service Commission is appointed by the president.

The other members are a judge nominated by the chief justice; the attorney-general, with the solicitor-general as the alternate; the permanent secretary responsible for public service management; a magistrate nominated by the chief justice; a representative of the Law Association of Zambia nominated by LAZ and appointed by the president; the dean of a law school of a public higher education institution, nominated by the minister responsible for justice; and one member appointed by the president.

The members of the Judicial Service Commission elect the vice-chairperson, although they may not elect a judge nominated by the chief justice, or the attorney general or a magistrate nominated by the chief justice.

It is worth noting that the head of the Judicial Service Commission is appointed directly by the president, while the judge nominated by the chief justice would also have initially been appointed as a judge by the president.

The attorney-general and the permanent secretary are also presidential appointees, as is the unaffiliated member. The representative of the Law Association must be approved by the president, while the dean of a law school of a higher institution of learning is not appointed by the president but is instead nominated by a minister appointed by the president.

All members of the Judicial Service Commission are either appointed directly by the president or nominated by someone appointed by the president. The interrelated nature of the appointments does not guarantee that the commission's recommendations are as diverse as may be desirable in a country such as Zambia.

If Zambia had a titular rather than an executive head of state, the current appointments structure would be less problematic because the appointments would be made by a nonpartisan authority. It may be advisable to reduce the president's influence on these appointments in the country's current circumstances. It is reasonable for the president to appoint one member to the commission., but other members of the commission should include the president of the Constitutional Court, a representative of the Law Association of Zambia supported by two-thirds of the members attending the meeting at which such representative is selected, a representative of the Zambia Congress of Trade Unions supported by two-thirds of the members attending the meeting at which such representative is selected, and a representative of the Zambia Chambers of Commerce and Industry supported by two-thirds of the members attending the meeting at which such representative is selected. In addition, there should be one member representing all the accredited law schools in the country selected like the members representing the Law Association of Zambia.

A Judicial Service Commission with the representation suggested above would attract a diversity of backgrounds and views, leading to more representative candidates for the Bench.

Removal of Senior Judges

The appointment of judges is just one side of the judicial independence coin. The other is termination. Article 98 of the Zambia Constitution Act of 1996 required senior judges to vacate office upon attaining the age of 65. There were two exceptions to this. The first was that a judge could continue beyond the age of 65 to complete a judgment. The second allowed the president, on the advice of the Judicial Service Commission, to appoint a senior judge who had attained the age of 65 for a further period of seven years.

That provision was problematic. The prospect of appointment for an additional seven years after the official retirement age could be used to press a judge about to retire to render decisions favourable to the executive branch.

The 2016 Zambia Constitution Act improved on its predecessor by raising the retirement age to 70, although a judge may still choose to retire at 65 without losing any retirement benefits. The chief justice and the president of the Constitutional Court are now also barred from holding office for more than ten years, although they may continue serving as ordinary judges of the Supreme Court or Constitutional Court.

Fixing the term of service for a judge is an improvement on the previous regime, but putting the age of retirement at 70 is problematic. This relatively early age of retirement has the potential to deprive Zambia of judicial talent, deprive it of many educated, reasonably fit, and mentally agile middle-class persons.

Consider the case of England's most celebrated judge in the 20th century: Lord Alfred Denning. He became a high court judge at the age of 45 and served in the Court of Appeal at the age of 58 and, five years later, in the House of Lords. He did not like the House of Lords because, as he explained to me once, it just was not intellectually challenging enough. He, therefore, asked to go back to the Court of Appeal where he became Master of the Rolls.

Throughout his 38-year service as a judge, Denning demonstrated a particularly sharp intellect. His imagination led to accusations of excessive judicial activism. When I spoke to him about this, he dismissed the accusations and explained that he merely ironed out the 'creases' when the law was unfair or unclear.

Denning did not step down from the Court of Appeal until he was 84. His last judgments were as lucid as the first ones. The loss to English jurisprudence would have been immense had Lord Denning been forced to retire at 70.

For a society whose traditional values include respect for elders and reliance on their wisdom, 70 as a retirement age for judges seems low.

There are of course circumstances which justify removing a judge prior to the mandatory retirement age. The 2016 constitution is clear about mandatory grounds of removal of a judge. They are mental or physical disability that makes the judge incapable of performing judicial functions; incompetence; gross misconduct; or bankruptcy.

The procedure for removing a judge has also been improved upon in some respects. For example, the removal of a judge is no longer initiated by the president but by the Judicial Complaints Commission or by a complaint made to the Judicial Complaints Commission based on the grounds mentioned above.

The Judicial Complaints Commission is duty-bound to determine whether a prima facie case has been established against a judge. When that happens, the Commission is obliged to submit a report to the president, who has the power to suspend the judge within seven days of receiving the report. Thereafter, the Commission has 30 days to hear the matter.

The power given to the president in suspending a judge and triggering a hearing by the Judicial Complaints Commission, is concerning. This power and the ease with which a judge can be removed threatens judicial independence. It should not be up to the head of the executive branch of government to determine if a judge ought to be suspended and then tried by a body appointed by the same president.

A better process would be for the Judicial Complaints Commission, after making a prima facie finding to refer the matter to the speaker of the National Assembly for a hearing by a special court. National Assembly members not involved in the prosecution or defence of the accused judge would then act as the jury and have the ability to remove a judge on a majority vote.

These are just broad principles that should guide the formulation of specific procedural rules for the removal of senior judges for cause.

Prosecutorial Independence

The office of the Director of Public Prosecutions (DPP) continues by virtue of Article 180 of the 2016 constitution. The DPP is appointed by the president, subject to ratification by the National Assembly. The holder of the office is constitutionally the chief prosecutor for the government and serves as the head of the National Prosecutions Authority.

The director may institute and undertake criminal proceedings against a person before a court, other than a court-martial, for an offence alleged to have been committed by that person; take over and continue criminal proceedings instituted or undertaken by another person or authority; and enter a *nolle prosequi* and thus discontinue, at any stage before judgment is delivered, criminal proceedings. Wisely, the constitution does not permit the DPP to enter a nolle prosequi in relation to an appeal by a convicted person, a case stated or a question of law reserved at the instance of that person.

The Constitution seeks to preserve the independence of the DPP by providing that she cannot be subject to the direction or control of a person or an authority in the performance of her duties. The DPP is required, however, to regard the public interest, administration of justice, the integrity of the judicial system, and the need to prevent and avoid abuse of the legal processes in the discharge of her duties.

The constitutional guarantee of the DPP's independence is however, undermined by provisions pertaining to retirement and removal from office for cause. At 60, the retirement age is very low for this kind of office. In order to be eligible for appointment as the DPP, the person must have been a legal practitioner for a minimum of ten years. Thus, a mature student qualifying as a legal practitioner at the age of 50 has no hope of becoming a DPP, however good he may be at undertaking criminal trials.

The DPP may also be removed even before reaching the age of 60 on the same grounds as a judge may be removed. The deficiencies of the current regime for removing judges for cause has already been discussed. These deficiencies apply equally to the removal of the DPP.

The ease with which a DPP can be removed threatens the prosecutorial independence of the office. It should not be up to the president to determine that the DPP ought to be suspended and then tried by an institution appointed by the same president. The perception that prosecutions are influenced by the executive branch are made credible by the reality that too often prosecutions seem to coincide with the interests of politicians in power.

A Hasty Prosecution

Within two years of leaving office, President Rupiah Banda's immunity from prosecution was purportedly lifted. He was charged with corruptly concluding a government-to-government oil contract between Zambia and Nigeria while in office. The prosecution alleged that the oil contract was entered into to benefit the former president and his family to the tune of USD2.5 million.

The press reports of the case were not easy to follow. Not infrequently, impartial observers of the trial wondered why the prosecution had been commenced at all because no explanation was ever given about how Banda benefited from the contract.

Joshua Banda, a magistrate who had previously convicted President Banda's son, Andrew for corruption, saw little merit in these particular charges. On June 29, 2015 he acquitted the former president. He said, 'there [was] no evidence tendered regarding the proof of the transfer of the money and that Banda and his family benefited'. The magistrate found the evidence laid before the court insufficient to warrant a conviction. He asked why, in a contract of this nature, no official from Nigeria had been called to testify.

It was a reasonable question. Why did no one in the government make arrangements for key witnesses from Nigeria to testify? Could it be there were no such witnesses and Rupiah Banda's prosecution was simply a form of harassment? Given the thinness of the legal basis for commencing the prosecution, many Banda supporters answered the question in the affirmative.

The People versus General (Dr) Brian Chituwo

While immensely inconvenienced, Rupiah Banda was more fortunate than others targeted in the anti-corruption campaign. Brian Chituwo was one of the most respected cabinet ministers to serve in both the

Mwanawasa and Banda governments. The Copperbelt-born medical doctor, who also served in the armed forces and earned the rank of brigadier general, is known for his calm demeanour and integrity. He was seen by many as a future president.

Three years after the MMD was defeated at the polls to give way to the Patriotic Front government, Chituwo was charged under the Anti-Corruption Act for failing to declare a conflict of interest.

The allegation was that Chituwo, as a Member of Parliament, 'on dates unknown but between 1st December 2013 and 31st December 2013' in Mumbwa where his constituency was, attended and participated in a Mumbwa District Council meeting during which the funding of a private radio station was discussed. Chituwo was a director and shareholder of Blue Sky FM Ltd, the company that set up the radio station. It was alleged that Chituwo had failed to declare his interest in Blue Sky FM Ltd.

Altogether, the magistrate heard from nine witnesses; six from the prosecution and three from the defence. The first witness for the prosecution explained the procedure for disbursement of constituency funds. According to this witness, projects to be funded are identified by the Area Development Committee, which then makes recommendations to the District Council Secretariat.

The District Council Secretariat compiles the recommendations from the Area District Committee to the Constituency Development Committee, which transmits the recommendations to the District Development Coordinating Committee. The undisputed evidence from the testimony was that Chituwo did not sit on the Area Development Committee which identifies projects for funding. He did not sit on the District Council Secretariat either. Thus, he was not involved in the formal identification of projects or the compilation of projects for transmission to the Constituency Development Committee.

Chituwo did, however, by virtue of being the area's Member of Parliament, sit on the Constituency Development Committee. The CDC is responsible for prioritising projects. In this regard, the first prosecution witness was categorical that Chituwo, although a member of the committee, '[did] not take part in the deliberations when prioritising projects'.

The first prosecution witness also testified that the application to fund the radio station submitted by Mumbwa Blue Sky FM and its community partner Kutenda Community Development Limited was approved at a meeting held 'earlier than the meeting of 12th December, 2013'. This was a District Council meeting in which Chituwo did not participate. This meeting, according to the prosecution witness, was held 'sometime in 2012'.

Significantly, the application for funding was approved 'based on the public-private partnership agreement between Mumbwa Blue Sky FM and Kutenda Community', because private sector entities cannot access constituency funds on their own.

The second witness for the prosecution confirmed that the approval to fund Mumbwa Blue Sky FM was given at the meeting held before 12th December, 2013. It is worth repeating that this approval was given by the District Council Secretariat, whose meetings Chituwo did not attend.

At times, prosecution witnesses sounded like defence witnesses. For example, the second witness for the prosecution testified that Chituwo, although a shareholder in Mumbwa Blue Sky FM, had never been paid any dividends. Unlike 'other shareholders,' Chituwo was not on the company's payroll either. On the contrary, Chituwo, according to this prosecution witness, would often 'use his personal money to run Mumbwa Blue Sky FM' with a view to 'helping the community'.

It was established that since constituency funds could not be used to fund private sector projects, a private company wishing to benefit from these funds could only do so through a partnership with a community organisation. The suggestion then was perhaps Dr Chituwo had influenced the signing of the memorandum of understanding between Mumbwa Blue Sky FM and Kutenda Community Development Limited.

But the fourth witness for the prosecution, who had actually participated in the signing of the memorandum of understanding, testified that Chituwo was not present when the memorandum was signed. The last witness for the prosecution said, among other things, that 'there were several meetings that took place whose minutes he did not have and that the accused could have declared interest recorded in the several other minutes that he did not have'.

Chituwo's testimony was consistent with evidence from some of the prosecution witnesses. He was categorical that he did not attend a meeting where funding for Mumbwa Blue Sky FM Radio was discussed. He did, however, attend a council meeting on 13th December, 2013 where his only contribution was responding to a councillor who wanted to know why the money spent on the radio station had not been used instead to fund a health post. Chituwo also testified that he did not attend the council meeting at which funding for the radio station was ratified. Since he was not present at the meeting, he could not declare his interest in the matter.

Despite this evidence, the magistrate found Chituwo guilty as charged. In so doing, the magistrate ignored Chituwo's evidence and evidence from the prosecution. Specifically, the magistrate ignored evidence by the first and second witnesses for the prosecution who confirmed that the approval to fund Mumbwa Blue Sky FM was given at a meeting not attended by Chituwo and held before 12th December, 2013.

The magistrate also ignored evidence by the last prosecution witness, who testified that there were several meetings where Chituwo could have declared his interest in Mumbwa Blue Sky FM. Most adjudicators would have been concerned by the testimonies of these two witnesses who were in fact in court to testify against Chituwo, and may well have considered the testimony sufficient to raise a reasonable doubt.

Instead, the Mumbwa Resident Magistrate sentenced Chituwo to one year in prison, suspended for two years. The directorate of public prosecutions and the National Prosecutions Authority suffer from a lack of personnel and other resources. For this reason, the DPP is always obliged to prioritise cases for prosecution. Despite this, prosecutorial agencies try to counter the general perception that the National Prosecution Authority is ineffective in prosecuting cases that involve influential people. Could this have motivated the prosecution of Chituwo?

This is a fair question because even if we assume that there was a basis for trying Chituwo, the question arises as to why this victimless 'crime' from which the accused never benefitted was prioritised for prosecution. Whatever the reasons for prosecuting Chituwo, the consequences were dire for both the good doctor and his family.

While relieved that he was spared a jail term, the Fellow of the Royal College of Surgeons of Edinburgh who, as Zambia's minister of health, handled a multi-million dollar budget without a whiff of scandal, was shocked to be burdened with a criminal record. After consulting his family and lawyers, he decided to put the whole matter behind him and not appeal. A reading of the case does suggest an injustice which can now only be fixed by a presidential pardon. We must hope a time will come when individual reputation and justice will matter sufficiently to warrant a pardon for Dr Brian Chituwo.

CHAPTER NINE

From Neglect to Responsibility: A Necessary Cultural Shift

Constitutional change is most effective when accompanied by cultural change. The way Zambians behave matters as much as the constitutional framework they establish for themselves. Zambians need to move away from a culture of neglect and embrace a culture of personal and collective responsibility. Firm embrace of this new culture would be an important tool in the arsenal of weapons to fight vices such as corruption.

Over the past forty years or so, the number of Zambians with a demonstrable sense of responsibility for fellow nationals, other than direct blood relatives, has declined noticeably. Similarly, not enough Zambians have a sufficiently deep sense of proprietorship over public assets. This means there are relatively few nationals willing and able to play the necessary custodial role with respect to public money. The neglect evident in Zambians' personal and communal lives coupled with the country's dependency on government and the international community is both excessive and embarrassing.

When society gives up its role as overseer of public spending, politicians and other officials inclined to do so, are given a freer hand in misappropriating public funds. The result of this corruption is that Zambia, a country with arguably the most placid people in world, an abundance of water and other natural resources, not to mention an agreeable climate and fertile land, has a GDP per capita (Purchasing Power Parity) of USD3,999. This is only a fraction of what Zambia's GDP per capita should be.

In contrast, the Bahamas, with 14,000 square kilometres of territory and fewer tourist sites than Zambia, has a GDP per capita of USD32,377. Bermuda, which is even less endowed in terms of natural resources, has a GDP per capita of USD52,547. Botswana, whose territory borders Zambia's, has a GDP per capita of USD17,110.

These figures are from the 2020 edition of The Economist's Pocket World in Figures. The same publication identifies Zambia (tied with

Nigeria) as the most entrepreneurial country on earth. The average percentage of the population who were either a nascent entrepreneur or owner-manager of a new business between 2013 and 2018, was 39.9. The figure for runner-up Senegal was 38.6.

Zambia's entrepreneurial spirit is an asset that can be used to transform the country's culture. Entrepreneurs are masters of productivity because they improve upon products and services without a proportionate increase in either labour or capital. Since the turn of the century, it has been understood that new job creation is driven by new and young businesses.[46] This is surely because these businesses do not have an abundance of resources and they have to make the most of the little that they have. An analysis of any small Zambian business will bear this out. Therefore, the Zambian government and the people must constantly look for opportunities that support entrepreneurs.

Education is the Key to Sustainable Development

Without education, however, neither entrepreneurship nor any other advantage Zambia may have will fully contribute to the country's effort to realise its enormous potential for socio-economic development. The country needs to become better educated to realise this potential. Education is a critical precondition for unmitigated success.

In this regard, the failure to invest adequately in the nation's education, especially the children, constitutes gross irresponsibility. Education is vital to prepare children for the future. Zambia has no future unless it can invest in young people and give them a strong sense of civic responsibility and skills to enable them lead valuable lives and contribute meaningfully to the country's development.

Early Education

The formal learning journey for Zambians must start as early as possible. Therefore, Zambia must aim to have all children from the age of four in full-day learning programmes. Investing in the education of young

---

[46] Davis, Steven J and Haltwanger, John, Gross Job Creation, Gross Job Destruction, and Employment Reallocation
The Quarterly Journal of Economics
Vol. 107, No. 3 (Aug., 1992), pp. 819-863 (45 pages)
Published By: Oxford University Press

Zambians would give the children a firm foundation for success in life and have long-term benefits for the entire economy.

In the paper, Schools, Skills and Synapses, the US National Bureau of Economic Research, shows that investment in early childhood education improves cognitive abilities and critical behavioural traits like sociability, motivation, and self-esteem. Children are thus given the opportunity to develop interpersonal skills and to learn to manage diversity and differences of opinion early in life, something sadly denied to the pickaninny bwanas. They are also exposed to rational thinking early so that by the time they reach adulthood, logical analysis becomes second nature to them. In a young country, getting the youngest citizens in a learning environment early also promotes national awareness and national pride.

Therefore, it is concerning that in April 2017, UNICEF reported that 377,482 children in Zambia, nearly 74 percent of Grade 1 entrants, started school without any formal early childhood education experience. Eight months after the UNICEF report, the Policy Monitoring and Research Centre reported that the Zambian government had given higher priority to early childhood learning. The report distinguished early childhood learning, which targets children able to receive instruction between the ages of three and six from child care.

The Ministry of General Education put in place specific measures, including standardisation of early childhood curriculum; raising of early childhood teacher qualifications; and introducing postgraduate degrees in early childhood learning.

Primary School and Beyond

While early childhood education focuses on developing a child's social, emotional, cognitive and physical needs, primary education and beyond introduces the child to content and intellectual values. This is not to suggest that social, emotional, cognitive and physical well-being cease to be important when the child advances to primary school and beyond. They do not. The primary school does, however, introduce the child to more disciplined learning, which continues into university.

The Zambian curriculum at primary and secondary school levels maintains a balance between the arts and the sciences. The teaching of these subjects would be enhanced by both content and a conducive physical environment. The education must teach children as early as possible, the ability to argue a case coherently without viewing opponents of that case as enemies. Children must be taught to defy orthodoxy and learn to avoid being epigones. A country that encourages this teaching is less likely to fall prey to such evils as apartheid or fascism.

When teaching Zambia's unfortunate colonial history, children must at all times be encouraged to see the humanity of colonisers. It is only when the adversary's humanity is acknowledged that progress in accommodation can truly be made. This applies to both historic and contemporary adversaries. In a diverse society such as Zambia, empathy and acceptance of difference is also something children should be taught at the earliest opportunity.

Zambian history should be taught as a stand-alone subject designed to capture the events that led to the country's creation. This history should start with the Bantu migration of the 4th century. The history of the Kongo and the evolution of the Luba-Lunda Empire should also be prominent so that Zambian students are as familiar with the Battle of Mbandi Kasi as they are with the Battle of Hastings. Mbemba Nzinga's efforts as King of Kongo to reduce slavery in his kingdom should be as well known to Zambian students as William Wilberforce's campaign to end the transatlantic slave trade.

Properly taught, history could add to national pride, in addition to increasing knowledge stock. Zambian children would be exposed at an early age to the historical successes of their people, and this may just fortify the idea in their minds that, in light of its history, Zambia has the right to be extraordinarily successful. In addition to formal lessons, history should be dramatized through film and stage acting.

In addition to content, however, pupils need to receive their education in a conducive environment. This means creating child-friendly schools which are hygienic and safe. For example, schools must have adequate water and sanitation facilities and healthy classrooms. The basic facilities must include separate toilets for boys and girls, and ramps for persons with disabilities. The infrastructure must also include lighting, safety and security equipment, communication facilities, and kitchens and eating places.

School lunch must be offered, without charge, to all pupils to ensure that children have the necessary nutrition to learn. This is beneficial to all children and critical for learners from low-income households. School lunches are also known to reduce food insecurity. Providing meals to school children need not be an expensive proposition as a nutritious meal can be as simple as a bowl of tomato soup, a few slices of whole wheat bread, and a glass of milk. The cost of the daily meal per child would amount to cents rather than dollars.

Class size is also important. Overcrowded classrooms undermine quality education in many Zambian schools. This is what Kansanshi Foundation, First Quantum Minerals Ltd.'s main corporate social responsibility arm, found in the Zeros in north-western Zambia where many schools in the Solwezi area had classes with more than 70 pupils each, and just one textbook for all the children. The Foundation has since built and rehabilitated schools to achieve a lower teacher-pupil ratio.

For the country as a whole pupil-teacher ratio in primary schools was 42.06 in 2017. The highest ratio since 1970 was 57.01 in 2006. The best ratio was in 1996 when, on average, one teacher had 38.19. In contrast, Finland's Ministry for Education and Culture recommends 20-25 pupils per class for grades 1 to 6. Therefore, Zambia should aim to bring its teacher to pupil ratio to this level.

Traditional Zambian education was conducted in small groups with most pupils getting their theoretical education at the Nsaka and the practical education in the field. Thus, traditional education focused on training and skills development to guarantee gainful employment for all able-bodied members of the community. As Walter Rodney, the prominent Guyanese historian, observed: among the Bemba people, children by the age of six could name 50-60 species of tree plants without hesitation. In this way, children were prepared for careers in the Chitemene agricultural system and herbal medicine.

Most of the skills valued in traditional society no longer guarantee employment in modern Zambia and might even be irrelevant. But the need to provide an education that maximises employment opportunities still remains. In the first quarter of the 21st century, new strategies need to be adopted to ensure that the education provided to Zambians leads to sustainable development.

Education for Success

The starting point in devising an educational system that guarantees success is accepting the truth that the country's most valuable resource is its population. Zambia also needs to understand that while high-quality education may not be cheap, it is infinitely less expensive than widespread ignorance. Democracy itself is not sustainable in an illiterate society where voters cannot analyse salient issues and cannot, therefore, make informed choices. When illiteracy is combined with its dependable ally, poverty, electoral success can mean no more than a political party's ability to bribe voters.

When the ruling Patriotic Front party won both the Nakato ward and Imalyo ward by-elections in Mongu District in June 2020, in a province considered an opposition stronghold, the area member of parliament had no doubt about the reason for his opposition party's loss. Mwilola Imakando accused the ruling party of bribing voters with maize meal at a time when the region was experiencing food shortages.

An educated population with a capacity to earn significant income, would be less susceptible to the kind of bribery alleged by Imakando.

Even in the post-colonial era, the importance of skills enhancing education has been known for a relatively long period. For example, in 1907, the Barotse-Mongu Trades School was established to provide training in construction and poultry farming skills. Eight years later, the famed Mabel Shaw formed a skills training institution for women at Mbereshi. This was the beginning of a girls' boarding school, which later gave the country many leaders. Yet another example of a skills training institution was Lukashya in Kasama, which now focuses on teaching agricultural science.

We are a long way from the 1900s. We live in a world where we cannot be sure of precisely the kind of labour force needed in the future without exhaustive analysis. Some of the jobs that will be considered critical in, say 2030, may not even exist yet. We know from the research, however, that an increasing proportion of the jobs that will exist at that time will require a post-secondary school education. This reality makes innovation all the more important. It is the ability to constantly look at old challenges in a new way that will help create a culture of innovation.

Zambia must create a vibrant higher education sector to prepare a new generation of leaders capable of making the necessary cultural shift that will lead to hitherto unimagined prosperity. While the education sector should continue to teach the humanities, the new focus must be on science, technology, engineering, and mathematics (STEM). Unfortunately, Zambia allowed the colonial neglect of STEM education to continue after independence.

To the country's credit, however, citizens, in concert with their government, did at least establish a university that came into being one year after independence. Despite the recent decline of the University of Zambia and the doubtful standards of many of the younger universities, Zambia is nonetheless in a position to create an enviable education sector. To do so, Zambia must engage nationals in the diaspora such as Kelly Chibale, the founder and director of the Drug Discovery and Development Centre (H3D) at the University of Cape Town. Chibale, like Misheck Mwaba in Canada, is a highly respected scientist keen to help his homeland.

And the homeland does need help. There are 21 universities and 11 colleges in a country of nearly 18 million people. In comparison, Ontario is home to 19 universities and 22 colleges for 14.7 million people. It is not clear what percentage of the Zambian population has university degrees, but a 2017 Afrobarometer survey suggested 13 percent. The Afrobarometer team, led by RuralNet Associates Limited, interviewed 1,200 adult Zambians. According to Afrobarometer, the sample was large enough to yield country-level results with a margin of error of +/-3 percentage points at a 95 percent confidence level.

By way of comparison, in 2016, 31.9 percent of Ontarians aged 25 to 64 had a university degree, the highest proportion among Canada's provinces and territories. In 2019, almost half of the Zambian population (44.4 percent) was aged 14 or under. Those aged between 15 and 64 made up 54.42 percent of the population. Zambia must ensure that its youthful population becomes a demographic dividend rather than a burden by developing talent. Some lament the fact that a relatively large number of young Zambians sent abroad for education never return. This 'brain drain' is, however, not necessarily a bad thing. Zambians who never return home after completing their studies still support their country through financial remittances.

In 2019, the World Bank estimated remittances from Zambians in the Diaspora at USD 128 million. That is almost certainly an underestimate because significant sums of money are sent to Zambia informally rather than through the banking system. The true figure is probably closer to USD 200 million.

If the Zambian educational system were to increase opportunities to acquire STEM skills, this figure would increase even further since workers with STEM degrees tend to command higher pay than those without.

Zambia did not record any inflows in the World Bank's Migration and Remittances Factbook until 2003, when USD 36 million was sent to the country. Had the colonial government paid more attention to the education of Zambians, the country would have participated in the global workforce earlier and benefited from the remittances of its international workforce.

Instead, the colonial government discouraged the education of black people, especially in STEM subjects, as the case of Valentine Musakanya illustrates. He graduated from Kutama College in Southern Rhodesia with solid performances in Latin, English, Physics, and Chemistry. With these results, he could easily have pursued a STEM career, starting with an apprenticeship with one of the mining companies. Despite the policy of African Advancement, however, the mining companies still adhered to the policy of not allowing black people access to apprenticeship positions, and so Musakanya was unable to pursue his dream of becoming a scientist. Little wonder that Andrew Kashita was the sole indigenous engineer in the entire country at the time of independence. The total number of medical doctors in the territory was three!

Unfortunately, while expanding educational opportunities in general, the post-colonial government did not focus on STEM subjects either. For many years after independence, indigenous people remained scarce in the technology sector. Fortunately, things are changing, as evidenced by the emergence of outfits such as BongoHive, Zambia's first technology and innovation hub. It is telling that BongoHive co-founder, Lukonga Lindunda, obtained his IT degree from South Africa's Nelson Mandela Metropolitan University, rather than locally. Unfortunately, Zambia has not been as aggressive as, for example, Rwanda, in promoting the study of STEM subjects in universities and prioritizing the development of IT infrastructure.

Zambia needs more BongoHives and a more aggressive approach to promoting STEM subjects. Failure to do that will result in a disproportionate number of knowledge-based jobs going to foreigners rather than Zambian nationals.

Zambian universities and colleges need to produce the scientists, technicians, engineers, and related professionals required to realise the Zambian economy's potential in the way that, for example, the tiger economies of Asia did a quarter of a century ago. The educated labour force needed to turn the Zambian economy into what it needs to be will not appear magically. It will need to be birthed and nurtured.

Superb colleges for superb students

None of Zambia's universities are ranked in the top 500 in the world. The top university in Zambia, UNZA, was ranked at 2,500 in 2019. Zambia should be concerned because the low rank isolates Zambian academics from the global knowledge generation from collaborations between the top 500 global universities. Zambian academics are largely absent at tables that identify the global talent pool.

One consequence of this is foreign dependency in domains such as science and technology, allowing outsiders to exercise significant control over the country's economic and even political behaviour.

Zambian universities must join the rank of the world's top 500 universities. The five categories by which universities are assessed give a clue as to what Zambia needs to do to turn its institutions into world-class universities. The core missions of all world-class universities are teaching, research, citations (research influence), industry income, and international outlook. Teaching, research, and citations carry the most weight when universities are ranked.

As of October 2020, the best universities in Africa, according to the 2021 Times Higher Education's World University Rankings, were in Egypt, Morocco, Nigeria, South Africa, and Uganda. The top universities in all these countries were among the world's best 500. The Universities of Cape Town and Witwatersrand in South Africa featured in the top 250.

There seems to be a correlation between a university's ability to provide quality teaching and the salary paid to lecturers. The average monthly salary for a university lecturer in Zambia at the time of writing is USD 440. An Egyptian lecturer can expect to earn USD 8,753 per month. A lecturer in South Africa earns USD 2,881, while a lecturer at Uganda's Makerere University earns USD 1,897. The average salary for Kenyan lecturers is USD 1,652. The figure for Botswana is USD 1,496, while the one for Nigeria is USD 1,212.

The African countries with the highest global university rankings pay their lecturers considerably more than Zambian universities do. With low pay comes low-quality teaching. Even when Zambian universities attract excellent lecturers, these professionals either leave for greener pastures or find a way to supplement their meagre income outside the university. The latter means they cannot devote all the time necessary to teaching.

The end result of all this is a low score in the teaching category of global rankings. The other categories are affected too because pay affects research capability, and therefore the likelihood of researchers being cited in external journals of note.

This is particularly serious for Zambia where the research tradition, especially in STEM subjects, is so limited. This limitation has the effect of isolating the country from global talent and knowledge generation. Without knowledge and resources, Zambia simply cannot turn herself into a significant player in the global economy.

It is telling that BongoHive does not have a robust relationship with any of Zambia's universities. In fact, the hub attracts little attention outside ICT and entrepreneurial circles. This is unfortunate because BongoHive is the kind of innovation and technology hub that both the government and the universities need to collaborate with to enhance the country's talent profile. This is especially true because BongoHive has established connections with international bodies adept at developing young scientists.

Among institutions with which Zambia should collaborate more is the African Institute for Mathematical Sciences, a pan-African network of centres of excellence whose aim is to enable Africa's talented students to become innovators and drive the continent's scientific, educational, and economic self-sufficiency. AIMS was founded by Neil Turok, a South African physicist who later served as director of the Waterloo, Ontario-based Perimeter Institute for Theoretical Physics from 2008 to 2019. Neil specializes in mathematical physics and early-universe physics, including the cosmological constant and a cyclic model for the universe. He is a valuable resource not just for his homeland of South Africa but also for the entire continent.

It is not just research limitations that undermine Zambian university performance in global rankings. The industry income category is also affected because without robust research, Zambian universities cannot make discoveries that can be commercialized by industry. Moreover, neither foreign students nor international lecturers will be attracted to universities without a stellar record for teaching. The absence of foreign students and international lectures undermine the performance of any university in the International Outlook category.

The automotive industry, which we shall discuss shortly, can contribute to the establishment of excellence in institutions of higher learning. It can help Zambian universities boost their research capability and make discoveries that have practical uses for the populace.

Universities that teach automotive engineering and collaborate closely with the auto industry tend to be ranked highly. Indiana State University, University of Michigan, University of South Wales, and Shanghai Jiao Tong University are just a few examples. Successful universities also invest in suitable environments for teaching and learning.

On January 16, 2018, the Zambia Daily Mail reported that although the University of Zambia had about 3,000 bed spaces, it accommodated more than 7,000 students. Allowing this to happen is irresponsible. The 7,000 students at the university were not so much exposed to education as they were to disease. This is not an environment conducive to study.

The new Zambian culture must include an absolute commitment to high-quality education. There must be an understanding that while education may appear expensive, its absence is even more costly. Therefore, education must be the number one development priority, followed by health care and food security.

All Laws Matter

Development cannot take place in a lawless environment. A stable legal regime is a major requirement for domestic and foreign investors who need assurance that the country will respect all laws. Sadly, the culture of neglect has led to a disregard of laws and regulations and the abandonment of the culture of personal responsibility, widely evident in Zambia until the mid-1970s. In many towns and cities today, zoning laws are ignored with impunity, even at the expense of public health.

In January 2018 illegal street vending was banned because the unhygienic practices it involved contributed to a serious outbreak of cholera in Lusaka. Between October 2017 and May 2018, more than 5,900 cholera cases resulted in 114 deaths.

Observing Lusaka City Council bylaws would have avoided the outbreak and the subsequent deaths. The excuse for allowing informal markets is that there is not enough room for all aspiring vendors in formal markets. In any event, these markets charge fees that some aspiring traders cannot afford.

Despite the absurdity of the excuse, local authorities tend to turn a blind to street vending, however unhygienic it may be. Turning a blind eye to the violation of any bylaw is unwise. The claim that local authorities would prevent many people from earning a living by enforcing bylaws is dangerous, disingenuous, and unimaginative. This is no different from excusing home burglaries on the ground that the burglars need to earn a living!

A cultural shift is necessary to ensure respect for the law and create legitimate opportunities to resolve issues that lead to illegal street vending. The first step is to identify the basic need of the vendors. That need is income generation. The next step is to devise ways in which the vendors could earn an income without breaking the law and endangering the community's health.

The vendors affected by the January 2018 ban mostly sold tomatoes. A tomato street vendor can sell as little as one box of the fruit in a day. According to Selima Wamucii, the online platform that helps global businesses buy and import food from African countries, the 2020 wholesale price for tomatoes was USD1.05 per kilogram. A box of tomatoes weighs roughly 25 kilogrammes and would therefore cost USD26.25.

The retail price for a 25-kilogramme box of tomatoes is about USD32.02. The vendor will therefore make a gross profit of USD5.77. The net profit, out of which the vendor is expected to support their family, will be significantly less than this. In the end, most vendors are lucky to take home two or three dollars after a long day's work. At this level of income, the vendor has little chance of escaping poverty. A society that cares about its citizens must be concerned about this.

Wholesalers buy their produce from farmers and, in this way, provide an important service. Even so, selling the produce to illegal vendors in the current fashion is unacceptable. Supposing we opened our minds to possibilities other than street vending. How about shifting the focus to food preservation?

Ideally, Zambia should have food processing facilities throughout the country where buyers who purchase produce from farmers can sell the produce in bulk, either directly or through intermediaries. Current illegal street vendors can fulfil the latter role splendidly after basic training in hygiene. These facilities would be able to buy everything available because of their ability to preserve food. For example, tomatoes could be processed into puree, jam, frozen tomato, ketchup, sauce, or soup.

Before the 1991 reforms, Zambia had food processing companies such as Copper Harvest Foods Ltd and Lyons Brooke Bond Zambia, which always had a market for fresh food producers. Unfortunately, the reforms of 1991 led to a regime that undertaxed imports, and these

Ndola-based companies closed because they could not compete with artificially cheap imports.

It is time to revive the food processing industry.

A commercial small-scale tomato jam- or paste-processing plant costs close to USD60,000. A large one with a five-year warranty will cost about USD200,000. These are not large sums of money. As demonstrated by the late Halina Ravensdale, self-styled 'Lala Princess' of Ndola, it is possible to establish a credible food processing outfit for relatively little capital investment. She did this at her smallholding off Misundu Road, with a lot of discipline, hard work, and an initial investment of less than USD10,000 in the 1980s. She sold bottled jam, mayonnaise, and many other products to shops on the Copperbelt. With the right incentives, Zambian entrepreneurs would invest in establishing a sustainable food processing industry.

The government could aid the establishment of an indigenous food processing industry by inviting Zambian entrepreneurs to participate in public tenders to provide food to government institutions. Then, knowing that they had a ready market, entrepreneurs would make the necessary investments to process and distribute food throughout the year.

This would end the all too frequent occurrence of food wastage during harvest times and food shortages the rest of the year. This would also significantly address street vendors, who would now have a more reliable and profitable market for the produce they buy from wholesalers.

Enforcing bylaws is both responsible and beneficial

Trading bylaws are not the only codes flagrantly violated by both citizens and local authorities. Zoning bylaws are also routinely violated. For example, municipal plots of land are routinely granted to political supporters even in areas designated as public spaces. Almost without exception, all local governments in Zambia have been negligent in this area of town planning.

Zambia's comprehensive zoning laws must be enforced consistently, not just when it is convenient for the local authority (or an individual in local authority) to do so.

The Copperbelt town of Chingola always prided itself as the cleanest town in Zambia. The entrance to the town is dominated by a well-manicured large roundabout with a perimeter marked by aesthetically pleasing flowers and plants. Until the late 1970s, the famous roundabout was surrounded by neatly painted houses, with manicured lawns. The city streets were broad, well maintained, and signposted. This was certainly the case in the low-density area. But even the high-density housing areas had order, and the houses there more often than not had a patch of lawn at the front and possibly a small vegetable garden at the back. The main streets in Chiwempala, one of the high-density areas, were paved and well maintained.

In the early 1970s, Town Clerk Tunji Fahm, perhaps influenced by the standards set by the colonial era mayor Nackson Longwe, made it a personal mission to ensure that his beloved Chingola was kept clean and well maintained at all times. The Chingola Municipal Council had an entire department dedicated to maintaining roads. The department took its responsibilities seriously. Both the low-density areas and the high-density areas had land reserved for parks. No one could build on these pieces of land.

One such designated park was at the southern end of the mall, in what the British colonial government called the second-class trading area along Zambezi Road. The road serviced a strip mall consisting of a butchery, shops, supermarkets, and two lounge bars.

In the late 1990s, the mall's character was entirely ruined by the construction of illegal stalls on the western side and by allowing 'development' on the designated park in the form of a shack that violated the most basic building code. Furthermore, the land allocation was done in violation of the Council's zoning bylaws. It is incomprehensible how this could happen. It is equally mindboggling that no one was held accountable. The councillors who allowed this defacement of Chingola must have known they were violating the law even if they were unaware of the extent of the damage they were doing to the community.

Parks are crucial to modern urban living. Their destruction harms the community in profound ways, with much of this harm being felt disproportionately by children, the most important segment of any society with a future.

It is no coincidence that in the 1990s, some established residents of Chingola noticed that the strip mall on Zambezi Road had become more susceptible to stormwater. This is related to the fact that unpaved ground in parks absorbs water, while trees and grass manage stormwater more efficiently than sewers and concrete drainage ditches. Given the scientific evidence that climate change has given rise to more extreme weather patterns, the benefits of parks cannot be overstated. Put differently, the destruction of parks increases the cost of managing stormwater.

This is the science which persuaded Ethiopia, for example, to adopt a plan to plant five billion trees in 2020 as part of an ambitious plan to plant 20 billion seedlings by 2024. The point of the exercise is to build a green climate-resistant economy.

For example, the Urban Heat Island effect makes urban neighbourhoods noticeably warmer than other areas. Planting more trees can reduce UHIs. In other words, increased park space combats the urban heat island effect.

Trees need not be confined to parks to produce beneficial effects. Planting them strategically with branches hanging over sidewalks, for example, provides shade, in addition to reducing the impact of heat on denizens.

In a Zambia desirous of promoting communal spirit, well-maintained parks would also provide space for neighbourhood residents to meet and get to know one another, either individually or through community events. It is far easier for one to feel a sense of responsibility for people one knows rather than for people one does not know. When neighbours know one another, the likelihood of communal responsibility increases.

It was common knowledge in Ndola during the 1980s that more crime was committed in newer areas compared to older areas such as Chifubu. The reason for this is that older areas were established communities where most families knew one another, whereas newer townships tended to be dominated by recent arrivals with no historic connection to the city.

All townships would benefit from more parks and recreational facilities. The evidence is also clear that increasing the number of parks and recreational facilities in neighbourhoods, has the positive effect of reducing crime rates among youth. When young people are given safe places to meet and enjoy themselves, they also have an additional incentive for keeping out of trouble.

Parks, however, benefit all age groups and are absolutely essential at this particular time in world history. Trees can absorb a wide variety of pollutants from the air and reduce air pollution, which decreases the risk for certain types of cancer. Particularly vulnerable in this regard are people with underlying respiratory problems.

In 2012, there was concern about the shortage of green spaces in Kigali, Rwanda. The concern was taken seriously and despite the cost of doing so, a commitment was made to build the Nyandungu Park scheduled to open in 2022. The rehabilitation of Nyandungu urban wetland will provide urban recreational space, restore hydrological functioning, and increase biodiversity. So far, four artificial lakes have been created as part of a plan to protect wildlife and increase leisure diversity in the 130-hectare sanctuary. The Rwandans are confident that the benefits of the park will outweigh the projected cost of USD5 million. Their calculation appears to be correct.

Writing in the Elsevier Journal of Environmental Pollution, David J. Nowak, Satoshi Hirabayashi, Allison Bodine, and Robert Hoehn acknowledged that urban pollution is a serious health issue. They stated that trees within cities can remove fine particles from the atmosphere and improve air quality and human health. The tree effects in their study were modelled on 10 cities from the United States. Focusing on particles formed as a result of burning fuel and chemical reactions that take place in the atmosphere, with a diameter of less than 2.5 micrometres, the authors found that the total amount of these particles removed by trees varied from 4.7 tonnes in Syracuse to 64.5 tonnes in Atlanta, with annual values varying from USD1.1 million in Syracuse to USD9.17 million in Atlanta. The largest annual value associated with removing pollutants was USD60.13, in New York City. Most of these values were from the effects of reducing human mortality. Mortality reductions were as high as 7.6 people per annum in New York City. The average annual percentage of air quality improvement ranged from 0.05 in San Francisco to 0.24 in Atlanta.

In addition to their ability to absorb air pollutants, strengthen stormwater management, contribute to a more climate-compliant economy, mitigate UHIs, and strengthen the social health of communities, parks also contribute to the mental health of inhabitants. A study from the Netherlands found that people living in residential areas with the least green spaces had a 44 percent higher rate of physician-diagnosed anxiety disorders than those living in the greenest residential areas. A study by Finnish researchers found that even ten minutes in a park or urban woodland area could tangibly reduce stress.

The phenomenal economic growth recorded in Zambia from the late 1990s to 2013 brought about an increase in obesity levels as more Zambians led sedentary lives. The downside is this lifestyle is not necessarily conducive to good health and can cause several health challenges such as cardiovascular diseases and cancer. Parks contribute to the fight against these diseases by offering spaces where people can walk and safely engage in physical activities. This is important in a country where only a minority of people have access to fitness centres.

Local government officials and others who believe that destroying areas designated as parks and subdividing these areas into plots to be given to political cronies is harmless, should reflect on the preceding paragraphs. As they do that, the rest of us must look forward to a time when those who have undermined society by flagrant disregard for zoning laws are held accountable for the harm they have done to society.

The Benefits of Zoning Laws

Every town in Zambia has bylaws that require buildings to conform to zoning laws and to be maintained. In addition, many properties in urban areas are acquired by way of underleases from municipal councils. These underleases specify minimum standards of maintenance that must be adhered to. In residential areas, these standards usually include maintaining manicured lawns.

Like other older cities and towns in Zambia, the City of Ndola has some historic buildings of interest. Government House on Buteko Avenue is an example. The other example is the building on President Avenue which houses a famous pharmacy. Apart from their colonial charm, now quite hidden, the two buildings have one other thing in common: they are both poorly maintained. A coat of paint may not be enough to fully restore these buildings to their former glory, but it might be enough to uncover their external aesthetic beauty.

The failure to maintain these buildings is a good example of the culture of neglect that has afflicted Zambia over the past 40 years. There were indeed visible signs of a change in culture in the early 1990s as homeownership increased and new owners took a greater interest in their properties. But this enthusiasm for property maintenance has not significantly affected the guardians of publicly owned buildings. The appearance of publicly owned buildings such as those referenced here can be improved very easily. They can, for example, be whitewashed at very little cost. Three ingredients, all locally available, are needed to make whitewash paint. They are lime, water, and salt. The salt allows the paint to stick to the walls. It does not take too much imagination to see how local authorities could encourage young people to make whitewash and engage them to paint public buildings. This approach would help address youth unemployment, in addition to beautifying the city.

Although Zambia has anti-litter legislation, arresting anyone for littering is extremely rare. In March 2018, the Minister responsible for Lusaka Province threatened that henceforth persons littering the province would be arrested. Nothing appears to have come out of this initiative.

That is a pity because a strong signal needs to be sent that anti-litter laws are as important as other laws and necessary for the health of inhabitants. This is the approach that Singapore has taken since 1968, when the Keep Singapore Clean campaign started. The idea at that time was to discourage littering through heavy fines. Lee Kuan Yew, the first prime minister, justified this because a clean Singapore would also be good for the economy. Punishing littering is now part of Singaporean culture. The BBC reported in 2018 that the minimum fine for littering in Singapore that year was USD217. Litterers in Lusaka would certainly take note of a ZMW4,500 fine for littering.

The fine for littering in Rwanda ranges between 10 and 100 USD. The City of Kigali District has also placed waste bins all around the city to reduce littering. There is a strict garbage collection system in place, with trash being collected every Tuesday. Each household pays the equivalent of two American dollars per month for the service, while corporate entities pay around USD10. A system such as this would create opportunities for entrepreneurs in Zambia who would surely be interested in the manufacture of garbage bins and the actual collection of garbage.

If all towns and city councils insist on a minimum standard of cleanliness for households within their jurisdictions, all houses would have lawns and gardens. The result of enforcing this bylaw would be a mushrooming of small-scale gardening businesses across the country. These businesses would obviously increase employment, especially among the youth. Towns and cities enforcing this standard of cleanliness would be wealthier in addition to being nicer places to live in.

Unfortunately, enforcing bylaws and attending to town planning matters is not a priority for many local authorities in Zambia. Instead, the priorities seem to centre on pomp and prestige. This has led to reduced expenditure on services and disproportionate expenditure on emoluments and unproductive activities.

With less money being spent on services, more Zambians have found themselves living in unsanitary conditions. The excuse that local authorities have no money to perform their basic duties rings hollow when all relevant circumstances are considered. For example, in 2019, the Lusaka City Council was owed an accumulated historic debt of USD1.5 million. When presenting the 2020 budget, the Council was content to collect only 10 percent (USD150,000) of that amount. It is unsettling that any Zambian local authority would write off USD1.35 million, so easily.

There is a price to be paid for lack of financial prudence.

Kanyama Township is an entirely unplanned habitat south of Lusaka. The growing settlement occupies 15 square kilometres and is home to about 400,000 people. Only half of the population has access to clean water. Since the late 1970s, Kanyama has experienced flooding in each year that Zambia has had anything resembling above-normal rainfall. The first recorded serious deluge occurred in 1978. Times were different then, and the country was more responsive to suffering than it is now. Businesspeople and ordinary men and women were joined by the international community in raising money for what came to be known as the Kanyama Disaster Fund. The purpose of the fund was to help accommodate, feed and otherwise help the victims of the flooding.

Since it was clear from the start that the flooding could have been avoided had the authorities constructed an appropriate drainage system, the hope was that drainage infrastructure would now be put in place to avoid similar calamities in the future. Sadly, that did not happen.

There was no public explanation either of how the local authority used the huge amount of money raised. Virtually every rainy season brings deleterious flooding to Kanyama, with the deluge of 1978 proportions repeated frequently in the recent past. This was certainly the case during the 2009 rainy season that caused widespread flooding, described by The Post newspaper as a 'death trap'. The death trap returned in 2020. This time, the Disaster Management and Mitigation Unit described the situation as 'serious and [requiring] urgent attention'.

The DMMU national coordinator, Chanda Kabwe, then delivered welcome news by promising that a team of engineers would be constituted to undertake a case study on Kanyama to find a lasting solution. In the meantime, the ministry of health undertook to prioritise the provision of clean drinking water and ensure there was no outbreak of water-borne diseases.

While the promise of building suitable infrastructure for Kanyama is welcome, it is a matter of regret that this was not done earlier as it could have saved lives. Furthermore, constructing suitable infrastructure would have been much cheaper in 1978 than in 2020. The most important resource in building a drainage system is labour. In addition, piping, stone, sand, cement, and excavation equipment are also required. All these are available in Zambia. Why then has the Kanyama drainage system not been built, as required by Zambian town and country planning law? Given the regularity of the flooding and its predictability, why are the authorities always taken by surprise when floods occur? There has been no lack of opportunity for both levels of government to end Kanyama's vulnerability to flooding. The problem has been ignored because Zambia has accommodated a culture of mediocrity, which normalises laxity.

There are hopeful signs that many people in Zambia, especially informed youth, will no longer tolerate the culture of neglect. In these changing times, it should be easier to make the case that all laws matter and sustainable development depends on a robust and respected legal regime.

Generally, the benefits of property ownership disappear in the absence of a credible legal regime that ensures, for example, that bylaws are universally obeyed. For example, when land title is issued fraudulently, that title may afford little or no protection to the holder if it is issued in violation of zoning laws. For this reason, it may not enhance economic development, as prudent lenders will decline to use the title for collateral purposes, fearing that it may one day be revoked on the ground that it was issued illegally. The holder of the title wishing to use it as collateral to start a business, will thus be unable to do so.

Disregarding bylaws undermines legitimate regulation of society and invites anarchy. This is not to advocate excessive regulation but rather to call for the enactment of necessary laws enforced universally. For example, it is necessary to have town and country planning regulations; it is necessary to regulate the sale and purchase of farming land so that farmers can have secure title and be able to borrow against that title; it is necessary to regulate occupation of residential properties so that people can be secure in their ownership of homes; and it is necessary to regulate the conduct of people in residential areas so that citizens can be safe and live in dignity.

The reasons for bylaws are numerous and form a critical part of the framework for sustainable economic growth.

Celebrating Zambian Citizenship

There is more to citizenship than simple possession of the national registration card or the Zambian passport. There are attributes that collectively constitute 'good citizenship'. Zambians seem to have a good sense of good citizenship, even though it may not be actively promoted by the authorities.

Obeying the law, for example, is an attribute the vast majority of Zambians would recognise as a characteristic of good citizenship. Related to this is the duty to pay taxes. Although in this instance, many would add the qualifier, 'reasonable'. So, as long as taxes are reasonable, Zambians would see support for the exchequer as an attribute of good citizenship. Voting is also seen as an attribute of good citizenship. It is interesting how quickly people disillusioned with politics and expressing a lack of interest in voting change their minds when it is pointed out that a failure to vote takes away their right to complain.

Less articulated but nonetheless equally important attributes are community engagement and commitment to diversity. Traditional Zambian values place a huge premium on community engagement as a way of attaining societal goals. In addition, the multi-ethnic nature of the country and the diversity of religions, despite Christianity being the official religion, makes promoting diversity a good citizenship attribute, particularly important.

A conscious effort to promote good citizenship encourages good behaviour in the population and promotes individual pride connected to national achievement. Nonetheless, more can be done to promote good citizenship in Zambia.

Honours and Awards

Driving along Independence Avenue in Lusaka, from Woodlands toward the High Court, there is a road on the left-hand side called Yotam Muleya Road. I have asked many Zambians below the age of 50 to tell me who Yotam Muleya was. Unfortunately, only about 30 percent of respondents have given the correct answer.

This is actually a higher percentage than I would have expected and may be due to the fact that one of the national newspapers featured the long-distance runner in a reasonably comprehensive article in November

2019. It is not good enough, however, and indicates how undervalued good citizenship and achievement are in today's Zambia.

Yotam Siachobe Muleya was born in 1940 and lived only to the age of 19, having died in Mount Pleasant, Michigan, on 23 November 1959 in a motor vehicle accident. Muleya had attended Hodgson Training School in Lusaka where he enrolled as an apprentice motor vehicle mechanic the year before his death. In his short life, Muleya brought much pride to his people, who were then fighting for statehood.

Muleya's name is closely associated with Douglas Alistair Gordon Pirie, better known simply as Gordon Pirie. Born on 10 February 1931 in Leeds, West Yorkshire, Gordon Pirie represented Great Britain in 1952, 1956, and 1960 Summer Olympics. On all three occasions, he featured in both the 5,000 and 10,000 metres races for men. His best performance was at the 1956 Olympics when he won the silver medal, after narrowly missing the bronze medal in the 1952 edition.

Towards the end of 1958, Gordon Pirie set off by ocean-liner from Britain with his sprinter wife, Shirley, for a seven-week tour of southern Africa. They were joined there by Murray Halberg of New Zealand, who held the three-mile Empire Games championship. The tour included Southern Rhodesia, where Yotam Muleya was also scheduled to compete in the three-mile race on December 06.

For a while, it appeared Muleya might not be allowed to compete. A week before the race, a Rhodesian Athletics Association official ruled that Muleya could not run with Gordon Pirie and Halberg because of his skin colour. It appears however, that public opinion was ahead of the RAA official. Furthermore, seven founding members of the Northern Rhodesia Athletics Association, which was less racist than its Southern Rhodesian counterpart, sent a telegram to the British Home Secretary, Sir Malcolm Barrow, expressing 'disgust and humiliation' at the ban. According to Pirie's autobiography, Running Wild, he and Halberg also decided that if the ban stayed, they would race with Muleya at a meeting run by the Africans, if necessary.

In the end, the Rhodesian Athletics Association overruled the recalcitrant official and allowed Muleya to run. By all accounts, the public was supportive of this decision. On the day of the event, the 4000-strong crowd was almost unanimous in cheering Muleya on as Pirie succumbed to the Northern Rhodesian hero, who won by 200 yards in 14:48.3 minutes, beating his previous best of 14:57.0.

In the autobiography, we glean something of Muleya's character from Pirie who describes his competitor as 'a quiet, charming fellow and an excellent runner'. Muleya is remembered for running this race barefooted. Apparently, it was Pirie who had suggested that Muleya race barefooted. Pirie's reasoning was that since Muleya had not worn spikes more than once, doing so now would disadvantage him.

In the end, Muleya won the race and established a new Rhodesian record. In The Impossible Hero, Dick Booth, Pirie's biographer, says although Pirie lost the race, he was still declared the official winner. Pirie, however, handed the prize over to Muleya.

This is the story of Yotam Muleya. He deserves to be remembered by more than a street name in the Zambian capital. There should be an annual national award for students demonstrating courage and discipline in the way that Muleya did. This award would be in the category of sports and athletics.

Diversity of Achievement

Not everyone is capable of outstanding athletic prowess like Muleya, but non-athletic persons can excel in other areas and bring just as much pride to the nation. In addition to sports and athletics, Zambia should look at arts and literature, bravery, community leadership, education, entrepreneurship, philanthropy and volunteering, science and technology, and youth leadership.

Needless to say, this list is not exhaustive. There should also be different fora for celebrating citizen achievement. Some awards would be granted by schools and colleges, others by local authorities, and others by the central government. How the recognition of an achieving citizen is expressed is less important than the institution of a culture which encourages and praises citizens for good work. Both living and deceased citizens should, as appropriate, be honoured.

Arts and Literature

There is no road named after Stephen Mpashi and Dominic Mulaisho, yet these individuals contributed significantly to the growth of literature in Zambia.

Stephen Mpashi was born on December 03, 1920 and obtained the bulk of his early education at Lubushi Major Seminary in Kasama, before proceeding to the University of Exeter in England, where he read creative writing. Between 1950 and 1978, Mpashi wrote 19 books, and almost all of them have more than one edition. Thus *Mnzako Akapsa Ndebvu* has seven editions while *Abapatili bafika ku baBemba* has eight. The book in which Mpashi shared his experiences as a soldier, *Cekesoni aingila ubu soja*, was first published in 1950, and has ten editions. Mpashi had a keen eye and an excellent memory. Both attributes are evident in this part-biographical work about the Second World War.

When that war ended, Mpashi took an appointment as a teacher at Central School in the mining town of Luanshya. When his teaching career ended, however, Mpashi moved to Lusaka where he fraternised with Zambia's future leaders in Chilenje Township, home to such luminaries as Kenneth Kaunda, Patrick Chella, Adam Ndalajani Banda, and Simon Kapwepwe.

Many expected Mpashi to join the political bandwagon and become a cabinet minister at independence. Indeed there are suggestions that Kaunda had been keen to name Mpashi minister of education. Mpashi, however, followed the example of his friend Adam Banda and stayed clear of politics. While Banda became a successful but unassuming businessman, Mpashi became a humble literary giant.

Mpashi's best-known work, *Pio Na Vera*, was reprinted in 1996, almost forty years after the storyline was first developed. The novel depicts life on the Zambian Copperbelt in the 1960s. The book is a perfect candidate for a big-screen adaptation in the romance category as *Cekesoni Aingila Ubu Soja* would be in the action genre. The dramatization of Zambian literature is an excellent way of teaching the country about itself and promoting Zambian values.

Dominic Mulaisho was a senior civil servant in the Zambian government. He is not as prolific as Mpashi but wrote two very different books in his spare time. The Smoke that Thunders fictionalises the campaign for independence and gives the reader not just an insight into what the issues were, but also allows the reader to get inside the mind of the settler community and the indigenous people. Tongue of the Dumb has a traditional village setting. The plot highlights the danger of propaganda and heresy and how these can be used to suppress even legitimate dissent. The novel's commentary on the relationship between evangelising Christians and local spiritual leaders and their followers is sharp. It is possible Mulaisho was influenced by Chinua Achebe in his analysis of this relationship.

Both books are candidates for dramatization, with The Smoke that Thunders better suited to the big screen while Tongue of the Dumb may be better suited to the stage.

In addition to his contribution to Zambian literature, Mulaisho was known for promoting education among young Zambians. As permanent secretary of education, he went out of his way to promote excellence in schools. Mulaisho, like Stephen Mpashi, is deserving of recognition for his contribution to arts and literature.

Bravery

Recipients of awards for bravery would be those individuals who risk their lives for the greater good. Many recipients in this category would probably get their awards posthumously with security personnel probably dominating, although civilians would also be recognised for saving others.

An obvious candidate for this award from recent Zambian history would be Elliot Mulenga, the labour rights activist killed on the 3rd of April 1940. The reader will recall that during the second African Mineworkers Union strike, 17 unarmed Africans were killed and 63 seriously wounded by shots fired by white law enforcement officers. Elliot Mulenga was initially shot in the arm and received treatment at the mine dispensary. After treatment, he returned to the demonstration to support his striking colleagues. This time he was struck with a bayonet that cut his bowels open, resulting in his immediate death.

Community Leadership

Those who persuade others to follow them in implementing an agenda designed to bring positive change to the community are leaders to be celebrated. The community leadership category would probably overlap with other categories. The recipients of community leadership awards may also attract attention beyond their immediate communities.

One example of a community leader whose work went beyond her immediate community is Julia Mulenga Nsofwa Chikamoneka, better known either as Mama UNIP or Mama Chikamoneka. Julia Mulenga Nsofwa was born in Kasama in 1910 to a British Army African sergeant who served in the First World War.

In 1938, Julia and her husband left Kasama for Lusaka in search of employment. It was here that she came face to face with the harshest aspects of colonial rule. It was inevitable that such an irrepressible character would soon find herself embroiled in nationalist politics. She concluded early on after arriving in Lusaka that the solution to social injustice was independence for Northern Rhodesia. She also believed she could best contribute to this by organising women into a potent force for the nationalist movement.

The women, however, worked closely with the men. Within a decade of arriving in Lusaka, she helped form the Northern Rhodesia Teachers' Welfare Association, led by Dauti Lawson Yamba, an astute campaigner for justice whose immense contribution has unfortunately been largely forgotten.

The Northern Rhodesia Teachers' Welfare Association was the forerunner of the Northern Rhodesia African Congress (initially led by Godwin Mbikusita-Lewanika), whose leadership Harry Mwaanga Nkumbula assumed on his return from the United Kingdom where he had been studying.

In 1951, Julia Mulenga Nsofwa, now known as Julia Chikamoneka, became a founding member of the Women's Brigade supporting the nationalist cause. The name Chikamoneka translates roughly to 'it will come to pass'. The 'it' was the independence of Northern Rhodesia.

The sense of urgency conveyed by the likes of Julia Chikamoneka led to a faction of the Northern Rhodesia African National Congress breaking away and forming a rival political party committed to achieving independence more quickly than the ANC appeared prepared for. The new party was known as the Zambia African National Congress.

Julia Chikamoneka lost no time recruiting women members for the new party, which was later banned following the state of emergency declared by the colonial governor, Sir Arthur Benson. But banning ZANC did nothing to quench the thirst for independence. On the contrary, two principal movements arose almost immediately after the ban.

The first was the African National Independence Party, led by Paul Kalichini. The second was the United National Freedom Party, led by Dixon Konkola. The highly regarded Mainza Chona did not immediately abandon ANC, but by September 1959, he had had enough. He and his friend Titus Mukupo joined ANIP, which merged with the UNFP to form the United National Independence Party.

Julia Chikamoneka and her supporters transferred their allegiance to UNIP. She remained prominent in the campaign for independence until UNIP won the election leading to the birth of Zambia.

Julia Mulenga Nsofwa has not been forgotten, unlike so many genuine Zambian heroes. Instead, she is remembered through the Julia Chikamoneka Awards organised by the Zambian media. One of the Julia Chikamoneka honourees is the late Mama Chibesa Kankasa, who played a crucial role in establishing the Women's Brigade. She later served at very high levels in the government.

Education

The education category may well have more unsung heroes than any other class of citizens. Education awards should be granted to outstanding teachers and leaders who may not necessarily teach but who promote education in unique and exemplary ways.

By being the first university graduate in the country and also the first principal of a secondary school, John Mupanga Mwanakatwe is better known than most other educators. But there were other similarly outstanding pre-independence secondary school teachers such as Vincent Nsomi, Pete Paul Banda, and Nayoto Kopano Mushasho, who would be worthy of consideration for honour in this category. In addition, those who were not famed for teaching but nonetheless made a huge contribution to education in Zambia include Stephen Andrea Mpashi and Patrick Chella.

Not surprisingly, most educators before independence were men. Ambitious women were rarely recognised on account of their skin colour, gender, and ambition. Those who made it were truly remarkable individuals. Consider the case of Gwendoline Chomba Konie.

Konie was born in Lusaka on the 9th of October 1938, to two dedicated educators. She showed exceptional aptitude and independence from an early age. She attributed her independent spirit to the fact that she had gone to boarding school at the tender age of eight. Years later, when she gained admission to the University College of South Wales (later called Cardiff University), no one was surprised. Her graduation from Cardiff gave her the honour of being Zambia's first indigenous female university graduate. She later attended the American University in

Washington D.C., and obtained a doctorate in Sociology from Warwick University in England.

Konie's academic progress was not sequential. She was only one of a handful of university graduates when she returned home. With the colonial era coming to an end, Konie was under pressure to serve in a public capacity. For this reason, her post graduate degrees were obtained quite a while after graduating from Cardiff.

In 1959, a forward-looking and enlightened man called Sir Evelyn Dennison Hone became governor of Northern Rhodesia. He immediately reached out to key players in the nationalist movement to prepare the country for what he saw as the inevitability of independence.

Three years after becoming governor, Sir Evelyn encountered the impressive Gwen Konie. Apparently, Sir Evelyn was impressed by Konie's 'guts'. In his view, this was precisely the kind of person Northern Rhodesia would need as it transitioned into Zambia. Thus, in 1962, Gwendoline Chomba Konie became a member of the Northern Rhodesia Legislative Council at the instigation of the governor. Before taking the appointment, she consulted Kenneth Kaunda in his capacity as head of the coalition government that had brought the ANC and UNIP into the pre-independence administration.

Konie received formal training in diplomacy as the country was approaching independence. Thereafter, she worked as a diplomat, rising to be Zambia's Ambassador to Sweden and being accredited to Denmark, Norway, and Finland from 1974 until 1977. Thereafter, she was appointed Zambia's permanent representative to the United Nations. She returned home to serve as permanent secretary in the ministry of tourism after a two-year stint in New York.

During the Third Republic, she served as Zambia's ambassador to Germany. That assignment ended in 1997. Four years later, she retired from the civil service and ran for president under the banner of the newly formed Social Democratic Party, which promoted child and women issues and called for an overhaul of the Zambian educational system. She was unsuccessful in her bid, but she continued to use her post public service life to educate through literature. Her poem, In the Fist of your Hatred, was included in The Penguin Book of Modern African Poetry in 2007. Not surprisingly, the poem addresses male arrogance, pointing out, accurately, that postures of superiority are usually a manifestation of inferiority. She had discovered this truth in her many encounters with different people over her illustrious career.

Gwendoline Chomba Konie died in Lusaka in 2009. She was given a state-sponsored funeral.

Entrepreneurship

Although the estate of Gwendoline Chomba Konie did not establish a memorial scholarship, Konie herself did establish the William Konie School to honour her parents. By setting up a school, she may well have inspired Mwansa and Lydia Folotiya, the founders of Rhodes Park School, to do the same. The estate of the enterprising couple established the Folotiya Memorial Scholarships in 1997 to give promising children free or subsidised secondary school education based on their performance in the final primary school examination.

The successful candidates typically receive tuition-free education from Grade Eight to Grade Twelve. This is a fine example of honouring both the entrepreneurs who started the Rhodes Park School and the bright students who attend the school.

As with education, there is no shortage of entrepreneurs in Zambia's past who are deserving of recognition. Names such as Adam Ndalajani Banda, Chileshe Chilaka, Robinson Chisanga Puta Chekwe, Safeli Hannock Chileshe, Anna Chilombo, Mpande Chilulu Boxer Chirwa, Abraham Benson Chungu Kazembe, Anne Lengalenga, Luka Mumba, Lameck Mwenso, Brian Nkonde, Philip Musekiwa Nekhairo, Patrick Mwanawasa, Tom DM Mtine, Justin Simukonda, Pascale Sokota, Tom Mwelwa Kashimbaya, Wilson Kapikila, Jeremiah Chizema, and many others, should be remembered and honoured as pioneers of modern Zambian entrepreneurship.

Of these giants, Anna Chilombo and Anne Lengalenga deserve special mention because, in addition to the challenge of skin colour, they also suffered gender discrimination. As a result, they had to work much harder than their male counterparts to succeed.

Anna Chilombo started her career as a teacher before deciding to go into business 'to work like a man'. She got a job with a company as the first step in her quest to gain trading experience. It did not take long before she became Northern Rhodesia's first travelling saleswoman. She saved as much of her earnings as possible and was, within a few years, in a positon to buy a delivery van and set up a fish trading business. The work was hard. Since her main market was on the Copperbelt, she travelled day and night, often sleeping by the roadside, between Lakes Bangweulu and Mweru and the Copperbelt towns. It was all worth it as in the end Anna established the first grocery store to be owned by a woman, in Fort Roseberry (now Mansa). She also married her supportive husband at about this time. Kenneth Little estimated her annual turnover toward the end of the 1950s in African Women in Towns: An Aspect of Africa's Social Revolution (1960) at more than £3,500. That is today's equivalent of USD62,000.

Mrs Chilombo moved on to other ventures, eventually settling in Kabwe where she bought a small farm just outside the town, while running Mike's Café, reputed to be one of the best hamburger bistros in the Commonwealth of Nations. On some estimates, Mrs Chilombo had become a millionaire at this point.

Anne Lengalenga's route to success was not too different from Chilombo's. She also started as a teacher, instructing pupils in home craft at a mission school near Ndola. She also tried her hand at nursing, leaving after having saved £60. When Lengalenga heard that there was a shop for sale, she quickly put in a bid and won. The work that followed was hard.

Twice a day, she cycled 18 miles to buy goods for her shop. It was not easy to fit boxes of soap, canned foods, and other items on a bicycle, but somehow this determined woman managed it. By 1956, Lengalenga had made enough money to buy a used car. The following year, she built a large flat-roofed property with six rooms at the back and transferred her business there. According to Kenneth Little, Lengalenga's next goal was to construct a double-storey building.

As with their male counterparts, Chilombo and Lengalenga must have experienced a huge sense of satisfaction building successful businesses from scratch by following the rules, even when those rules disadvantaged them. These business pioneers should never be forgotten. Their memory should be allowed to stand as a reminder of the value of hard work, dedication and transparency in business. In addition to honouring these entrepreneurs, the country should unambiguously commit itself to universal and unbiased enforcement of laws to encourage budding entrepreneurs. When entrepreneurs know that they can always count on the law, they will do whatever is necessary to succeed. And their success will benefit the country.

Philanthropy and Volunteering

Philanthropists and volunteers are motivated by a desire to pay back and make society a better place. Their typical profile includes a successful career and a burning desire to give back to a society that made this success possible. Indeed, the 'giving back' could be to persons resident in foreign lands, not necessarily in the country where the philanthropist's success was achieved. In this instance, philanthropists simply recognise that their privileged position places a responsibility on them to help those less fortunate, wherever they may be.

Volunteers too may have had a successful career before volunteering, but this is not necessarily the case. Many young volunteers help others even before their careers have properly commenced. These volunteers rely on their skills and compassionate nature. An example of an organisation that depends on such volunteers is the Denmark-based Ubumi Prisons Initiative, which works to improve the health of particularly vulnerable groups in Zambian prisons.

Education attracts both philanthropists and volunteers. Thus, the Mwansa and Lydia Folotiya estate depends on volunteers to administer the Folotiya Memorial Scholarship. Volunteers also made the establishment of the Munali Old Boys Association possible. Unfortunately, Munali alumni, many of whom benefited from great tertiary educational opportunities and wonderful careers from the 1950s until the 1970s, do not appear well represented in Zambia's small club of philanthropists.

This privileged group does not appear to be following the example of pre-independence Zambian businesspeople who were keen to use their financial resources, skills, and experience to address societal challenges. Many of these businesspeople not only advocated for the creation of a local university, they actually took steps to ensure the university was built.

Writing about those days, Douglas Anglin, the first vice-chancellor of the University of Zambia, said of Robinson Chisanga Puta Chekwe: 'Perhaps, his most significant contribution to the University was as a member of the [University Provisional] Council's innovative Fund-Raising Committee as well as in personally canvassing for small and large contributions, especially in Chingola.'

The spirit of philanthropists and volunteers who contributed so much to the creation of Zambia's first university should be allowed to grow. It would be gratifying, for example, to see a similar commitment from the early graduates of Munali expressed in the form of, say, a scholarship of excellence for current students at their old school. There would be many volunteers to help manage such a scholarship as Zambians already have a tradition of helping extended family and friends with no expectation of monetary compensation.

Scholarships established to support excellence need not be confined to study at local institutions. Opportunities exist to establish scholarships to enable young Zambians to study at some of the world's most prestigious universities. If Zambia is going to have a meaningful voice at global tables where consequential decisions are made, the country needs to have a cadre of young people studying, at any given tine, at institutions where these tables draw the bulk of their talent. Oxford University offers excellent opportunities in this regard. For GBP1 million or USD 1,350,000, Oxford will create a scholarship in perpetuity. If Zambia had set up such a scholarship at the time of independence, there would be 56 well-educated and highly connected Zambians able to advocate for the country, globally.

Sadly, there is not a single Zambian endowed scholarship at Oxford. The only Zambian-supported scholarship outside Zambia may be the Zambia Cambridge Scholarship initiated by Andrew Sardanis. Earlier, Sardanis had established the Sotiris Scholarship at the University of Zambia in honour of his then recently deceased father.

A million British pounds is not a huge amount to layout for a scholarship that guarantees unusually high-quality education for one student every year in perpetuity. The benefits of such a scholarship would easily outweigh its cost. Yet, successful Zambians with resources have been shy to commit to the creation of such a scholarship.

When former president Kenneth Kaunda considered running for the presidency again in 1996, he reportedly had USD5 million at his disposal for this purpose. If that amount of money can be raised for an election campaign, surely USD1.3 million can be found for the very worthwhile exercise of establishing a Zambian scholarship at the world's most prestigious university.

To his credit, Zambia's fourth president, Rupiah Bwezani Banda, did look into the possibility of establishing a merit-based scholarship for Zambian students at Oxford. He could not provide the money required, but he was interested in starting a campaign to raise the necessary funds.

Unfortunately, Banda was diagnosed with cancer and could not continue with his laudable efforts.

Thanks to data revealed by a former HSBC employee, we now know that as of February 2015, there were 69 Zambia-connected individuals among the 100,000 clients of the bank's Swiss subsidiary who had a combined USD48.3 million in their accounts. This evidence, in the context of the opulent lifestyles of many Zambian millionaires, provides a clear indication that if wealthy Zambians were serious about exposing the country's brightest young people to the best education in the world, the money for Zambian-endowed scholarships at Oxford and other first-rate universities could be found.

One last word about volunteerism. Anyone who doubts the value of volunteering may wish to consider that in Ontario, a jurisdiction with a population similar to Zambia's, 58,000 not-for-profit organisations and charities operate in communities across the province. These organisations employ over one million workers. They also engage 5.2 million volunteers, contributing 2.6% of Ontario's GDP of USD730 billion. 45% of the organisations' income is earned independently of government funding and donations. Imagine this in the context of the new Zambia and you begin to see the financial benefit to the nation of promoting volunteerism and philanthropy.

Science and Technology

Advancement in science and technology starts with an idea such as the one Mukuka Nkoloso had about creating a Zambia space programme. The idea is then given practical application. In Zambia, few ideas reach practical application for various reasons, including insufficient human resources and infrastructure.

The absence of human resources is, however, exaggerated. While there may be insufficient human capital in the science and technology sector within the country, there are many Zambians in the diaspora who possess this capital. Unfortunately, as Dr Misheck Mwaba and Professor Kenneth Mwenda have observed, key decision-makers in Zambia are reluctant, even unwilling, to engage the diaspora. In this way, they deny the country access to critical human capital and global connections.

In early November 2020, Dr Misheck Mwaba was named president and CEO of Bow Valley College in Alberta. In this role, he continues to champion the College's robust Open Doors - Open Minds strategy. Mwaba's basic responsibility is to ensure that the College continues to provide educational excellence to students, grows the College's highly skilled community of alumni, creates value for the College's stakeholders and partners, and contributes to shaping the future of post-secondary education in Alberta. Consider these responsibilities in the context of the global ranking of the University of Zambia and you begin to appreciate the contribution that Mwaba can make to the advancement of higher education in his country of birth.

As a pupil at Kabulonga Boys' Secondary School in the late 1960s, I participated in the first Junior Engineers Technicians and Scientists awards. My friend, Inambao Francis Muyoyeta, and I did a joint project in chromatography. I also had a solo project on the manufacture of rayon in a laboratory. The joint project was supervised by Professor Dawson Nkunika, a renowned University of Zambia chemist. Once or twice a week, he would pick us up at the school and take us to his lab at the University to show us the intricacies of chromatography. Later, Dr Nkunika became head of the National Council for Scientific Research.

While in England, I was informed that Professor Nkunika had died in a car accident. The news was obviously shocking, but it also made me realise that the opportunity to be tutored by such an accomplished scientist, whose understanding of chemistry surpassed that of my teachers in England, contributed to my confidence in Zambians. I know that my late friend Inambao felt the same way. He told me so before his own untimely demise.

If scientists such as Mwaba were allowed to engage young Zambians, these youth would be as positively affected by these encounters as Inambao and I were by our encounter with Professor Nkunika.

Equally inspiring would be Dr Patrick Chilufya Chimfwembe, the Canada-based communications technology inventor with at least seven patents to his name. Chimfwembe is a modest man with a deep sense of loyalty to Zambia. Sadly, his overtures to help the country in the science and technology sector have been largely ignored. If the Zambian government is unwilling to work with the likes of Chimfwembe, the country should at least encourage the creation of citizen-led fora through which young Zambians could be exposed to these scientists.

In general, Zambian scientific achievements are better publicised outside the country than within it. On occasion, however, the local press takes an interest and Zambians know about their foreign-based achievers.

When Kelly Chibale, founder and director of Africa's first and only integrated drug discovery centre, was recognised as one of Fortune magazine's World's 50 Greatest Leaders for 2018, the Lusaka Times took note. They had good reason to.

Professor Kelly Chibale is an organic chemist at the University of Cape Town in South Africa. His Drug Discovery and Development Centre (H3D) at UCT pioneers world-class drug discovery in Africa. The professor is also known for his pivotal work on malaria. By being recognised by Fortune magazine as one of the 'influential figures we admire most', the South African National Research Foundation A-rated Zambian scientist found himself in the company of such global leaders as Bill and Melinda Gates, the presidents of France and South Korea— Emmanuel Macron and Moon Jae-in—tennis player Serena Williams, Apple CEO Tim Cook, and the MeToo movement.

In keeping with traditional Zambian humility, Chibale said that his inclusion on the list was 'totally unexpected and overwhelming. I am so grateful to God for this recognition on the global stage'. These words barely hint at the hard work and discipline that brought Chibale this far. He was selected for his pioneering work in developing infrastructure to support scientific research, which led to his founding H3D at UCT in 2010 and officially launching it in 2011.

At inception, H3D only had a handful of researchers. That number has grown to 65. In addition, there are around 20 postgraduate (PhD) research students and postdoctoral fellows in his separate academic group as of November 2020. H3D is an example of entrepreneurial science that has great potential for job creation.

More than 2,000 malaria deaths are still reported annually, even as the Zambia National Malaria Elimination Centre shows these deaths to have decreased dramatically over the past decade. Africa-wide, the disease kills a child every 30 seconds and leaves some survivors with physical and mental diabilities.

Chibale is acutely aware of these statistics. Not surprisingly, malaria is a key focus area at his Drug Discovery and Development Centre, alongside tuberculosis and antibiotic-resistant microbial diseases. He is hopeful H3D will contribute to a global pipeline of new medication for malaria and tuberculosis. Although this would be good for Zambia and the world, Chibale has never been formally approached by the Zambian government to use his immense talent and global influence to help the homeland.

The only academic institution to have formally approached Professor Chibale is the young Apex Medical University in Lusaka, which expressed an interest in opportunities for staff members at his centre. It is telling that the approach was made by the respected Professor Evariste Njelesani, a former member of the Zambian diaspora. In addition to teaching internal medicine at Lusaka's Apex Medical University, Njelesani is also an honorary lecturer and consultant physician at the University Teaching Hospital and Levy Mwanawasa Teaching Hospital.

Njelesani is also the founding president of the Zambia College of Physicians. Before his return home, Njelesani served as World Health Organization Representative in Sierra Leone, Nigeria, and Zimbabwe.

Clearly, Professor Njelesani has an appreciation of genuine Zambian talent and the value of global connections. We can only hope that as Zambian culture evolves, this appreciation will become the norm and the likes of Kelly Chibale will be allowed to render the help their homeland so desperately needs.

Youth Leadership

Recognition of good deeds in young people early in life tends to solidify good citizenship instincts in them. The earlier this recognition is given, the better. For example, it is well known that exposing very young people to volunteer work tends to turn them into lifelong volunteers. So, Zambia needs to revive the traditional value of volunteering, albeit in the modern context.

There is no sharp cut-off point as to when one becomes or ceases to be a youth. The 2006 Zambia National Youth Policy, for example, defines youth as those between the ages of 18 and 35, while the 2010 census defined youth as the segment of the population between 15 and 35 years. The United Nations defines a young person as someone aged 10-24 years. Within this category, adolescents are identified as those between 10 and 19 years, and youth as persons between 15 and 24 years.

Perhaps we do not need a precise and universal definition of 'youth' as the categories for which young people are honoured tend to make obvious the segment of the population being honoured. For example, a young person honoured for promoting good citizenship through the Boy Scout movement will almost certainly be between the ages of 10 and 18. What matters is that young people are recognised and encouraged to be good citizens. Early recognition also engenders passion in young people to combat real dangers such as climate change. This passion often leads to leadership roles.

One such youth leader is Brighton Kaoma who won the 2016 Worldwide Fund for Nature International President's Award for his efforts to educate and give youth a voice about the environment. The award recognizes outstanding leadership in young conservationists from around the world.

Kaoma's work started when he was 14 and living in the Copperbelt town of Kitwe. He responded to rising levels of pollution in his community by running a weekly radio programme, Environmental Watch, which educated the local population on the dangers of pollution and deforestation, and how they could protect themselves from climate change. He believes strongly that giving the community a voice creates a springboard to a world of broader opportunities. And his community was given a voice! Shortly after his broadcasts commenced, the programme was inundated with questions and suggestions from listeners, all interested in improving their environment.

The response from the community fortified Kaoma's resolve, emboldening him to use radio to emit even stronger messages on climate action. He collaborated with different youth community organizers to establish Agents of Change Foundation, and offered radio skills training to children across Zambia. He further collaborated with UNICEF and other stakeholders such as Children's Radio Foundation to train more than 1,250 young Zambians, aged between 12 and 19, in radio production and broadcasting.

Now a graduate of Columbia University, Brighton Kaoma and his collaborator Karan Jerath, himself a global youth leader, are building the technology to improve reliability and efficiency in Zambia's logistics ecosystem under a new social-good transportation venture appropriately named KARTON.

Although Brighton Kaoma, who is also a Mandela Washington Fellow, has received a leadership award from Her Majesty Queen Elizabeth II at Buckingham Palace and granted an exclusive audience with former US President Barack Obama, there is no record of him being similarly honoured in his homeland.

Investiture Ceremonies

Zambia does have investiture ceremonies that typically honour citizens who have contributed to the country's political and economic development. It is at these ceremonies that honours such as the Companion Order of Freedom are conferred. The honourees go to State House, the official residence and office of the head of state, on Independence Day to receive their medals from the president of the Republic of Zambia. In addition, the president confers honours on Africa Freedom Day, notably the Insignia of Meritorious Achievement. It is gratifying that on May 25, 2019, Prof Kenneth Kaoma Mwenda, the noted academic, was recognised in this fashion.

While the investitures of the late 1960s caused no controversy because of the obvious suitability of the recipients, some recent awards have raised eyebrows. Equally, the failure to consider manifestly qualified citizens for these awards has caused angst in citizens respectful of meritorious achievement. This is because Zambia does not have an honours and awards secretariat with a nonpartisan secretary-general and staff to assess nominations and administer the programme.

Things do, however, appear to be changing.

On Independence Day in 2019, President Edgar Lungu honoured eight people for their distinguished service to the nation. Among them was Andrew Sardanis, founder of the ITM International group, whose holdings in its heyday included an innovative international banking group. Sardanis should have been honoured much earlier than 2018, but it is better late than never.

Although essentially a businessman, Andrew Sardanis also played an important role in the liberation of Zambia from British colonial rule. As a white-skinned person championing (black) majority rule, he incurred the wrath of white Northern Rhodesians who saw him as a traitor. It has sometimes been suggested by people unfamiliar with Sardanis' philosophy and history that in supporting the nationalist cause, he was simply being opportunistic and securing the interests of his business in a future Zambia.

This suggestion is absurd. Sardanis did not need to risk his life to secure his business interests in post-colonial Zambia. He could have secured his future under a future black government by simply remaining quiet and not taking sides.

Many white business owners did precisely that. Many who loudly opposed independence prospered in the post-colonial era. Furthermore, when Sardanis chose to publicly support the nationalist movement, life in Northern Rhodesia was so settled, and the British rulers so secure that few actually believed the country would one day become independent.

In addition to supporting the independence movement, Sardanis gave business opportunities to indigenous Zambians at a time anti-black racism was the order of the day.

The Order of the Eagle of Zambia, third division, conferred on Andrew Sotiris Sardanis was well deserved. We can only hope that there will be more merit-based awards such as this in the future.

In May 2018, Vice President Inonge Wina launched the National Policy on Honours and Awards to bring about a well-administered national honours and awards system in Zambia by improving transparency and accountability and enhancing stakeholder participation. According to the vice president, the new policy will also enhance the coordination of different national awards programmes, such as the Ngoma Awards which are administered by the National Arts Council of Zambia. Properly implemented, the new policy could create a vehicle for coordinating private and public sector awards, and encouraging merit in the granting of honours and awards.

A transparent system of nominations from members of the public is critical to the credibility of any awards programme. It is encouraging that Vice President Wina has committed to simplifying the nomination procedures and guidelines for honours and awards to encourage greater public participation.

As proposed by the vice president, it is indeed a good idea that this new regime be established by new comprehensive legislation. By the vice president's own admission, the current law only focuses on the prevention of abuse of honours and decoration, and has minimal provision with respect to the actual administration of the awards.

Media

One of the reasons Zambian achievements are under-appreciated is that the local media is under-resourced and unduly dependent on foreign news outlets. In his paper, Perceptions of Media in Zambia by Public, published by the International Journal of Multi-Disciplinary Research, Kwesi Atta Sakyi found that the public consider state radio and television stations under the umbrella of the Zambia National Broadcasting

Corporation as nothing more than megaphones of the ruling party, with most news items focusing on government functionaries. Insufficient space is given to independent reporting or coverage of activities of the opposition political parties.

Although the survey had a relatively small sample (120 participants), its conclusions confirm the general perceptions Zambians have about their media. According to 38 percent of the respondents, ZNBC is not innovative and tends to repeat 'boring' content. Of even greater concern, almost all the respondents agreed that ZNBC has a relatively poor calibre of staff. Because of this, Zambians rely heavily on Western news outlets. This is not healthy for the country as reporting accurately on Zambia and other African countries has never been a priority for the foreign media. The obvious exceptions are the BBC and The Economist. Western media often portrays the African continent as a single entity with nothing to offer but poverty, corruption, disease, and conflict. This stereotype is actively promoted even by Zambians who have never known conflict by virtue of living in one of the most peaceful countries in the world. In this regard, these Zambians take their cue from the white ghetto, which never misses an opportunity to disparage the country. To reinforce the stereotype of African hopelessness, virtually every negative foreign media report on Zambia describes the country as 'the African nation of Zambia' even when the story in question has no continental implications. The local media then mimics this, as if there would be anyone in their readership unaware of Zambia's geographic location.

The Zambian media needs to undergo a cultural shift in their reportage of events in the country and highlighting the country's successes. They should also report failures, but in an informed way. To undergo this cultural shift, the Zambian media needs to strengthen its independence and self-regulatory capacity. Equipped with confident, well-trained, and ethical journalists, the Zambian media will then be able to convincingly challenge the flawed reporting from uninformed and indolent foreign journalists.

In 1991, as Zambia anxiously awaited the first democratic election after nearly 20 years of dictatorship, Jonathan Manthorpe, a writer for Southam News, confidently told his Canadian audience that Zambians were extremely worried about the forthcoming election and that foreigners were leaving the country in droves in anticipation of the inevitable violence. He then added that locals too would like to leave but were too poor to do so. Had Manthorpe not relied on the aloof white ghetto for information, he may have realised that ordinary people in landlocked Zambia have a long tradition of traveling to neighbouring countries regardless of economic status. More importantly, he may have learned that Zambians were actually looking forward to the election and had no concerns about their safety in exercising their right to vote.

In the end, Zambians showed up in record numbers to vote in an election declared by all concerned as free, fair, and peaceful! Zambians were not surprised by this. After all, they are only one of a handful of diverse young nations in the world never to have experienced civil war or military rule. Zambians cherish peace. Unfortunately, few people outside Zambia had the opportunity to learn about this encouraging news because Manthorpe's assertions were never challenged and remained on record as the truth.

But not all was rosy after the re-establishment of democracy. Within two years of taking office, President Chiluba reacted to what he considered politically motivated violence in Lusaka by invoking the hated Preservation of Public Security Act and imprisoning seventeen opposition leaders without trial. Those detained include Rupiah Bwezani Banda who at the beginning of November 2008 became president of the Republic, following the untimely death of President Mwanawasa. Later, Banda had no difficulty in forgiving Chiluba whom he understood had acted on bad advice. In the best Zambian tradition, Banda and Chiluba reconciled and strengthened their friendship, remaining close allies and collaborators until Chiluba's demise.

Chiluba's state of emergency lasted 90 days and the Preservation of Public Security Act was never invoked again.

President Chiluba's imprisonment of suspects without trial was rightly condemned by the recently liberated local press. The British media joined in the condemnation and warned that the invocation of a law that permitted detention without trial marked the beginning of the end of democracy in the country. This warning would have been taken seriously had the British Parliament not renewed a law, applicable only to Northern Ireland, at about the same time that Chiluba's state of emergency was invoked, which allowed for detention without trial of suspects. Under British law, suspects could be detained, not for 90 days, but for one year. The hypocrisy of the British media was startling, but the Zambian press never challenged it.

The local media has a critical role to play as Zambian democracy and nationhood evolve. The media should give civil society and political parties the means by which these important institutions can reach large numbers of people and inform them on important issues to the nation. One of the weaknesses of Zambian democracy is that the bulk of the electorate does not have sufficient information on the issues they are expected to vote on at election time.

It is the duty of both the media and the nonpartisan institutions in government to provide this education to the population. Democracy cannot thrive in ignorance. And ignorance thrives when the press is oppressed, uninformed, and incurious.

The lack of media confidence probably goes back to the One Party State days when newspapers were heavily regulated and curious journalists persecuted. Before the third republic, the church-owned National Mirror served as the country's only independent newspaper with a national reach. It was not, however, a daily paper and had to be careful about what it published.

The government of the day was so intolerant of departures from officially sanctioned opinions that astute journalists resorted to reporting in code. They had to avoid biting satire when they did this because political humour was not tolerated. Under the one-party system, the United National Independence Party reigned supreme. The phrase 'the party and its government' was coined to emphasize the party's supremacy over the government.

In one opinion column, The National Mirror suggested that the phrase 'party and its government' should be abbreviated to PIG. The paper then cautioned that whoever was found referring to Freedom House, the party headquarters, as the Piggery 'should be made to feel the wrath of the PIG'! The party and its government were not amused and threatened the independent newspaper with closure unless an apology was issued. The National Mirror apologised.

Not all 'erring' journalists got off so lightly. On the morning of January 15, 1976, about 500 of the University of Zambia's 2,800 students responded to the power struggle in neighbouring Angola, where Portuguese rule was coming to an end, by demonstrating in favour of the People's Movement for the Liberation of Angola, one of the protagonists in the struggle. The demonstration included a general meeting addressed by student leaders at the Great East Road campus.

Armed policemen were sent to the university, but there was no physical altercation between the police and the students guided by the demonstration's largely peaceful nature. At about 1pm, the protesting students dispersed and returned to classes. Despite the end of the protest, paramilitary units entered the campus later in the afternoon. The purpose of entering the campus was not clear as the demonstration had ended. It did, however, cause confusion resulting in at least one lecturer being denied access to the campus. Two weeks after the demonstration, the government purported to declare a state of emergency. This was odd as Zambia was already in a state of emergency and had been in one since shortly before independence.

When making this declaration, President Kenneth Kaunda referred to 'deteriorating security' both internally and on the country's borders. He attributed the demonstration and other disturbances to foreign interference in Zambia's affairs. There were the usual rants about colonialism, fascism and racism undermining Zambia, Angola, and the region, but there was also something new. Kaunda referred to a 'marauding tiger, with its deadly cubs' bent on entering Angola through the back door.

Kaunda's remarks clearly referred to the Soviet Union, which had intervened in the conflict on behalf the MPLA, using Cuban surrogates. Kaunda then linked this to foreigners using Zambians to infiltrate vital Zambian institutions, including institutions of learning. The presence of armed police at a peaceful demonstration at the University of Zambia was now beginning to make sense. Kaunda was setting the stage for a round of politically motivated detentions of academics and students.

On January 31, 1976, a detention order under the notorious Preservation of Public Security Regulations was issued against Lionel Ronald Cliffe, a British lecturer in Politics at the University of Zambia. Shortly after his detention, the law firm in which I was articling received a visitor in the person of Mrs Cliffe. I remember her as a calm and level-headed woman with an ability to see the big picture. Etched in my memory is her response when Ali Hamir, a partner at the firm and future attorney general of Zambia, advised her on her husband's rights as a political prisoner: 'That is more than we ever had in South Africa!' she exclaimed.

From this encounter, I realized Cliffe was an intellectually honest and principled person who had inevitably had run-ins with the apartheid regime when he worked in South Africa. He had done a huge amount of work in developing countries. For example, he had taught at the University of Dar es Salaam and written about Tanzania. He was also a member of the editorial working group which produced the respected journal, The Review of African Political Economy. Therefore, it was not surprising that a man with this profile would have had conflicts with the apartheid South African regime. President Kaunda saw in Cliffe a foreigner—possibly backed by apartheid South Africa—intent on misleading Zambians and causing them to commit acts of sabotage against their own government.

Also detained were a lecturer, Younus Gulam Lulat, and several students such as Munyonzwe Hamalengwa, Alex Kamanga, Gilbert Mwiya Mubita, Derek Chewe Mulenga, Vincent Musakanya, Guy David Stokes and others linked to pro-MPLA demonstrations. When I visited the detainees, Mubita, with an above-average height, appeared proud of the fact that he had been able to plant a VIVA MPLA poster quite high up on the billboard at the entrance to the campus. The students were in high spirits, and that was encouraging. None of the detainees was charged with any offence, although they spent several months in prison. Later, the Kaunda regime reversed itself and decided to recognise the MPLA government in Luanda, the very thing the students had been asking for. With tongue in cheek, Guy (aka Chisanga) David Stokes asked if President Kaunda would now apologise for not having taken the students' advice earlier.

The saga, which had started in January 1976, continued. On March 15, Robinson Makayi, the features editor of the Times of Zambia, was detained under the Public Security Regulations and held at Lusaka Central Prison until August 4. Reflecting the times, Makayi's arrest was reported in the Zambia Daily Mail on 17 March, but not in his own newspaper, the Times of Zambia.

Makayi's 'transgression' was that he had been curious enough as a journalist to actually travel to Angola and report on the conflict there. He visited Luanda, after the city was proclaimed as the MPLA capital. The Zambian government was concerned that Makayi had not obtained its permission to visit Angola.

Makayi was never charged with any crime and it appears his detention without trial was a consequence of the witch-hunt for MPLA sympathisers. The experience obviously had an impact on Makayi. In early 1991, when the country was demonstrably fed up with the one-party dictatorship and the Movement for Multiparty Democracy had been formed, Makayi took advantage of the opening space for independent reporting and became editor of the newly formed Weekly Post. Commenting on politics and the prospects for the MMD, which had now become a political party, Makayi said, 'I can't see us ever going back'.

But the country can slide back to a regime resembling a one-party state where the press is ineffective at carrying out its most basic duties. Zambians need to examine traditional ways of ensuring free public discourse to prevent this slide into a de facto one-party state with a compliant press.

Let the king know

Zambia needs a credible free press that is uncompromisingly committed to the truth. While a sycophantic press may keep a particular government happy in the short term, it will also deprive that government of vital information for planning and delivering services. A sycophantic press will also undermine accountability by failing to report on official misdeeds. Independent-minded journalists such as Makayi are necessary to expose high-level corruption and other abuses of power.

Traditional society understood this. The office of Ing'omba has evolved since the founding of the Kongo Kingdom in 1390. The Ing'omba's basic role is to bring matters of concern to citizens to the king's attention. In the early days of the office, this role was almost as risky as being Speaker of Parliament in contemporary England.

Sir Peter de la Mare, the first Speaker, had the unenviable duty of telling the king and the lords (the most powerful people after the king) what the House of Commons thought of them and their proposals. Inevitably, Sir Peter soon offended the monarch and was imprisoned. As for his successors, seven were executed, killed in battle, or murdered between 1394 and 1535.

The first Ing'ombas had reason to reflect before accepting the appointment. In general, however, they fared better than the English speakers. Nonetheless, guarantees had to be put in place to ensure that suitable candidates could be found to perform this role. Thus Ing'omba were granted immunity from prosecution or other forms of harassment while carrying out their duties. They were also given a free hand in the training of successors.

It was natural that Ing'ombas would turn to their own children to continue the profession when they retired. As time went by, the typical Ing'omba would have learnt his trade as his father's apprentice.

Recognising the importance of objective news, Ing'ombas were given the status of royal household members. Furthermore, the accuracy of the information relayed by the Ing'ombas could be tested by ceremonies such as the now-abandoned Luba-Bemba annual assembly of Ilamfya, which gave everyone (commoner and noble) in the kingdom the right to air concerns and have those concerns debated.

The role of Ing'ombas, however, went beyond narrating citizens' concerns. They also played a role in intelligence gathering, often reporting on the plans of potential external enemies. Thus, when Diogo Cão's ship found itself in Nzeri River, in Kongo territory, the unusual arrival was spotted by unseen scouts, trained to blend in the forest, who reported the matter to the Ing'omba. Using talking drums, whose message was transmitted from village to village until it reached the capital, Mbaza Kongo, the scouts alerted the Ing'omba of what they had seen. The scouts only surfaced after receiving word from the king that they should apprehend the intruders and take them to the capital.

The Zambian media should be seen as an objective deliverer of news committed to evidence-based analysis. Sensationalism must give way to intelligent, professional, and responsible reporting. That would be good not just for the public but for the media itself. The public is more likely to come to the defence of journalists and media outlets when they know they can count on the veracity of the news and the integrity of the journalists.

On 21 June, 2016, Zambian authorities ordered the closure of Post Newspapers Limited, the company that published the popular Post newspaper, successor to the Weekly Post. The stated reason for the closure was that the publishing company owed the Zambian treasury USD6.1 million in tax arrears. The company did indeed owe the tax arrears but it was not the only entity to be indebted in this way to the treasury. Although the Post did from time to time engage in gratuitous vitriol, for the most part, it provided the country with an alternative viewpoint to that promoted by the government-owned media. It is not unreasonable to conclude that the tax arrears were used as an excuse to shut down an independent paper with a wide following in the country. It is poignant that a year earlier, police had arrested Fred M'membe, publisher of The Post newspaper, as well as journalist Mukosha Funga, in connection with an article that discussed the investigation by the Anti-Corruption Commission of a presidential aide accused of soliciting a bribe from a Chinese businessman who wanted an appointment with the President. Amnesty International was certainly persuaded that the tax arrears were used as a ruse in the matter. Deprose Muchena, the organisation's director for southern Africa, responded to the closure thus:

> The closure of The Post newspaper is a disturbing development clearly designed to silence critical media voices. The shutting down of one of Zambia's main independent newspapers in the run up to an election is an affront to media freedom and the authorities should immediately reverse their decision.

With respect to how tax arrears should be addressed, Muchena reflected the thinking of many in Zambia when he suggested that there were alternatives to shutting down the newspaper. He could have added that closing the newspaper was in fact counterproductive because it reduced the likelihood of the company ever paying the arrears. It would have made more sense to allow the company to continue generating an income and agree to a payment plan.

The government's action clearly undermined freedom of the press and the idea of diversity in disseminating the news. Despite the mandate of the Independent Broadcasting Authority, including the promotion of 'a pluralistic and diverse broadcasting industry' in Zambia, the IBA appears to have accepted the closure of this independent newspaper without protest.

The apparent indifference of the IBA to the closure of an independent newspaper fortifies the view of many in Zambia that the IBA itself is a tool of the government. This perception is unfortunate as media reform in Zambia will depend on the strength of institutions such as the Independent Broadcasting Authority to succeed.

The process of ensuring that Zambian media is an objective deliverer of the news committed to evidence-based analysis must include an IBA with unimpeachable credentials and commitment to these goals. For that to happen, there must be a transparent and credible process of appointment of members of the IBA.

At the moment, IBA members are appointed by a cabinet minister. At the very least, the minister should be required to appoint on the advice of an independent self-regulatory body such as the Zambia Media Council. Ideally, the minister's role should disappear altogether over time.

Media reform cannot, however, take place in a vacuum. In a country where journalists are generally underpaid, it is easy to bribe reporters into distorting news. Therefore, economic reforms guaranteed to raise general income levels in the country must be implemented. How this can be done is the subject of the next chapter.

CHAPTER TEN

Turning Zambia into an Economic Powerhouse

While 56 years is a long time in an individual's life, that time is minuscule in the life of a nation. Zambia, having just celebrated this milestone, is therefore a very young nation. At this stage of development, most nations are beset by conflict, often leading to civil war and economic uncertainty.

At a comparable time in its history, the United States, for example, was embroiled in what seemed to be unending conflicts between Native Americans and white settlers over western land, the best known of these conflicts being the Black Hawk War in 1832. Even more devastating was the civil war that started in 1861, lasted four years, and took 750,000 lives.

England was founded in July 957 when the Anglo-Saxon kingdoms united to form the new country. Fifty-six years later, the king of Denmark, who also ruled Norway and Sweden, invaded England. After a brief campaign, the Danish monarch secured the submission of all English people living outside of London. In due course, however, the Londoners, fearing that they would be destroyed, capitulated and submitted.

The 1013 invasion by Sweyn Forkbeard lasted less than five weeks. But in 1016, Forkbeard's son, Prince Cnut the Great, successfully invaded England. Cnut was on the English throne for 19 years. He governed without significantly disturbing English governance structures and his rule was largely peaceful. After Cnut's death, however, England was involved in some 40 wars before the civil war (1642-1651).

Although England has been largely peaceful at home in recent times, over the past 100 years, Britain has experienced two world wars, significant conflicts in Korea, Iraq, Kenya, Egypt, Aden, Malaysia, Falklands, Bosnia, and other countries. With maturity has come the ability to defuse potential military conflict.

Zambia can be proud that despite its age, it has succeeded in avoiding the kind of armed conflict experienced by both the United States and England at comparable stages in their development.

Maturity has not, however, shielded the United Kingdom from economic woes. The global recession of the 1970s highlighted the vulnerability of the British economy as it failed to grapple with both stagnation and inflation. The stock market reacted haphazardly, causing confusion in the minds of both domestic and foreign investors. For the first time since the Second World War, shops were unable to provide all the goods required by customers. There were long queues at petrol filling stations, and commercial television struggled to attract advertising customers.

The recession of the 1970s brought into sharp focus the fact that for most of the 20th century Britain has been struggling with an ailing economy. There was a view at the time that the economic decline was a consequence of Britain losing her colonies and no longer being able to command cheap raw materials and labour. This view encouraged many to support Britain's entry into the European Economic Community (now known as the European Union).

With the United Kingdom leaving the EU at the beginning of 2021, it will be interesting to see how the country copes on its own once again. Will history repeat itself and force the UK to look for outside help as it did in 1976, when the minority government of Prime Minister James Callaghan was obliged to borrow USD3.9 billion from the IMF to stabilise the British pound?

The loan conditions included public spending cuts and increased interest rates designed to reflect the true cost of borrowing. These conditions caused a split within the government, with the left-wing of the Labour Party loudly opposed to cuts in social spending. In the end, the IMF programme was implemented, resulting in an improvement in the current account, a reduction in the budget deficit, and an appreciation of the pound sterling.

As Zambia contemplates another bailout from the IMF, it too can expect the same conditions as those attached to the 1976 IMF loan to the UK. Zambia faces a similar dilemma to that confronting the UK in the 1970s and needs the same decisiveness and discipline shown by the Callaghan government.

Whether or not help comes from the IMF or a homegrown economic recovery programme, public expenditure will have to be cut to give the economy room to grow and generate wealth.

Importance of sound economic policy

The traditional saying, *Buchete nkuyanda*, translates roughly as, 'People choose to be poor'. A deeper meaning of the proverb, however, suggests that anyone can be wealthy as long as they think innovatively and work very hard.

While acknowledging the neglect of the colonial era and the negative impact that colonialism has had on the confidence of many Zambians, it must be said that Zambian poverty today is more a result of contemporary policy failure than colonial history.

Quite often, a policy is influenced more by emotion than data and sound economic judgment. For example, at independence, Zambia had a string of schools and hospital wards previously reserved for white people. These facilities charged fees for the services they offered. The tuition fee for attending Chingola Primary School was £8 a term. The school provided an excellent education and extra-mural activities. Because of this, many middle-class black parents who could afford the fee enrolled their children in the school.

Understandably, the new government wanted as many of their black supporters to have access to these schools as possible. The same was true of hospital wards. However, the reality was that there were not that many members of black society who could afford the fees in what was now being referred to as fee-paying schools and hospital wards. So, the government acted to remove what it saw as financial barriers to high-quality education and health care. Initially, the government responded by halving tuition fees. Then, about three years later, they abolished tuition fees altogether.

It did not take long for the schools and hospital wards to decline and lose their value. With increased demand and no money to expand the attractive facilities, the infrastructure soon collapsed. Whereas, in 1963/64 the teacher pupil ratio at Chingola Primary School was 1:20, by 2008 the Zambian ministry of education put the ratio at 1:43. Students were no longer guaranteed desks, the sick bay disappeared, the swimming pool no longer existed, the playing fields were unmaintained, and to this day the school struggles to paint its buildings. The quality of teachers has also declined significantly.

The decision to abolish fees at these schools and hospital wards was undoubtedly a popular one, at least in the short term. But, it was a financially reckless one in the longer term. The fees abolished allowed Chingola Primary School to support its high quality of education. More generally, the fee-paying schools and hospital wards collectively made significant contributions to the government budget for education and health. By abolishing fees, the new government deprived itself of this contribution at precisely the moment the people of Zambia needed it most.

There is a tendency in Zambia to react to problems rather than respond to them. In other words, 'solutions' are implemented without the necessary investment in analysis and policy discussion. For example, in the mid-1970s, the entire land tenure regime of the republic was changed because the head of state was upset that a 'profiteer' had bought a piece of land in Lusaka only to turn around and sell the same piece of land for considerably more than he had paid for it just a few days earlier. The head of state failed to understand that sometimes this is how the market works. From the inefficiencies that followed the new land tenure regime, it was clear that no meaningful policy discussions had taken place prior to the abolition of the old system. Long-term solutions cannot be found without robust analysis and policy discussion. The country's current financial crisis has its history in policy failure and a reluctance to engage in robust analysis to find sustainable solutions.

In November 2020, Zambia became the first African country to default on its debt since the pandemic. While the coronavirus pandemic did not help, it cannot be said to have been the sole cause of the default. As both the International Monetary Fund and World Bank observed, Zambia took on more debt than it could manage. Even before the pandemic, which played a role in the November default by forcing unplanned expenditure on healthcare, Zambia was liable to pay USD1.5 billion in debt servicing per annum.

Zambia first missed a USD42.5 million coupon payment on its bonds in October 2020 and was placed in a technical default position shortly after that. Zambia was in fact in a position to pay the USD42.5 million but doing so would have resulted in favourable treatment for Eurobond holders at the expense of other creditors that the country was negotiating with at the time.

The default inevitably triggered a blame game between Zambia and the banks and asset and fund managers. The latter group could have been more helpful but that does not answer the question of the wisdom of incurring the USD12 billion public debt in the first place.

At the time of writing, Zambia and the IMF are preparing to hold talks on a possible USD1.3 billion loan. That loan would have to be repaid and, based on past experience, would come with conditions that would restrict the country's ability to make independent economic plans.

Turning to the IMF, which may indeed help Zambia, may have been avoided had the country invested in an honest analysis of the growing debt, especially after the issuance of the first Eurobond.

It is remarkable that, until recently, the government refused to recognise the relationship between excessive expenditure and debt and acknowledge that the current debt burden is largely a result of profligacy. For example, the government has allowed its bureaucracy to grow uncontrollably to the point where it is not even sure about the number of persons legitimately on the public service payroll.

When Dr Bwalya Ng'andu was appointed minister of finance in July 2019, one of his major tasks was to eliminate 'ghost workers' from the government payroll to reduce government expenditure. The Public Service Management Division estimates that the country has more than 4,000 ghost workers on the public service payroll.

Building on the work of his predecessor, Margaret Mwanakatwe, Ng'andu's ministry announced that the accounts into which the pay of ghost workers were deposited would be frozen. Ng'andu has also stated his commitment to effective expenditure control, debt management, and enhanced domestic revenue collection. He is reportedly interested in introducing blockchain identity technology, which would decentralize data storage and deny central actors the ability to own, control or manipulate such data. In addition, this technology would link the registration of births, deaths, and employment so that the death or resignation of a civil servant would automatically result in that civil servant's removal from the payroll.

That belongs to the future. For now, steps need to be taken to control public expenditure on salaries of persons who should not be on the public payroll. The effect of paying a ghost worker is the same as paying a person formally and legally on the payroll who does not add value to the enterprise. In short, not everyone on the government payroll works for the government.

The emoluments trap

Since the one-party state era, the amount of money spent on emoluments has been a cause for concern to all who believe in prudent fiscal management. The one-party state doubled the size of government by creating a full-time Central Committee paid by the taxpayer, even as the cabinet, also paid by the taxpayer, continued to be responsible for day-to-day government operations. Although the Central Committee ceased to exist after the return to democracy in 1991, the government has continued to spend excessively on emoluments.

The result is that emoluments and debt servicing now make up the largest component of the budget. While acknowledging that the 2020 budget performed better than expected in the first quarter of the year, the Policy Monitoring and Research Centre data also showed that 73.5 percent of the government's total expenditure went to debt servicing and personal emoluments.

Quantifying precisely how much of the budget goes to emoluments is a challenge because many areas of expenditure not categorised as 'emoluments' nonetheless have significant emolument components. The practice of paying public servants additional amounts in the form of sitting allowances, travel allowances, and even training allowances, further complicates the picture.

A comparison between Ontario and Zambia shows how abnormally large the Zambian civil service is. The two jurisdictions have similar populations. Ontario has 14.73 million citizens while Zambia has nearly 18 million. Ontario has a landmass of 1.076 million km² while Zambia's territory is 752,618 km². The Ontario civil service performs more transactions than the Zambian civil service. Ontario has 60,000 civil servants while Zambia has 200,000.

The Zambian civil service has doubled since 2001 when it employed 109,611 people.[47] The civil service costs the Zambian taxpayer USD2.2 billion a year. Reducing the size of the civil service by 50 percent would still leave the country with a relatively large public service but potentially save the Zambian government USD 1.1 billion a year and create the needed breathing space to service debt and increase investment in social services.

---

[47] Valentino R, Theodore, A Medium Term Strategy for Enhancing Pay and Conditions of Service in the Zambian Public Service, May 2002, Dar es Salaam.

Such a reduction cannot be arbitrary. The focus must be on ghost workers and underemployed civil servants. Regard must also be had to the pay gap between permanent secretaries and the lowest-paid members of the service. In the paper, Civil Service Reform in Indonesia, Prijono Tjiptoherijanto, estimated that permanent secretaries in Zambia earned more than 50 times what the lowest-paid civil servant earned. When reducing the size of the civil service, it would be necessary to pay attention to this reality.

The argument against reducing the civil service to manageable levels is that this increases the number of unemployed people in the country. This argument misses the point. The Zambian civil service's ineffectiveness is clear evidence that while people may be on the public payroll, not all these people actually work for the public. Those on the payroll who do not add value to the civil service simply get in the way of dedicated professional civil servants and succeed only in undermining the overall performance and morale of the enterprise.

It is fair to say that persons removed from the payroll would need alternative sources of income. In this regard Dr Mwilola Imakando, a Member of Parliament, who has studied the Zambian civil service and written about its reform, says international institutions and countries supportive of Zambia's development effort would support cutting the size of the civil service by contributing to redundancy payments to civil servants removed from the public payroll. A solution that is less dependent on international institutions would involve outsourcing services to private sector companies owned by competent former civil servants. For example, private sector companies could process applications for passports and drivers' licences with the government being responsible for regulatory enforcement and document issuance. Furthermore, the economic reforms proposed in this book would create other opportunities in the private sector for civil servants laid off after the reforms.

Private sector growth and the civil service

Evidence from World Bank data supports most economists' conclusion that the size of a country's government can negatively affect economic growth and prospects for economic development. There is a correlation between an expansion in the size of a government (reflected by an increase in its expenditures) and a decline in private investment and economic growth.

James D. Gwartney, professor of economics at Florida State University and holder of the Gus A. Stavros Eminent Scholar Chair, avers that an excessively large national government can have a negative effect on economic growth. The reason for this is clear. As a government grows in size, it tends to crowd out investment, leading to a decline in productivity growth and a slowdown in its real GDP growth rate. Robert Barro, a Harvard professor of economics, found that a ten percentage point increase in government expenditure as a share of a country's GDP is associated with a decline of approximately 1 percentage point in real GDP growth rate.

The 2021 Zambian budget shows total government expenditure amounted to approximately 30 percent of GDP. This is higher than the figure for most successful economies. In 2019, government expenditure in Singapore amounted to 14.32 percent of the country's GDP, 16.19 percent in Rwanda, and 31.64 percent in Botswana, which bucks the trend for fast-growing economies. Historically, total government expenditure in fast-growing economies tends to be below 30 percent. For example, from 1980 to 1995, Hong Kong, Singapore, South Korea, and Thailand had total government expenditures averaging 20.1 percent of GDP. According to World Bank figures, from 2000 to 2016, when Ethiopia was the third-fastest growing country with 10 million or more people, total government expenditure as a percentage of GDP was consistently below 20. In 2018, Ethiopia's total government expenditure was 16.08 percent of GDP. In 2019 it was 15.32 percent.

The relatively small percentage of government expenditure relative to GDP in Rwanda probably contributed to the country's government being rated 7th for the efficiency of its public management in the 2014-2015 edition of the Global Competitive Report. In 2015, the percentage of Rwanda's total expenditure relative to GDP was 14.52. It was 14.98 the previous year.

Harnessing government spending to create value chains

Expanding the Zambian public service payroll has created the illusion of employment and undermined Zambia's ability to generate real jobs. The basic role of government is to protect both individual and collective rights, protect citizens from all forms of external attack, and maximise citizens' socioeconomic well-being and happiness. The government should perform its role by creating a policy environment that encourages entrepreneurs to generate wealth from which social services and the necessary government structures can be financed. One of the necessary government structures is a law and order apparatus operated by an efficient and trustworthy police and security service.

While successive Zambian governments have promised to revitalise the economy and create sustainable employment, little has been done to turn this wish into actionable policy. The country has a high level of unemployment and a huge amount of work that need to be done. This work must be turned into jobs through innovative thinking and value chain creation.

When opening the recently built Mpelembe House in Ndola in 1968, Simon Mwansa Kapwepwe declared that while he was happy to open the building, which signified progress, he had to take the opportunity to warn the nation of over-dependency on copper and called for economic diversification. The dependency on copper has continued, and the mining industry's health continues to determine the health of the Zambian economy. In tough times, the industry is under pressure to pay excessive taxes and provide social amenities at a level that undermines some mining companies' ability to survive prolonged downturns. Diversifying the Zambian economy would make the country less dependent on the copper mining industry, whose revenues would become the icing on the cake. How does Zambia diversify her economy?

Manufacturing has to be a key part of the Zambian economy because it has a history of building strong middle classes by being a major source of stable, high-wage employment. The starting point to building a strong manufacturing sector is for the Zambian government to commit to buying, whenever possible, only goods and services made entirely or partly in Zambia. For example, school desks, public service uniforms, processed food for consumption by schools, colleges, universities, the army, air force, police, and other security organs; and anything else consumed on a large scale by the government should be produced in Zambia or have significant Zambian content.

Using the auto industry to create jobs

The Zambian government should announce at the earliest opportunity that it will henceforth consume only goods and services produced entirely or in part in Zambia. This policy would increase investment in local manufacturing capacity as Zambian businesspeople prepare to meet increased demand for goods and services due to the government committing itself to procure locally. With this policy, the Zambian business sector can also plan more effectively based on a guaranteed market.

Consider the automotive industry. It is conservatively estimated that the Zambian government imports about 12,000 motor vehicles for its various arms each year. The exact number is difficult to ascertain because many of these vehicles are bought for the intelligence network, which is understandably unwilling to divulge information. The research does suggest, however, that the figure of 12,000 is on the low side.

If Zambia were to adopt a policy that required all these vehicles to be assembled locally, both local and foreign entrepreneurs would be interested in participating in the ensuing tender to secure the government contract, especially if that contract was for a long period.

The guaranteed market of 12,000 vehicles would give the successful bidder a sound economic basis to make the necessary investment. The successful bidder would also pursue non-government sales both in Zambia and the southern African region. The successful bid should, however, include an undertaking to introduce local content in the vehicles assembled up to an agreed level. The requirement for Zambian content would speed up the creation of value chains because motor vehicle manufacturing has a particularly high multiplier effect. There is much more to the automotive industry than just designing, building, and selling cars. The industry has a deep reach in the supply chain. It is a consumer of both finished products and raw materials. If Zambia were to prioritise the manufacture of hybrid vehicles, for example, the local automotive industry could become a significant purchaser of copper. These purchases would increase as the automotive industry advances to the manufacture of electric vehicles.

A successful automotive industry could spur a tannery industry to supply seat covers for luxury cars. It could also lead to the establishment of manufacturing companies for tyres, wipers, windscreens etc. Former president and CEO of the Alliance of Automobile Manufacturers, Mitchell Burt Bainwol estimated in 2015 that the multiplier effect for the auto industry in the United States is eight, meaning that for every job created in the industry, eight more were created in the rest of the economy.

Because of the automotive industry's deep reach into the supply chain, it is difficult to give a precise number of jobs that would be created in the economy by assembling vehicles in Zambia as proposed here. We can, however, have a reasonably good idea by examining the South African automotive industry. In 2019, South Africa produced 631,983 motor vehicles. The industry employs directly 110,000 people. Therefore, on average, it takes 5.74 workers to produce one vehicle. The total number of jobs created by the automotive industry in the economy is 457,000, suggesting that each job in the automotive industry leads to the creation of 4.15 jobs in the broader economy.

Assuming an average of five people would be needed to build one vehicle, the annual Zambian government requirement of 12,000 vehicles could be satisfied by a plant potentially employing 60,000 people. The number of vehicles produced by this plant would, however, be much greater than 12,000 because of demand from non-governmental consumers.

According to Working Paper No. 1 produced by the Zambia Institute for Policy Analysis and Research in December 2014, there were 50,000 new vehicle registrations in Zambia each year from 2006 to 2013. Therefore, if the government imported 12,000 of these vehicles each year, the private sector imported 38,000.

The bulk of the vehicles registered by the private sector are used automobiles, as confirmed by ZIPAR, which found that the average age of Zambia's motor vehicle fleet increased from 13 years in 2006 to 17 years in 2014. In 2020, the average age was estimated at 20 years.

The roadworthy life span of an imported used car is, according to ZIPAR, less than four years, and the proportion of Zambian motor vehicles without roadworthiness certification stood at 32 percent in 2013, helping to explain Zambia's relatively high rate of motor vehicle accidents. In addition to that, older cars are obviously less environmentally friendly than newer ones.

It makes eminent sense to discourage the importation of used cars in Zambia through high import tariffs. The argument against discouraging the importation of old used vehicles is that restricting access to these cheaper vehicles would leave many Zambians without transportation as they would be unable to purchase newer vehicles from a local assembly plant or abroad. This argument understates the danger posed by older cars: car accidents that are costly both in human life terms and financially.

The point that Zambians need access to relatively inexpensive transportation is, however, well taken. There are at least three ways to mitigate the negative impact of discouraging the importation of used vehicles. In the first place, a stronger economy would result in lower interest rates, making hire purchase and leasing more affordable for average consumers. Secondly, in recognition of the fact that many people choose to drive because of the absence of reliable public transport, bus operators could be required, as a condition of the licence to operate a public service vehicle, to ensure their buses were safe, clean, on time, and roadworthy. The safety requirement would include buses being fitted with firefighting equipment and seat belts. Overcrowding would also be banned and buses would be subject to random inspections. An important feature of this new world of public transportation would be to publish individual bus routes that would then be consolidated into a city bus route by the local authority. In this way, a resident of, say, Avondale who works in downtown Lusaka, would have more confidence using public transport, knowing the bus would be on time, clean, and safe. The pressure on this resident to buy her own car would obviously be eased.

The third response to mitigating the cost of new cars for average consumers is to encourage the establishment of government-approved vehicle scrappage companies, like the Retire Your Ride system in Canada. This would be a national programme under which authorized auto recyclers would pay cash to owners of old cars. The money thus paid to the seller of an old car could be used as part of the deposit to purchase a new vehicle.

Phasing out older and environmentally harmful motor vehicles creates a huge market for our motor vehicle assembly plant. In addition to the 12,000 vehicles the government would be obliged to buy, there is now a potential market of 38,000 vehicles from private citizens. If all these vehicles were to be replaced at once, potentially 190,000 people would be required to build the replacement models. Whether this happens or not would depend entirely on government policy.

Assuming a ten percent vehicle replacement rate in the private sector, future demand from this market segment would be about 3,800 a year. This conservative figure does not take into account natural growth in the consumer population. Even on this basis, however, the plant would require a workforce of 19,000 to meet annual production for the private sector alone. The total workforce required to fulfil the government and private sector vehicle orders could be as high as 79,000. With each job in the automotive industry generating a further 4.1 jobs in the broader economy, the country could expect 323,900 additional jobs created from the automotive industry.

There is also the very real prospect of some orders coming from the region, especially the COMESA and SADC areas. The precise number of orders from these regional blocs is hard to ascertain at the moment, but all it would take is for the region to buy another 12,000 vehicles for Zambia's auto industry to potentially generate an additional 60,000 jobs for the Zambian economy.

These figures can only be indicative because labour requirements will not increase proportionately with increases in demand, at some point in the production process. The figures would also need to be tested against other factors. Nonetheless, they do demonstrate the wisdom of Zambia investing in motor vehicle manufacturing.

The skill level required for most of the jobs in the automotive industry would be equivalent to the skills of mechanical fitters, forklift operators, environmental officers, electricians, and heavy-duty mechanics. Following the recent huge devaluation of the Zambian Kwacha, the average salary for these jobs is now only USD2,720 per annum. In 2017, the average salary for the same jobs was over USD5,000. That figure is likely to increase as the Zambian economy recovers. But even at the lower figure of USD2,720 and assuming that this number would apply only to 90 percent of the auto industry, total salaries in this category would come to USD193,392,000. At the current tax rate, the Zambian exchequer would receive USD58,017,600 per annum in the form of Pay as You Earn (income tax) from people employed directly by the automotive industry.

As for the jobs resulting from the multiplier effect, we shall use the average salary in Zambia to get a flavour of the impact these jobs might have on the economy. Depending upon how the multiplier effect is calculated, there would be at least 244,900 of these jobs. Based on 39 job categories identified by Paylab.com, the average annual salary in Zambia is ZMW75,792 or, at the current rate of exchange, USD3,789. Thus, the potential total earnings from the 244,900 jobs would be USD927,926,100. The tax rate for incomes over USD3,720 is 30 percent. The Exchequer could therefore expect to collect USD278,377,830 in taxes due to these jobs being created.

Governance and economic performance

Zambia needs to take a holistic approach to development to avoid policy confusion and inconsistency. While colonialism dealt Zambia a bad hand, the country can, with the right policies, overcome the trauma of colonialism and turn itself into a high-performing economy.

There are former colonies that have gone on to do well economically. A study of these countries shows that they took deliberate steps to ensure a functioning state. This explains in part the difference in the performance of countries with identical topography and demography.

Burundi and Rwanda are good examples.

The two countries were once a single country forming part of German East Africa. Under the 1918 Treaty of Versailles, Rwanda-Urundi was made a League of Nations protectorate governed by Belgium. Rwanda and Burundi were thereafter administered separately under two different Tutsi monarchs. On 1 July 1962, Belgium accepted United Nations demands and granted full independence to the two countries.

Burundi and Rwanda occupy roughly the same physical space: 27,834 square kilometres and 26,338 square kilometres, respectively. Burundi has a population of 11 million and Rwanda 12.2 million. Both countries have experienced genocide against the minority Tutsi population by the Hutu majority. In 1994, Burundi had a GDP of USD925 million compared to Rwanda's USD753.6 million.

Today, the two countries present very different economic landscapes. In 2018, Burundi's GDP was USD3 billion while Rwanda's was USD10 billion. By virtually all measures, Rwandans are wealthier than Burundians. The secret to Rwanda's success lies in governance. While neither Burundi nor Rwanda are yet to be classified as full democracies, Rwanda has a functioning government committed to combating corruption and enhancing the general welfare of its population.

The 2020 edition of the Mo Ibrahim Index of Governance in Africa ranked Rwanda 11th out of 54 countries for good governance. Burundi was ranked 47th. The top spot was taken by Mauritius, something which could never have been predicted when Mauritius gained independent statehood.

James Meade, a Nobel laureate in economics, famously predicted poor prospects for Mauritius in 1961. The prediction was based on the new country's vulnerabilities to weather, external price shocks, ethnic tensions, and lack of job opportunities outside the sugar sector. Despite these dire predictions, Mauritius has transformed itself from a poor sugar economy into a country with one of the highest per capita incomes in its region, with Mauritian GDP per capita standing at USD23,751 in 2018.

Mauritius' success is attributable to the country's firm commitment to a free enterprise system, particularly to policies that welcome foreign investment into its exports processing zones. The rule of law makes it relatively easy for Mauritius to attract investment.

While Zambia generally respects the rule of law, key players in government are often tempted to change the game's rules midway. In 2008, a Zambian member of parliament made the remarkable claim that the government was right to cancel the development agreements that had formed the basis upon which some foreign mining companies had brought capital into the country to salvage the industry. This member of parliament appeared incapable of understanding the importance of honouring contracts. He seemed to think that now that the investment was secured, it was perfectly legitimate for Zambia to insist on a unilateral revision of the contracts. This is precisely the kind of sharp practice that drives long-term investment away. The honourable member of parliament also seems to have forgotten how risky mining in Zambia was at the time of privatisation. At that time, the state-run mining giant, Zambia Consolidated Copper Mines, was losing a million dollars a day. Simply privatising the corporation stopped this leakage and provided the state with badly needed breathing space.

To attract investors to the industry, the Zambian government agreed to put incentives such as attractive corporate and royalty tax rates in place. In the case of First Quantum Minerals Ltd, which started new projects, these incentives set the royalty tax rate at 0.6 percent and the corporate income tax rate at 25 percent during a 'stability period' of 15 years. Mineral royalty tax is based on the price of copper and is payable whether or not a company makes a profit.

These incentives were codified in governing instruments known as Development Agreements, which helped the new investors raise money abroad for investment either in former ZCCM entities or in greenfield ventures. Thanks to this new investment, by 2010, Zambia was able to return to its 1972 copper production record of 720,000 tonnes.

There have been allegations that Zambia's reforming president, Frederick Chiluba, was responsible for the development agreements entered into with First Quantum Minerals Ltd., and that he acted with corrupt intent in doing so. While Chiluba was responsible for commencing the privatisation process, these particular agreements were signed in 2006, five years after he had left office. Furthermore, the incentives given to the mining companies were not unusual in the industry. For example, at the time, the royalty tax rates for Finland, South Africa, and Botswana were 0 percent, 1 percent, and 3 percent, respectively. The corporate tax rate in these three countries was 26 percent, 29 percent, and 25 percent, respectively.

After cancelling the development agreements, First Quantum Minerals was obliged to pay 3 percent in royalty tax and 30 percent in corporate tax. Then, a period of increases and frequent changes to the tax regime made planning for mining companies extremely difficult.

Michael Sata, the fifth president of Zambia, considered by many as a radical nationalist, took a sensible approach to the development agreements. He called on the government to reinstate them. Sata's fear was that cancelling these agreements would send a very bad signal to prospective investors. He also understood, at least prior to becoming president, that by cancelling the development agreements, Zambia exposed herself to a huge contingent liability that could cost the treasury billions of dollars.

Disputes under the development agreements are settled by international arbitration. Despite passage of time, it is understood that the mining companies have kept this action alive by notifying arbitrators of the existence of a dispute. If, for example, First Quantum Minerals formally instituted arbitration, Zambia would be liable for all excess tax paid over the 0.6 percent royalty tax rate and over the 25 percent corporate tax rate. The liability would run from 2008 until 2021, when the stability period should have ended.

The mining companies affected by the breach appear reluctant to commence proceedings because they prefer an amicable solution. That is a sensible position to take, but it only works if an equally sensible partner is on the other side.

As for the impact of the cancellation of the development agreements on foreign investors, Sata was right. Interest in investing in Zambia started to decline with the cancellation. The current debt crisis has done nothing to revive that interest.

Foreign direct investment goes to jurisdictions with independent and trustworthy law enforcement systems, and a stellar reputation for keeping their word.

Widespread prosperity is a precondition for a viable democracy

There is a relationship between prosperity and democratic governance. Thus the prosperity of the early independence days, which resulted in an expanded local middle class, also enhanced political space between 1964 and 1969. This progress was, however, thwarted as the country slid into a one-party dictatorship after 1972.

The middle class rebounded again after much sacrifice made necessary by the painful economic and political reforms of the early 1990s. By the mid-1990s, the chronic shortage of consumer goods that had characterised the one-party rule had ended. The chronic shortage of public transport was replaced by a surplus of passenger vehicles.

The reforms also strengthened freedom of the press as well as the rule of law. At the time of writing this book, advances are rapidly receding into distant memory, with the middle class beginning to shrink and poverty rising. The Zambian experience is consistent with evidence from other parts of the world that shows that poverty is a consequence of political action or inaction. While Zambia is now increasingly thought of as a poor country, for the first decade of this century, it was associated with what The Economist called 'stunning economic growth'. Now, inappropriate political decisions threaten Zambian prosperity just as good political decisions brought about the stunning growth praised by The Economist.

Zambia has generally held free and fair elections since 1991. But that fact alone is not sufficient to reduce, let alone eliminate, the alarming rates of poverty in the country. The Zambian Central Statistical Office published a report in 2018 showing that in 2015, 40.8 percent of the population was 'extremely' poor while 13.6 percent was 'moderately' poor. To eliminate poverty, greater attention needs to be paid to other aspects of good governance such as transparency, accountability, and a general capacity, with the full participation of citizens, to use public resources to promote the public good.

Promoting the public good often requires long-term planning. On the other hand, poor people require immediate help just to meet the daily needs of life. This makes poor people vulnerable to electoral bribery, as alleged by Dr Imakando during ward by-elections in Mongu District in June 2020. The immediate needs of poor people also encourage politicians to make unrealistic promises of salvation and, once in government, avoid long-term planning in favour of crisis management.

The official poverty rate in Zambia suggests that a majority of the electorate is poor. This segment of the population does not pay taxes and is therefore unconcerned about tax-raising policies that increase public spending astronomically, even at the expense of more productive investments. Zambian politicians must be cognisant of this and have the discipline to invest the time to plan for a future of sustainable jobs, even when that planning takes resources away from the immediate gratification of an important constituency.

Horticulture looks like manufacturing

As has been demonstrated with the automotive industry, manufacturing is a reliable generator of good-paying jobs. Moreover, most successful economies have used manufacturing as the principal tool for economic diversification. Zambia needs to understand that manufacturing covers a much broader area of activity than current economic discourse suggests. She needs to manufacture for both the foreign and local markets and look at other activities that generate jobs in a similar fashion to traditional manufacturing.

Given Zambia's climatic conditions, the Zambian floriculture industry has great growth potential. Between 2000 and 2001, when the industry was on the rise, the sector employed over 12,000 people and exported 9,928 tonnes of fresh produce valued at USD 68.5 million.

Out of the 3.8 million hectares of arable land in Zambia, only 195 hectares are dedicated to flower production, with roses taking up 74 percent of that (98 percent of these are sold at Dutch auctions). Because of financing constraints and high transaction costs, the local market for flowers is very limited, with relatively low returns.

An article in the International Trade Centre magazine of May 21, 2016 blamed 'bad policy and laxity' for the poor performance of the Zambian floriculture industry. These constraints include airfreight, which typically makes up 50 percent of the producers' direct costs. The high cost reflects aviation fuel cost, which other industries have also identified as a constraint. That same article pointed out that by 2016, employment in the sector had dropped to 5,500, significantly less than the 12,000 employed between 2000 and 2001.

In 2017, the Zambia Export Growers Association called on the government to promote investments in the horticulture industry and save it from collapsing. The warning came from the organisation's CEO, Luke Mbewe, who pointed out that underperformance of the horticulture industry had resulted in huge job losses between 2003 and 2017.

Mbewe was undoubtedly concerned that rather than offering help, the government introduced more crippling regulations and increased fees for services such as landing and handling at airports. The erratic power supply in recent years has not helped either.

With the right policy framework, horticulture in general and floriculture in particular, can make significant contributions to the economy. In Ethiopia, for example, horticulture provides 180,000 jobs. In Kenya, exports of cut flowers to Europe were worth USD134 million in 2000. In 2020 that figure jumped to USD700 million. Kenya's floriculture industry employs 70,000 people.

Without the policy constraints complained of, Zambia could outperform Ethiopia and Kenya in terms of revenues from horticulture and the number of jobs created by the industry. The labour-intensive floriculture industry is particularly suitable for Zambia, whose population is projected to increase to 25 million by 2030.

The global future for the floriculture industry is rosy. As Reportlinker.com announced in August 2020, the cut flowers market is projected to be worth USD41.1 billion by 2027. Zambia needs to wake up and smell the roses!

Don't forget the bamboo

The bamboo plant in Zambia and other parts of the world grows quickly and easily. While it can be farmed, Zambian bamboo furniture makers rely entirely on nature. This is understandable given that some bamboo species can grow up to 91 cm in one day.

Beyond furniture making, the ubiquitous Zambian bamboo is also a potential source of great revenue for the country. Taking advantage of the ease with which bamboos grow in Zambia, entrepreneur Mwewa Chikamba co-founded Zambikes, a company set up to make high-end, lightweight bicycles with frames made from locally grown bamboo.

This product should be encouraged in Zambia because it is environmentally friendly and serves all segments of society, particularly rural dwellers. As Chikamba said in a 2012 interview, this green product helps with climate change resilience. Chikamba was categorical that the process used to manufacture his bicycles was pollution-free.

The global bicycle market is enormous and creates huge opportunities for a company as innovative as Zambikes. Bicycle-Guider.com estimates that there are one billion bicycles in the world. The top five countries for cycling include the Unites States, Germany, and Japan, where Zambikes already have a market. Collectively, these countries have 244 million bicycles. Each year, about 36 million bicycles are sold in these markets. If Zambikes secured 0.01 percent of this market, its sales would increase by USD36 million. This is just one reason for Zambia to support this venture.

There is another important reason to do so. Making bamboo bicycle frames is labour-intensive. It takes 40 to 60 person-hours to build one bamboo frame. For this reason, within five years of establishment, the company was able to employ 40 people producing 500 hand-made bamboo frames. By 2015, the company, now led by Chikamba as managing director, employed over a hundred people. Zambike has an active international sales department that sells bicycles to customers in Singapore, Germany, Finland, Japan, and the United States, for USD1000 apiece. Zambikes also manufactures the Zambulance for use in underserved areas and the Zamcart, which helps small companies with limited capital to transport their goods to the market.

For more conservative and traditional Zambians, the company offers conventional bicycles. The future, however, lies in the production of predominantly bamboo bicycles, which are more environmentally friendly. It makes sense for the government to promote this product as part of the strategy to combat climate change.

Beyond bicycles, bamboo can be used to produce textiles. In 15th century Kongo, the bark of trees was used to produce textile. The bamboo pulp can be used similarly. There are many benefits to enhancing the technology used in Kongo all those years ago. For example, bamboo textile is antibacterial and keeps the body odour free, feeling and smelling fresh.

The material is sweat-absorbent and keeps the body dry by pulling moisture from the skin for evaporation. Another benefit for Zambian consumers is that the material keeps the body cool in the warm months but warmer in cooler weather. Add this to the fact that bamboo material is among the softest fabrics in the world, and you begin to appreciate the luxurious nature of the product. As if these benefits were not enough, the smooth-as-silk fabric is a natural UV protectant. It is also safe for use by people with allergic reactions. Few products could be more eco-friendly.

Zambia as a low-cost provider of services

Zambia need not wait to establish the services sector until the manufacturing base has been developed. While this has been the sequence in recently developed countries, in Zambia, both sectors must be promoted at the same time to maximise employment generation and rapidly expand the educated middle class, which is key to sustainable democracy.

Zambia has advantages that can turn the country into a more significant service provider. For example, the country could run call centres. This would obviously require further investment in the telecommunications and internet infrastructure. Some of this investment is already taking place as evidenced by the growth in mobile cellular subscriptions over the past two decades. Whereas the country had 100,000 subscriptions in 2000, the number of mobile connections in Zambia in January 2020 was equivalent to the total population, according to Datareportal.com.

A call centre is an office operated by representatives who manage telephone calls and keep track of pending cases and transactions. Obviously, the representatives need extensive and ongoing training about the affairs of the companies they represent. The offices use call centre software to allocate enquiries and engage customers all over the world. Zambia has two basic advantages in the call centre business. The first is geography, and the second is relatively low-cost skilled labour. In the Zambian winter, when the financial markets are opening in New York for core trading, it is 3:30 pm in Zambia. It is 9 am in Zambia when the markets open in summertime London. When the markets are closing in Beijing, the day is just starting in Lusaka. Zambia's geographic location makes it possible to interact with an international clientele relatively easily, with most call centre employees working regular eight-hour shifts.

Based on a survey of 124 salaries in Canada, a call centre agent with one to four years work experience is estimated to earn an average total compensation of USD 11.81 an hour. That would be a princely sum in Zambia, qualifying the recipient to membership of the middle class. The

African Development Bank regards any African with a daily spending power of between USD2 and USD20 to be in the middle class.

The Pew Research Center used a higher definition of USD10 to USD 20 in 2015. Either way, a Zambian earning USD11.81 per hour would easily qualify for membership in the middle class. Call centres would be of particular interest to unemployed or underemployed university graduates who would be ideal phone representatives capable of effectively engaging a global audience after basic training in enunciation. There are an estimated 2,784,500 customer service representatives in the United States. Employers struggle to fill CSR jobs because of the relatively low pay and often turn to call centres abroad where the lower cost of living makes the standard American pay for customer service representatives attractive. Zambia would be seen as an attractive source of skilled call centre representatives by most of these employers.

While the United States customer service representative job market is expected to grow by only 4.9% between 2016 and 2026, research shows that globally, customer service representative jobs are set to grow by 36% over the same period.

South Africa's experience gives us an idea of the contribution that call centres and the service industry, in general, could make to the Zambian economy. In 2017, South Africa sold more than USD16 billion worth of services to the world. Call centres alone contributed USD3.5 billion to GDP in 2018. The call centre industry employs 228,000 people, with 38,600 of them dedicated to international business. The country takes advantage of its hundreds of thousands of educated English speakers and a timezone that makes it relatively easy to engage businesspeople in Europe, Asia, and the Americas. Zambia has both these advantages, in addition to the virtue of even lower labour costs.

Growing the middle class and regional integration

The impact of a rapidly growing middle class on the economy is likely to be fortified by greater integration of regional markets. On October 26, 2020, the Zambian cabinet approved the ratification of the African Continental Free Trade Area (AfCFTA). This was a preliminary step to giving Zambia access to the proposed single continent-wide preferential market for goods and services. The African Continental Free Trade Area also aims to harmonize trade instruments across Africa's regional economic communities.

Integrating continental trade makes immediate sense, especially as the AfCFTA area boasts a market of more than 1.2 billion people. But the promise of the free trade area will only be realised when all member states are committed to democratic practices that maximise citizens' freedoms. It is also important that the inevitable bureaucracy which will result from trade harmonisation, does not threaten the sovereignty of member states. Africa is a large and diverse continent with diverse interests. While all countries may appreciate the benefits of regional trade, few will unreservedly accept edicts, from AfCFTA, with the potential to infringe on their sovereignty.

Lessons can be learned from Europe where the United Kingdom left the European Union, which offers a single market like that proposed under the AfCFTA. Polls are unanimous that there were two main reasons why British voters opted out of the EU. The first was that only by leaving could Britain guarantee that decisions about the UK would indeed be taken in the UK. The second reason was that a departure offered the best chance for the United Kingdom to regain control over immigration and its own borders.

Unless the African Continental Free Trade Area manages its affairs in a spirit of unqualified respect for the sovereignty of its member states, it could find itself disintegrating prematurely. Disintegration could also come from the real or perceived exclusion of ordinary citizens from the benefits of the free trade area. A perception of exclusion could fuel support for populist movements against regional integration, as has happened in the UK and other European countries.

On the other hand, if AfCFTA turned out to be meticulous in its respect for member-state's sovereignty and was seen as encouraging its members to apply public resources effectively for the benefit of citizens, it could play an unprecedented role in generating wealth for the continent and its citizens. AfCFTA certainly has the potential to create opportunities for Zambia's growing middle class and entrepreneurs. Most of the activity would probably be in the SADC/PTA regions because of limited continental infrastructure and connectivity. It is not possible, for example, to take a fast train from Lusaka to Accra or Lagos, but it is possible to travel from Lusaka by rail, road, and air to Harare and Johannesburg. Travelling to Abidjan from Lusaka is also difficult because of the continent's colonial history, resulting in Côte d'Ivoire being better connected to France than to Zambia.

Partly because of this reality, there has been talk of reviving a national airline for Zambia. This sentiment is understandable, but the Zambian government's idea of raising capital to invest in such an airline is deficient. The airline industry is extremely competitive. It is not known for treating new entrants kindly, and newcomers find it difficult to get established and make a profit.

The sensible option for Zambia would be to identify a successful international carrier with a reputation for innovation and superior industry knowledge and invite that airline to establish a subsidiary in Zambia. The minister of finance could take out a golden share in the subsidiary, giving the government veto power over changes to the company's agreed-upon objectives.

In return, the international airline would have the right to fly the Zambian flag, using Lusaka as the originating point for all its flights. In addition, incentives for a reputable international company establishing a subsidiary company in Zambia would have to include a reduction in the cost of jet fuel and a reduction in landing and handling fees. These incentives would also help Zambia's image as a friendly destination for other forms of foreign direct investment.

Economies of scale

As we have seen, aviation fuel costs and high landing and handling fees have undermined the Zambian floriculture industry. In the absence of a viable local market, the industry has been forced to reduce employment levels. The local market for flowers is simply too small to make up for the loss of access to international markets. In addition, lack of financing and high transaction costs contribute to the woes of the local market.

The floriculture industry is similar to other Zambian industries dependent on the local market. Firms in these industries cannot get the economies of scale that competitors, in say Europe, have. Zambia is also handicapped by the absence of value chains. The country is a huge exporter of copper but imports most of its finished copper products. Zambia grows cotton but the bulk of its clothing is imported.

Since the Zambian government is a large buyer of clothing in the form of uniforms for the army, police, air force, Zambia National Service, and immigration and customs services, a commitment from the State to buy only clothing made from Zambian cotton would go some way in developing value chains in this sector.

More broadly, the proposed AfCFTA offers an opportunity for economies of scale and value creation. While intracontinental trade in Europe makes up between 60 and 70 percent of all trade, the figure for the African continent is only 17 percent. The elimination of tariffs on Zambian goods seeking markets in neighbouring countries or even farther afield on the continent would create large enough markets to encourage specialisation and investment in quality, making Zambian goods and services globally competitive.

The USD838 billion aerospace industry is perhaps an unlikely example of how Zambia can benefit from economies of scale and market access. However, Morocco, Tunisia, and South Africa have shown how a successful aerospace manufacturing industry can be operated in African countries. Tunisia and Morocco have the advantage of proximity to key European aerospace powers. But this is not a precondition for success as South Africa's performance attests. In March 2019, Ethiopia committed to establishing its own aerospace cluster in East Africa. Ethiopia is following South Africa's lead. The country is aware of the aerospace industry's potential to create, directly and indirectly, large numbers of highly skilled jobs.

Ethiopia knows that despite its distance from Europe, South Africa's aerospace sector directly employs about 15,000 highly skilled engineers and is estimated to support an additional 60,000 skilled jobs in the broader economy. The number of people employed in the sector in Tunisia exceeds 9,000, while the aerospace manufacturing cluster, consisting of more than 110 companies, directly employs about 11,500 people in Morocco. South Africa's aerospace manufacturing sector is valued at USD1.8 billion, while Morocco's is worth USD1.1 billion. The figure for Tunisia USD430 million.

Ethiopia finds these data inspiring as it develops an aerospace manufacturing industry, in collaboration with global aircraft and engine manufacturers. Thinking ahead, Ethiopian Airlines has a plan to work with the Addis Ababa University Faculty of Science and Technology and other universities and technical schools to train young engineers in the envisioned aviation academy.

With the continental free trade area, opportunities exist for Zambian entrepreneurs to manufacture on a subcontract basis for the aerospace engineering sectors in South Africa, Ethiopia, Morocco, and Tunisia. The time may well be ripe for this kind of productive continental cooperation. Africa not only has a young population but apparently is also now home to the world's most optimistic people. This suggests that the trauma of slavery and colonialism may be on the brink of being banished as an impediment to progress. The African continent may be on the way to regaining her confidence and proceeding to make a huge contribution to global society, just as survivors of extreme trauma do.

A September 2017 IPSOS survey found that 48 percent of the world's inhabitants believed living conditions for them and their families would change for the better in the next 15 years. The figure was 28 percent in Britain, while only 23 percent of the French believed their living conditions would improve. At 48 percent, the Americans were rather more optimistic than both the British and the French. 54 percent of South Africans believed their living conditions would change for the better. They were far less optimistic than the Senegalese, Nigerians, and Kenyans, whose respective scores were 82, 79, and 78 percent. The African respondents surveyed showed similar optimism with respect to their countries' future prospects.

Agriculture

When Zambians talk about the 'copper curse', they typically refer to the country's failure to exploit its agricultural potential because of the 'easy' money provided by the copper mining industry, at least in good times. Zambia has 75 million hectares of land. 42 million hectares of that is classified as having medium to high potential for agriculture production. Only 15 percent of this land is, however, under cultivation.

Zambia has ample water resources, although it is an exaggeration to say that the country has 60 percent of all freshwater in the Southern African Development Community. Zambia does, however, have significant water courses that flow through the country. The totality of these watercourses, spanning several other countries, carry about 60 percent of SADC water resources.

Determining the quantity of freshwater in Zambia is not an exact science because the calculation relies on long-term annual averages. The term 'freshwater' is quite broadly defined and includes rainfall, groundwater, and surface water in lakes, rivers, and streams. Data from Africa Check and the Organisation for Economic Cooperation and Development (OECD) show that Zambia has 104.8 billion m^3 of 'renewable freshwater resources'. With the 1998 admission of the Democratic Republic of Congo into the SADC, which brought 1,283 billion m³ of water into the regional pool, this figure now represents 4.5 percent of regional freshwater.

The important point for our purposes is that Zambia does not have a water shortage but could do more to exploit her water resources by greater investment in water management systems.

Zambian farmers are said to fall into three broad categories: small, medium, and large-scale. Small-scale farmers have virtually no access to irrigation systems and are totally dependent on rainfall to produce staple foods. This categorization is not entirely satisfactory as it does not pay enough attention to emergent farmers who do not fit perfectly into any one of the three slots above. The government defines emergent farmers as those who cultivate between five hectares and 20 hectares of land. These farmers often occupy a transitional step between the three categories.

With that in mind, it will be noted that smallholder farmers are reasonably price efficient. In the 2019/2020 season, they contributed 93 percent of the total maize production in the country, with the remaining seven percent produced by large-scale farmers. The 2019/2020 crop forecasting survey shows that the country produced 3,387,469 tons of maize, an increase of 69 percent over the 2018/2019 season.

Maize production is, however, the only area in which smallholder farmers appear to excel, at least when weather conditions are favourable. Rarely do smallholder farmers produce enough of other crops for sale. And yet it makes sense for Zambia to encourage smallholder farmers to produce crops such as cassava, millet, and sorghum which are more drought-resistant than maize. It is estimated that with a population of 18 million people the total maize required for both industrial and human consumption is about 3,613,289 tons. It is risky to rely solely on seasonal rainwater for a requirement as large as this one.

Diversification of crops for consumption is as important as installing irrigation systems, making agricultural production for smallholder farmers more predictable.

Large-scale farmers, who have invested in irrigation systems, produce crops such as sugar, soybeans, coffee, groundnuts, rice, and cotton for the local market and export. Horticultural produce may also be added to this list. Altogether, agriculture contributes about 20 percent to the country's GDP and employs three-quarters of the working-age population.

According to the World Bank, 53.4 percent of the Zambian population in 2019 fell into 'working age' category. That means 9,612,000 Zambians were aged between 15 and 64. If three-quarters of the working age population is employed in the agricultural sector, the country has around 7,209,000 farmers and agricultural workers. Investing in the sector can directly raise the standards of living of more than seven million Zambians. In addition to investment in irrigation systems, smallholder farmers must also gain access to markets, requiring the development of a good transportation network.

Some of the infrastructure developed in recent years is already making a difference to smallholder farmers. For example, the construction of the 187 kilometre stretch of Mwenda-Kashiba road has, according to local residents, reduced travel time from Chipili to Mansa from over two hours when the road was in a state of disrepair, to 40 minutes. That means smallholder farmers in Chipili have greater access to the relatively large market in Mansa. In addition, these farmers can now get their produce to the even larger market of Mufulira on the Copperbelt within four hours.

To fully take advantage of reduced travel times, smallholder farmers need to have more produce to sell. To do so, they need access to affordable fertiliser and improved seed, in addition to irrigation infrastructure. Smallholder farmers in Zambia consistently complain however about the high cost of improved seed. Zambia cannot afford to deny her farmers access to this seed. The evidence is clear, for example, that improved sorghum varieties can produce a crop 40 percent larger than the usual variety.

With respect to irrigation infrastructure, a World Bank irrigation project in Ethiopia studied by The Economist, helped local farmers increase their potato harvest from eight tonnes per hectare to 35 tonnes.

Historically, Zambia has favoured subsidising urban consumption over investment in agricultural production. The result has been less food than one would expect in a well-endowed country with a good climate, good soil, and freshwater. This policy has also left smallholder farmers cashstrapped and unable to consistently invest in basics such as good seed.

The budget passed on September 25th 2020, included an allocation to the Farmer Input Support Programme. In 2019/2020 the allocation was USD70 million. The allocation for 2021 increased by over 300.0 percent, to USD285 million. Leaving aside the government's motivation for this drastic increase, recognition of the agricultural sector in this way is welcome. Since, however, the FISP is used mostly by maize farmers, it would have been even more helpful had the government taken the opportunity to reserve a significant portion of this money for producers of other crops such as cassava, millet, and sorghum.

Furthermore, the government could have used the budget to more effectively promote value addition to crops and livestock, which can generate jobs. For example, USD2 million could have been set aside to support entrepreneurs interested in establishing food-processing plants in each one of the country's ten provinces. Since a reasonably large food processing plant with a five-year warranty will cost about USD200,000, the government could have used the USD2 million to guarantee loans by entrepreneurs interested in establishing food-processing plants. In this way, the government would have aided the establishment of an indigenous food-processing industry able to employ many nationals.

Sufficiently supported, the 7,209,000 farmers and farm workers could be an engine for creating a large tax-paying middle class. Strategic investment in this sector would yield remarkable dividends for the country and end poverty as we know it. There are about 150,000 emerging farmers, 130,000 medium-scale farmers, and 2,000 commercial farmers. If we assume all commercial farmers are in the tax-paying middle-class bracket, we are still left with 6,927,000 rural Zambians awaiting elevation into this class. If Zambia made the necessary investments in this segment of the population, and incomes went up, all it would take is an average monthly income of USD310 (at the current exchange rate), for employees in the agro sector to collectively earn USD2.14 billion. At an average tax rate of 25 percent, this group of workers would contribute as much as USD536,842,500 to the treasury every month.

As farmers grow wealthier, their ability to mechanise operations will increase, and only a fraction of the 6.9 million farm labourers will remain on the land. Before that time comes, however, many farm labourers would have acquired new skills, increased their incomes, and performed other functions.

Agricultural opportunities from climate change

While the precise impacts of climate change are yet to be known, it is generally agreed that global warming represents a huge threat to African prosperity. This is because in parts of the continent, temperatures are rising more quickly than the global average. From this, it is concluded that heatwaves in Africa are likely to intensify and undermine agriculture. For example, The Economist estimated that about 40 percent of the land used to grow maize could cease to be suitable for that purpose, and maize yields could fall by 18-22 percent.

But before we get too depressed, let us remember once again that Africa is a large and diverse continent and that it will not be uniformly affected by climate change.

It is beyond dispute that the world's demand for water will surge in the next few decades. The doubling of the African continent's population by 2050 will certainly lead to a significant increase in water consumption. The strain on water resources will only increase with more people moving from rural areas into urban zones. But does this trend necessarily condemn Zambia to chronic food shortages, or can the country still be a regional food basket?

Using various tools, climate models, and socioeconomic scenarios, the World Resources Institute has attempted to measure more precisely the impact of water scarcity in the next few decades. Their findings are remarkably similar to those of a study I once saw as a member of Ontario's Deputy Ministers' Social Policy Committee.

In its August 2015 report, WRI found that 33 countries (out of 167 examined) will face extremely high water stress by 2040. WRI also found that, among others, Namibia and Botswana could face an especially significant increase in water stress. The degree of stress in Botswana and Namibia will be between 40 and 80 percent.

That means these countries will experience a 40-80 percent decline in the current water supply. This raises the real prospect of businesses, farms, and communities in Botswana and Namibia becoming significantly more vulnerable to water scarcity. This obviously threatens the trajectory of prosperity that the two countries are currently on, which could all but disappear unless these countries find a new source of water or reduce their water consumption by, for example, importing food previously grown by them from a reliable and friendly country.

Roughly two dozen African countries will be neither high nor medium water-stressed. One of these countries is Zambia, which is expected to be a low stress jurisdiction with less than ten percent water stress levels. As a dependable neighbour of Botswana and Namibia, Zambia could enter into agreements with the two countries to supply them with as much food as needed, thereby saving more local water for human consumption and industry. Zambia could also develop water bottling plants in places such as the environs of Lakes Bangweulu and Tanganyika, where the water supply may actually increase, both for export and local consumption.

There was much excitement when the British company Tullow announced commencement of oil and gas exploration in northern Zambia in August 2017. Successful exploration would certainly help diversify the Zambian economy, but it would also potentially threaten the natural environment. The region Tullow is interested in is also home to some of the country's large water bodies. Would it not be prudent to consider establishing bottling plants in these areas instead of oil fields? Consideration must be given to the declining value of oil, the rising value of water, global demand to reduce carbon emissions, and the emergence of alternative power sources.

The water demand will continue to increase. Bottled water produced in Zambia could be for both the domestic and international markets. Given the anticipated shortage of fresh water in countries such as the United States, a comparison of the price of bottled water and petrol may be enlightening.

The average price of a litre of bottled water in the United States is USD1.17. The average price of a litre of petrol is 67.5 cents. Globally, the annual cost of bottled water is USD60 billion. These data, combined with the fact that the United States and many other countries will be high water stress jurisdictions within the next two decades, make a compelling case for Zambia to consider investing in better water management and bottling plants for domestic and foreign consumption.

Other countries expected to be in a high water stress situation by 2040 include Australia, the Peoples' Republic of China, and the Republic of South Africa. These countries are not about to accept a reduction in the amount and variety of food available to their citizens in local supermarkets, just because the supply of water relied on by their farmers is threatened. This creates an opportunity to link Zambian farms to retailers of both fresh and processed foods in these countries. In 2018, United States supermarket food sales were worth an estimated USD447 billion. The value of food retailed in Australia in the same year was USD81.3 billion. Domestic market food retail sales in South Africa amounted to USD52.2 billion. In Australia, the People's Republic of China, and South Africa, the market for food sold in supermarkets is worth USD580.5 billion. These countries will be hard-pressed in the coming decades to produce this food domestically. They will need reliable foreign suppliers to meet this demand. As a low water-stressed country, Zambia should be well-positioned to take advantage of this market.

The total retail value of food sold in the three countries' supermarkets is greater than the amount paid to the producers of that food. The combined markup of food wholesalers and retailers is about 25 percent. Depending on volume and destination, transportation and other costs could push the total mark up to 30 percent. That means the amount paid to producers of food sold in Australian, US and South African supermarkets is about USD406 billion. Even a modest share—one percent—of this market would earn Zambia over USD4 billion per annum.

Zambia has less reason to be fearful of the future than most countries. Indeed the expected deleterious effects of climate change could work to Zambia's advantage. To exploit that advantage, however, Zambia must start investing sensibly in the agricultural sector now.

Tourism

The Smoke that Thunders is the translation of 'Mosi-O-Tunya', the indigenous name for the Victoria Falls, one of the world's greatest natural wonders. Between late November and early April, over 38,000 cubic feet of water cascade down the falls every second. This is perhaps the best time to view the falls. But even in drier times (May to early November), there is much to see and do at the Mosi-O-Tunya. Visitors may, for example, swim at the Devils Pool, a natural infinity pool accessible through Livingstone Island, which also serves as a superb dining site.

The luxurious Royal Livingstone Hotel, set in the lush riverine belt on the banks of the Zambezi River, is only a 10-minute walk away from the falls. The resort housing both the Royal Livingstone and the slightly less luxurious Zambezi Sun is a perfect example of how to combine luxury with nature.

Attached to the resort is one of Zambia's smallest public game parks, Mosi-O-Tunya National Park. After a drive of no more than ten minutes from the luxury hotel, the visitor enters a tutored wilderness that eagerly reveals Zambia's pristine countryside. This particular park has no predators because of its size but the visitor is likely to see giraffes, elephants, impalas, zebras, and baboons.

Victoria Falls is the best known of Zambia's waterfalls and features on every respectable list of must-see places in the world. It is not, however, the only waterfall in the country. Less well-known cataracts include Chavuma, Kalambo, Lumangwe, Ngonye, Nkundalila, and Ntumbachushi. Of these, Ntumbachushi is probably the most picturesque, although that is a difficult assessment to make given the beauty of all the sites.

Elephant at Kafue Game Park

Ntumbachushi is a series of water pools and rapids culminating in a 30-metre drop from the Ng'ona River. As with Kakabeka Falls in Ontario, there are myths and legends about Ntumbachushi. The best known of these is that the waterfall was a sanctuary of good spirits with the power to purify the waters of the Ng'ona River. For this reason, local monarchs are still bathed in the river's waters before installation on the throne. The bathing represents cleansing and protects the monarch from bad influences.

Ntumbachushi will likely become famous thanks to its location, the realisation that tourism needs to be promoted, and good provincial leadership in the person of Nickson Chilangwa, the provincial minister who pioneered the successful 2017 Luapula Expo.

The Expo was spread over five districts in the Luapula Province, namely Samfya, Mansa, the provincial capital, Kawambwa, a tea-growing centre, Mwansabombwe, and Nchelenge. The organisers were hoping to have a few hundred attendees. In the end, the expo attracted more than 1,000 local and foreign delegates.

Victoria Falls

All this is good news for Ntumbachushi Falls and Samfya, which boasts a little-known fine sand beach on the shores of Lake Bangweulu, a massive freshwater lake that looks more like a sea than a lake. Local people often describe the lake as the place where water and sky meet. The hustle and bustle experienced by Samfya during the expo may well be a harbinger of the prosperity to come when its beach becomes a popular tourism destination.

It's all in the game

Although the Mosi-O-Tunya is the best-known tourism site in Zambia, it is not the industry's sole driver. Consistently present on the lists of sophisticated travellers interested in Africa is the desire to see game in its natural habitat. Game competes favourably on these lists with the Victoria Falls, Egyptian pyramids, Namibian sand dunes, Cape Town, and Kigali. Zambia is more fortunate than most countries in having a global waterfall wonder and game. Sites such as the Nachikufu Caves, which contain 15,000-year-old rock paintings, are a bonus.

One of the enduring myths among many Zambians is that wildlife has suffered greatly as a result of poor mismanagement by post-colonial governments. This belief is strongest among black Zambians who have internalised racism and come to accept some of the negative stereotypes about their own people. They have been led to conclude that as

Zambians, they are incapable of managing affairs as well as other people. In fact, the greatest threat to African and Zambian wildlife arose during the colonial era. As Elizabeth Becker observed in Overbooked:

> The Europeans treated the immense continent as their private hunting ground, killing Africa's magnificent animals for trophies and sport at such a rate that some Europeans began to worry. Something had to be done to save the elephants, lions and native antelopes from European rifles and extinction. The authorities' solution was to set up vast parks where animals could roam free.

The parks established in this manner were often carved out of land also used for hunting by local people. Inevitably, the sudden restriction of hunting in these areas caused resentment, which could have been avoided had local communities, who had coexisted sensibly with these animals over centuries, been consulted. Many of these communities had strict regulations about how and when to hunt. They understood the importance of balancing the interests of both people and animals.

Pre-colonial and Colonial Conservation Practices in southern Africa and their Legacy Today

In his January 2002 paper, Pre-colonial and colonial conservation practices in southern Africa and their legacy today, Dr James Murombedzi, chief of the African Climate Policy Center of United Nations Economic Commission for Africa, found that pre-colonial society had effective ways of conserving wildlife. For example, places of worship and objects of spiritual veneration located in forests came with strict hunting rules. With the effluxion of time, these areas became conservation areas. In addition, adopting particular animals as spiritual symbols of ethnic groups and clans within these ethnic groups typically required these animals to be protected from indiscriminate killing. Thus, not all animals could be hunted. Especially protected were those animals considered to represent sacred societal values. With so many strict regulations about the kind of game that could be hunted, it was only a matter of time before there was general societal agreement that even animals without significant spiritual value could only be hunted under certain circumstances. According to Murombedzi, these pre-colonial ethnology and environmental management practices were so entrenched in the lives of indigenous people that they survived long into the colonial period because of their continued relevance in the conservation of natural resources. Without these practices, much of pre-colonial Zambian wildlife may well have gone the way of the American buffalo.

In any event, the parks carved out by European authorities concerned about the destructive behaviour of their brethren form the foundation of African wildlife tourism today. Becker estimates that the wildlife industry earns the continent USD76 billion per annum in direct receipts. When tourism-related expenditures are taken into account, that figure goes up to USD171 billion.

Zambia should be getting the lion's share of this market with its vast parks and peaceable people. South Luangwa National Park, for example, covers an area of about 9,050 square kilometres, three and a half times the size of Luxembourg. Altogether, 30 percent of Zambia's 752,614 square kilometres is reserved for wildlife. Owing to policy failure, however, Zambia earns only a fraction of what it should be earning from wildlife tourism.

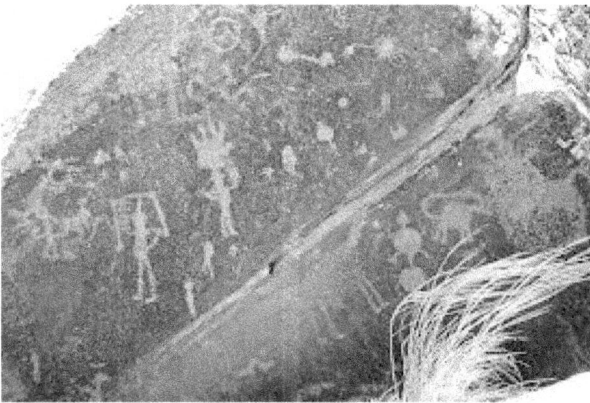

Nachikufu Caves

While Lower Zambezi National Park and South Luangwa National Park are beginning to get better ratings as places to see, Zambia continues to attract fewer visitors than it should. Statista, the German company specializing in market and consumer data, ranked Morocco first among African countries with the most international tourist arrivals. In 2019, Morocco had 12.93 million arrivals. In second place was South Africa, which received 10.23 million arrivals. Despite having an abundance of game and the Victoria Falls, Zambia did not make the top ten, but next-door Zimbabwe did.

It should be noted, however, that the number of arrivals in Zambia has actually been on the increase since 1999, reaching a record 1.07 million visitors in 2018. According to the International Growth Centre, international visitors spent USD849 million, representing 10% of Zambia's total exports, in 2019. Altogether, the industry contributed 7 percent to the GDP.

As encouraging as this trend may appear, Zambia could in fact do much better. With 237 mammal species and 700 bird species, not to mention Victoria Falls and other cataracts, Zambia has more to offer than its competitors in the region. Botswana, for example, has 170 mammal species and 550 bird species. Besides game, Botswana has little else to offer tourists. South Africa has 297 mammal species and 850 bird species. The country also has other impressive tourist sites such as Table Mountain, Cradle of Mankind, Robben Island, Cape Winelands, and the Drakensberg Mountains. Most visitors, however, go to the country for game, consistent with World Travel & Tourism Council research which shows that four of every five tourists to sub-Saharan Africa visit to view wildlife.

South Africa's largest game park is the Kruger National Park which covers 19,485 square kilometres. Zambia's largest game park is the Kafue National Park which covers 22,500 square kilometres, about the size of Wales. Whilst Zambia earns less than USD1 billion from tourism, South Africa earned USD 9.5 billion in 2019.

Zambia's advantages as a tourist destination are very difficult to replicate. While Niagara Falls may be a plausible alternative to Victoria Falls for Ontarians, the three-square-kilometre African Lion Safari near Cambridge, Ontario does not come close to the experience of roaming in the 22,500-square-kilometre Kafue National Park.

With better planning, investment, and more aggressive marketing, the country could relatively easily have the lion's share of global tourism income. Zambian wildlife is, however, threatened by poaching and the illegal global wildlife trade. This scourge can be defeated with education and better management. WTTC estimates that, annually, international wildlife tourism generates five times more revenue than illegal wildlife trade. If this fact were better publicised, would-be poachers may well be encouraged to conserve wildlife and earn their living from activities designed to do just that.

The size of the global wildlife tourism is enough incentive for informed people to abandon poaching and for enlightened governments to invest in the industry. In 2018, global wildlife tourism's direct contribution to global GDP was USD120.1 billion. In contrast, revenue attributed to global poaching of wildlife amounted to USD23 billion. More than nine million people worldwide were lawfully employed in global wildlife tourism. About half of these employees were in the Asia-Pacific region whose market is worth USD 53.3 billion. The Africa region was not too far behind the Asia-Pacific with 3.6 million people employed through wildlife tourism, worth USD29.3 billion. North America is the third largest wildlife tourism economy after Asia-Pacific and Africa, directly contributing USD13.5 billion to global GDP.

The total number of direct and indirect jobs created by the wildlife industry is 21.8 million. In other words, the number of people supported by the global tourism industry in the form of jobs, exceeds the current population of Zambia. When non-wildlife activity is factored in, tourism's total contribution to global GDP is USD343.6 billion. The last decade has seen significant growth in private game reserves and hotels in Zambia. This trend is consistent with the fact that, in general, tourism is growing rapidly in sub-Saharan Africa. WTTC forecasts that the number of tourists in the region will double to 134 million by 2030.

With better planning, education, and investment, Zambia could benefit substantially from this growth. As part of this planning and education effort, villagers living near game reserves and dependent on firewood for energy, and game meat for food, must be educated about the value of wildlife tourism. That means, for example, giving this segment of the population priority when employment opportunities arise in game parks. In the words of Gloria Guevara Manzo, President and CEO of the World Travel & Tourism Council, these people must be convinced that wildlife is worth far more alive than dead.

It also means educating them about the contribution that tourism makes to the national economy. But to truly eliminate poaching and illegal trade in wildlife and give people living close to game parks a sustainable lifestyle that encourages game conservation, more needs to be done. Solar energy, for example, could be used to provide a cleaner and less environmentally destructive source of energy for these households. In this regard, the government's efforts to promote solar power through reduced tariffs on imported inputs are welcomed.

In the longer term, there is a huge role for scientists in the conservation of Zambian wildlife. The country should invest in cultured meat research and production. Cultured meat is created by harvesting muscle cells from a living animal. These cells are then fed and nurtured to multiply and create muscle tissue, which is essentially meat. The meat so produced is biologically the same as the meat tissue from, say, antelope. If this meat were readily available, there would be absolutely no need to poach wildlife for food.

Communities on the periphery of game parks must also be given incentives to invest in the success of game parks. One way of doing so is to introduce community shareholding in companies that own or manage wildlife reserves. Incentives could include selling wildlife company shares to communities at a discounted rate. Communities owning these shares would not be involved in the management of the game parks, but they would be entitled to dividends when the game parks made a profit.

If these reforms occur, Zambia could receive at least two percent of the wildlife tourist arrivals of 134 million projected for the African continent by 2030. Research conducted by Acorn Tourism Consulting Ltd in 2018, shows that, on average, a tourist visiting Zambia spends USD446 a day. Assuming a ten-day stay, that amount comes to USD4,460. On this basis, if Zambia received 2.68 million visitors a year, a mere two percent of the projected number of arrivals in Africa in 2030, the country could expect to earn USD11.9 billion a year from tourism alone. That amount is equivalent to Zambia's current public debt.

Immigration

When Canada announced that 34,260 permanent residents had been accepted in the country during the second quarter of 2020, there was widespread concern about the impact this would have on the national economy. Many African and European countries would be surprised to learn, however, that the concern was not that too many foreigners had been let into the country. Rather, the concern was that not enough had come in!

During the same period in 2019, Canada welcomed 94,275 immigrants. The 2020 second-quarter figures, therefore, represent a 64 percent drop. The decline was a result of border closures designed to curb the spread of COVID-19. The number of permanent residents welcomed for the first six months of 2020 was 103,420. The fear was that at this rate, Canada's annual immigration levels would fall short of the government's target of 341,000 immigrants for 2020.

Immigration is one of Canada's key drivers of economic growth. This is a tested way of growing the workforce in a jurisdiction where 17 percent of the population is over 65 years. In addition, immigration has clearly contributed to Canada's robust housing market.

As a former Ontario deputy minister for citizenship and immigration, I can vouch for the value of immigrants to Canada. Immigrants are, however, disproportionately recognized for their achievements in research and the arts, as evidenced by their overrepresentation in the Canada Research Chairs Program which attracts and retains some of the world's most accomplished and promising minds. With respect to the arts, immigrants disproportionately win the coveted Scotiabank Giller Prize for literature.

They also contribute significantly to innovation in Canadian businesses, in part, by expanding Canada's trade relations. For example, a 1 percent increase in the number of immigrants to Canada corresponds to an increase in imports of 0.21 percent, and an increase in exports by 0.11 percent. It is not surprising, therefore, that immigration rates in Canada are linked to greater foreign direct investment

The data from the United States and Australia are similar. Despite the proven value of immigration, Zambian policymakers rarely connect immigration to economic prosperity. As a result, the country has been unable to benefit fully from the advantages of immigration.

Imported skills

With 44.4 percent of the Zambian population aged 14 or under, Zambia does not need immigrants to augment population growth. The country does, however, need immigrants who bring skills and capital. Since independence, Zambia has sourced foreign-skilled labour from countries such as the United Kingdom, India, and South Africa. Skilled workers are required to obtain employment permits before entering the country to take up employment with a duration of more than six months. These permits can be extended for further periods, up to a maximum of 10 years from the original date of issue.

This means that when a skilled worker cannot convert her work permit to a permanent residence permit, she will be obliged to leave the country and take her skills with her.

Before 1992, the expatriate community was the only group of workers allowed to remit money abroad. Many came on three-year work permits and they spent the first year learning about the country, the second year learning the job, and the final year, preparing to leave. The expatriate system was clearly inefficient, especially with respect to those who only worked in the country for three years or less.

With the abolition of exchange control regulations in 1992, Zambians may now also remit their earnings abroad. In that respect, Zambian skilled workers are treated equitably with their foreign recruited counterparts.

The abolition of exchange controls makes it even easier for expatriates to remit their earnings. From personal experience, few expatriates could justify the amount of money they were paid in the 1970s and 80s. As a practising lawyer, I met very few expatriates who genuinely made a net positive contribution to the country.

There were outstanding exceptions to this rule, such as a very committed Irish teacher called Anne Watts, who taught mathematics at a government high school in Ndola. Ms Watts was highly regarded by her Zambian headteacher, colleagues, and students, many of whom went on to be successful professionals.

After her contract ended in 1981, she returned to Ireland, only to be enticed back to Zambia ten years later by Simba International School, a prestigious multi-cultural school dedicated to providing a holistic education.

Few foreign-skilled workers had the good fortune to get satisfaction from their work as Ms Watts did. The majority of these workers never set out to take advantage of Zambia, but the system encouraged them to do so. They were well paid but generally did less work than their Zambian counterparts, who earned less than they did. The disparity in treatment of professionals persisted because too many Zambian leaders were prepared to exaggerate the value of foreign expertise relative to local talent. After all, local professionals were only Zambians.

Zambia certainly needed skills during the early days and continues to do so. Temporary work permits are not, however, the best way to attract these skills to the country. Skilled persons should come to Zambia through a well-thought-out immigration policy. In the first instance, they should come in as permanent residents after being screened for cultural and professional suitability. After working in the country satisfactorily for five years, these immigrants should be eligible for citizenship.

A skilled foreign worker entering Zambia on this basis will inevitably take a long-term view of his relationship with the country. As with most immigrants, he will want to buy a house at the earliest opportunity. The more enterprising ones will also think of starting businesses that will employ Zambians. Either way, the immigrant will be making an investment in Zambia.

This is not to suggest that there is no room for work permits. There is. It will from time to time be necessary to bring in specialists to, for example, install or repair specialised machinery at a mining company, or a mechanised farm. The permit required for this specific purpose would obviously be for a short period. It is imprudent, however, to rely on work permits for people bringing skills that are projected to be in demand for a long time.

Historically, this reliance on work permits has lost Zambia billions of dollars because work permit holders prioritised externalisation of their excessively large salaries over investing locally. Consequently, they spent as little of their huge salaries as possible in Zambia, especially given that most were entitled to free accommodation and transportation. Some contracts even contained a clause entitling the expatriate employee and his family to a vacation anywhere in the world, once a year! By no stretch of the imagination could the skills of most of the expatriates I met in Zambia have justified this. Among the few whose skills would have was Ms Watts, and she was not entitled, as a government school teacher, to employer-funded vacations.

Long-term capital importation

The crowd listened to Paul until he said this. Then they raised their voices and shouted, 'Rid the earth of him! He's not fit to live!'

As they were shouting and throwing off their cloaks and flinging dust into the air, the commander ordered that Paul be taken into the barracks. He directed that he be flogged and interrogated in order to find out why the people were shouting at him like this.

As they stretched him out to flog him, Paul said to the centurion standing there, 'Is it legal for you to flog a Roman citizen who hasn't even been found guilty?'

When the centurion heard this, he went to the commander and reported it. 'What are you going to do?' he asked. 'This man is a Roman citizen.'

The commander went to Paul and asked, 'Tell me, are you a Roman citizen?' 'Yes, I am,' he answered.

Then the commander said, 'I had to pay a lot of money for my citizenship.'

'But I was born a citizen,' Paul replied.
Those who were about to interrogate him withdrew immediately. The commander himself was alarmed when he realized that he had put Paul, a Roman citizen, in chains.

The commander wanted to find out exactly why Paul was being accused by the Jews.

So the next day he released him and ordered the chief priests and all the members of the Sanhedrin to assemble. Then he brought Paul and had him stand before them.

This passage from Acts 22: 22-30 generally shows the value placed on citizenship and the fact that the concept of citizenship by investment existed in Roman times. We are also reminded by Dr Jelena Dzankic, Professor in the Global Governance Programme at the Robert Schuman Centre of the European University Institute in Florence, that there was a link between wealth and citizenship in ancient Greece.

In the mid-1980s, the small Caribbean country of St Kitts and Nevis passed legislation offering citizenship to individuals who 'made a substantial investment in the state.' St Kitts was at that time largely dependent on sugar for foreign exchange earnings, and the new law was passed to diversify the economy.

After the disastrous sugar harvest of 2005, which followed many years of losses, the government closed its sugar industry. With tourism unable, at that time, to generate enough earnings to make up for the losses arising from the closure of the sugar industry, the government contracted the world's premier firm on citizenship planning, Henley & Partners, to promote its recently established Sugar Industry Diversification Fund. In 2011, Henley & Partners established a Citizenship by Investment Unit to handle applications for citizenship by investment. The Unit was responsible for screening and approving applications.

The citizenship by investment programme did succeed in returning the country to economic stability. St Kitts' public debt reduced from 154 percent of GDP in 2011, the year the CIP was formed, to 83 percent in 2013. In that year, 25 percent of GDP came from the grant of citizenship to foreign investors.

Capital transfer through citizenship

In August 2018, Henley & Partners wrote to the Zambian government to explore opportunities for a citizenship by investment programme. Based on the firm's 20-year track record of assisting countries in North America, the Caribbean, Europe and Asia in strategic consulting, design, set-up and operation of the world's most successful residence and citizenship programmes, the firm's chairman and CEO, Dr Christian Kaelin, was convinced that Zambia could benefit immensely from such a programme. Kälin told the government that he strongly believes that launching a citizenship by investment programme in Zambia would result in huge foreign direct investment.

Henley & Partners' claim was hard to dismiss given that the firm's Government Advisory Practice had at that point raised more than USD7 billion in foreign direct investment. After analysing global and regional dynamics in the industry, Henley & Partners concluded that Zambia was optimally positioned to implement such a programme and generate revenues for the country ranging between USD100 million and USD 250 million per annum for at least ten years.

In a departure from the St Kitts model, Henley's suggested that the offer of citizenship in Zambia should initially be confined to persons already resident in the country. As of 02 July 2019, Zambian citizens had visa-free or visa on arrival access to 69 countries and territories, ranking the Zambian passport 75th in terms of travel freedom according to the Henley Passport Index. Henley & Partners took the view that foreigners happily residing in the country would be motivated by these benefits in their quest to become citizens. The fact that Zambia now permits dual citizenship would also make Zambian citizenship even more desirable.

Estimates of revenue are based on the assumption that the required investment under the Zambian citizenship by investment programme would only be USD 50,000, significantly lower than the amount demanded by countries such as St. Kitts and Nevis, which require a minimum investment of USD 100,000. In the case of Zambia, this minimum investment would go into a government-designed development fund and used to finance pressing development priorities such as education, health care, and infrastructure. In addition to the USD 50,000, prospective investors would be required to pay an application processing fee to help pay for the running of the programme.

The most convincing aspect of Henley & Partners' offer is perhaps that the company put its money where its mouth was. The company was so confident its Zambia proposal would work, that it offered not to charge the Zambian government any upfront fees, relying instead on future proceeds from the programme for its fees. The proposal as presented bore no financial risk to the Republic of Zambia.

According to Fitch Ratings, Zambia faced approximately USD1.5 billion in external debt servicing in 2020. This represents 105 percent of current international reserves. If Henley & Partners are right, the proposed citizenship by investment programme would mitigate this obligation by as much as USD250 million. Yet the government has been reluctant to adopt the programme. The Zambian government's hesitancy is understandable. There have been instances of abuse of these programmes. For example, fugitive financier, Jho Low, was able to obtain Cypriot citizenship despite being sought by Malaysia, Singapore, and the United States for alleged corruption and money laundering. On this occasion, the Cypriot citizenship by investment programme brought much embarrassment to the country.

In the few countries where citizenship and residence programmes have been abused by international criminals, politicians have almost always interfered in the due diligence process designed to ensure that only persons of integrity acquire citizenship. For this reason, the best-run programmes are managed by independent agencies staffed by highly professional individuals. As Staying Ahead: Due Diligence in Residence and Citizenship Programmes, published in 2018 by the Geneva-based Investment Migration Council attests, the vast majority of citizenship by investment programmes are well run and ensure that neither residency nor citizenship is offered to persons who may in any way pose a security threat.

People seek a second passport under a citizenship by investment programme for a variety of legitimate reasons. These include the right to live, work and study in a different country; to secure visa-free travel to more places; or as a safe haven for family and assets in the event of one's country of origin becoming politically unstable.

The Zambian government may also be concerned that in the current politically polarised environment, it may be prudent to bring along the opposition before implementing such a programme. That too, is a reasonable position to take. In the end, a well-designed citizenship by investment programme for Zambia would be good for the country. Since the plan is to limit applications to persons already in Zambia, the risk of abuse by international criminals is minimal, especially if the kind of due diligence for which Henley & Partners are noted is employed.

CHAPTER ELEVEN

Epilogue

A respected and successful Zambian entrepreneur discussed Zambia's debt crisis in 2020 and neatly laid out reasons the crisis could be considered an existential threat. He then concluded by observing that, 'Zambia is a truly blessed country. Somehow it is going to get over this and proceed forward'.

Zambia is indeed a fortunate land which should, by most measures, be an extremely successful country. So well placed for success is the country that an impartial observer would be forgiven for concluding that the country's failures are by design. One of the reasons the country stumbles instead of marching to prosperity is that it has never adequately addressed its traumatic colonial past and gained the confidence to chart its own path to prosperity.

Just as individual trauma must be addressed, so too must collective trauma. The starting point for Zambia is for the country to learn to love and accept itself. Knowing the country's pre-colonial and post-colonial history is essential for this exercise. Knowing the purpose of colonialism is to dominate and emotionally demoralise the colonised, will explain why so many Zambians assume certain achievements are beyond them. So, in addressing the nation's trauma, it is necessary to know what happened and its consequences.

Without this foundational knowledge, most people will struggle to understand why they act the way they do and why they cannot let go of feelings of inadequacy. A failure to address the nation's historical trauma increases the likelihood of the nation being re-traumatised by future events.

While embedding this training in formal education syllabi is vital for national therapy, many other areas need addressing. For example, in the conduct of foreign affairs, the country must establish special relationships with other countries with a similar history. At the very least, these kinds of collaboration provide opportunities to formulate collective strategies to prevent future abuse.

This drives the close relationship between Israel and Rwanda, two countries whose peoples have experienced genocide. Unlike Zambia,

Israel and Rwanda publicise their trauma, actively work to overcome it, and seek justice for individual trauma victims. On this basis, the survivors of Elliot Mulenga, the unarmed protester who was brutally murdered for demanding fair pay, should have been conspicuously honoured shortly after independence. Indeed, there should be a national monument to his memory. Zambia does have the Freedom Statue in Lusaka, which serves as a memorial to all who fought for freedom. This statue, and the few other memorials across the country do not, however, compare to Israeli and Rwandan shrines.

The relationship between Zambia and OECD countries suggests that the country still sees itself as a victim rather than a survivor of colonial trauma. For example, the country is unduly dependent on foreign aid, which is actually costly to Zambia. Like individual trauma victims, the country generally lacks confidence in its dealings with the foreign countries offering this aid to the point where even the most basic questions are never asked when dialogue occurs between the 'donors' and Zambia. One such question might be: How does the United States intend to eliminate poverty among Zambian children when the United States has more poor children than Zambia?

This is an important question because nearly 11 million children live in poverty in the US, according to the Center for American Progress. The figure for Zambia is 3.4 million; a high figure for sure, but the question is still relevant.

Questions such as this are not meant to be provocative but to elicit valuable information and help craft appropriate programmes for Zambian economic development. As a result of this failure to analyse and ask necessary questions, more often than not, the aid given to the country does not achieve its declared purpose. This phenomenon reinforces the view (especially in individuals who have internalised racist stereotypes) that Zambians are incapable of managing their own affairs.

The assumption is made that success and Zambianness are mutually exclusive concepts. This may explain why high achieving Zambians in the Diaspora are rarely celebrated at home. Home-based high achievers are almost kept under lock and key and generally kept as far away from the levers of power as possible. This is not done consciously; it is a result of Zambian subliminal suspicion of excellence and achievement.

No one wants to belong to a 'loser' group, and the Zambians who struggle with self-acceptance and confidence do their very best to run away from their Zambianness, sometimes even through sad attempts to alter physical appearance. Attempting to run away does not, however, help because the very act of attempting to run away from oneself tends to confirm what one is.

Zambia needs a cultural shift that will lead to a more disciplined and confident nation more willing to use its numerous advantages to advance the welfare of Zambians. The country needs to behave more like a survivor determined to thrive and less like a perennial victim destined to fail. This cultural shift cannot occur without discipline (especially among leaders), a well-thought-out education system, good governance, and incorporating the best traditional Zambian values into all aspects of national life. Some unheralded leaders have the vision to do this. Conditions need to be created for these leaders to pilot the nation to prosperity.

Prosperity is easier to attain in Zambia than most other countries. To paraphrase Gwendoline Konie, the first Zambian woman to graduate from university, Zambia is a rich country that is poorly managed. The MIT-educated metallurgist, lawyer, and mining and metals consultant, Dr Silane Mwenechanya, puts it even more succinctly: 'Zambia has no business being poor'.

Many reasons have been advanced for Zambia's failure to realise her enormous potential. One of them is that the country's landlocked status denies it efficient access to trade-related networks available to coastal nations. While there are advantages to being a coastal nation, being landlocked does not necessarily close the door on prosperity. If that were the case, landlocked Switzerland would not have been ranked the world's wealthiest nation in 2019. Closer to home, landlocked Botswana has a GDP per capita income four times greater than Zambia's.

Zambia must invest in her people. In the past, this investment has been haphazard and conditional. For example, the early years of independence saw huge investment in the education of young Zambians, but with no plan to sustain this investment. The result was an eventual decline in educational standards and crumbling infrastructure.

At various points in the country's life, development has been conditional on support for the ruling party. Recent Zambian history is replete with warnings of denial or withdrawal of development funds to 'unfriendly' regions inclined to vote for the opposition. The most extreme form of political favouritism is perhaps found in pre-independence Zambia when the United Federal Party built an entire agricultural infrastructure for the benefit of 200 European farmers who formed the core of their support in the country.

There should be no such favouritism in the new Zambia. All people and all regions must have access to developmental opportunities. For this to happen, only mentally liberated and self-respecting individuals should be allowed to make significant decisions about the country's future. A decision-maker who lacks self-respect is not likely to respect 'ordinary' citizens. Such a decision maker would inevitably be dismissive of the needs of the citizens and is likely to misappropriate funds earmarked for human development.

Investing in people goes beyond providing money for projects meant to help citizens. It includes educating citizens about their civic responsibilities. With this education, citizens can make informed choices at the polls, and make Zambian democracy more viable. With democracy should come the strengthening of institutions that are uncompromising in their commitment to the rule of law and protection of human and property rights.

Thus Zambians must have access to capital and the ability to acquire land quickly. Without this, efficient business operations are almost impossible. An absence of clear ownership rules denies people and businesses the opportunity to produce, buy, and sell goods and services. On the other hand, secure property rights aid prosperity as they allow individuals to start businesses, using property as collateral for loans. No rational being will employ people to construct an expensive home on a piece of land to which she does not have a clear title.

While the government has a duty to protect the population through regulations, this duty should not be exercised to hinder the operation of free and open markets. Too much regulation can make business unprofitable and lead to unemployment, as the Zambian floriculture experience demonstrates.

Laws and regulations understood to be necessary for the common good are more likely to be obeyed than those considered a hindrance to growth and prosperity. The new Zambia must be governed more by law than individuals. Equity must always be present in the application of the law. There must not be selective prosecution, for example. The issuance of licences must not depend on one's connections to politicians or one's ethnicity or skin colour. Long-term capital, which Zambia yearns for, is more likely to materialise when investors are confident that the legal regime will be equitable and stable and not subject to the whims of uninformed individuals. Promises made to investors, be they domestic or foreign, must be kept.

Failure to provide stability and certainty for legitimate business will discourage investment and aid capital flight. Furthermore, once a country establishes a reputation for disregarding the rule of law, it becomes a haven for fly-by-night companies and international criminals. This must not happen in Zambia, where the people generally respond well to order.

Zambia is not held back because of its people. It is held back because of poor policies and the lack of consistently good leadership. To illustrate the importance of investing in people, developing appropriate institutions, and respecting the rule of law, let's compare North Korea and South Korea.

The two countries have a common culture, ethnicity, and history. When Japan surrendered at the end of World War II, Korea was divided at the 38th parallel, with the Soviet Union occupying the north and the United States occupying the south. At that point, the two regions were more or less at the same level of development. Since the division, however, North Korea has been run as an authoritarian nation where the rule of law exists only in the minds of people with generous imaginations. The country has no human and property rights to speak of, and free and open markets are largely absent. It is also among the poorest nations in the world, with a GDP per capita of USD1,700.

In contrast, South Korean institutions are robust and the supremacy of the rule of law is beyond question. The stability of South Korea's legal regime and the country's commitment to free enterprise has attracted copious investment, both domestic and foreign. South Korea is also among the richest countries globally, with a GDP per capita of USD39,548. South Korea also consistently outperforms North Korea on the UNDP's Human Development Index, which measures countries' average achievement in core areas of human development.

Let Zambia be a South Korea, not a North Korea.

Bibliography

Anta Diop, Cheikh,

The African Origin of Civilisation; Myth or Reality (Lawrence Hill & Co, Chicago 1974)

Baum, Steven,

The Psychology of Genocide: Perpetrators, Bystanders, and Rescuers. (Cambridge University Press, Cambridge 2008)

Bright, Jake and
Hruby, Audrey,

The Next Africa: An Emerging Continent Becomes a Global Powerhouse (St Martin's Press, New York, 2015)

Davidson, Basil,

Which Way Africa? The Search for a New Society (Penguin Books Ltd, Middlesex 1964, 1967)

Fanon, Frantz,

Black Skin, White Masks (Pluto Press, London 2017)

Harris, Russ,

The Confidence Gap (Published by arrangement with Penguin Group Australia, Boulder, Colorado 2011

Larmer, Miles (editor),

The Musakanya Papers, the autobiographical writings of Valentine Musakanya (Lembani Trust, Lusaka 2010)

Moyo, Dambisa,

Dead Aid: Why Aid is not Working and How There is another Way for Africa (Penguin Group, London 2009)

Mwanakatwe, John,

John Mwanakatwe: Teacher, Politician, Lawyer, My Autobiography (Bookworld Publishers, Lusaka 2003)

Parpart, Jane,

Labour and Capital on the African Copperbelt (Temple University Press, Philadelphia 1983)

Sardanis, Andrew,

Africa, Another Side of the Coin, Northern Rhodesia's Final Years and Zambian Nationhood (I.B. Tauris & Co. Ltd, London 2003)

Sardanis, Andrew,   *Zambia: The First 50 Years* (I.B. Tauris & Co.
                                    Ltd, London 2014)

Tanguy, F,   *Imilandu ya Babemba* (Oxford University Press,
                                    Oxford 1948)

Zukas, Simon,   *Into Exile and Back* (Bookworld Publishers,
                                    Lusaka 2002)

Index

A

Abrams, Stacy, 96
Addis Ababa, 113, 277
Adichie, Chimamanda Ngozi, 81
Africa Check, 95, 278
Africa Freedom Day, 242
African Advancement policy, 48
African Continental Free Trade Area (AfCFTA)., 274
African ethnogeography, 44
African Mineworkers Union, v, 20, 52, 55, 229
African National Congress, v, vi, 21, 22, 23, 55, 60, 129, 192, 230
African Representative Council, 129
Agents of Change Foundation, 241
Alliance for Community Action, 167
Alvaro III, Mani Kongo, 29
Anglo-Saxon kingdoms, 253
Atomic Energy of Canada Limited, 74
Axum, 110, 111

B

Banda,Rupiah,200,236,245
Bangweulu Regional Hospital, 188
Becker, Elizabeth, 287, 288
Beijing, 273
Belgian Congo, 49
Bemba, 19, 35, 36, 37, 38, 39, 40, 62, 126, 127, 128, 135, 136, 144, 209, 250
Bembaland, 125, 127
Berlin Conference, 17, 21, 40, 41, 42, 43, 44
Berlusconi, Silvio, 171
Bismarck, Otto von, 17, 40
Botswana, 43, 89, 90, 91, 95, 100, 121, 145, 163, 165, 170, 172, 173, 184, 205, 213, 260, 268, 282, 289, 301
Boundaries Review Committee, 172

British South Africa Company, 18
Brock University, Ontario, 58
Buhari, Muhammadu, 94, 95
Burton, Lillian Margaret, 59
Burundi, 266

C

Cairo, 99
Callaghan, James, 254
Canadian International Development Research Centre, 74
Cão, Diogo, 24, 34, 250
Central Intelligence Agency, 73
Cha-Cha-Cha, 154
Chibale, Kelly, 211, 239
Chibomba, Hilda, 194
Children's Radio Foundation, 241
Chilombo, Anna,233,234
Chiluba, 31, 151, 152, 155, 185, 245, 267
China, 89, 97, 113, 118, 122, 283
Chingola, xii, 51, 54, 57, 66, 67, 70, 77, 139, 175, 192, 193, 217, 218, 235, 255, 256
Chitemene system of agriculture, 125
Chituwo, Brian, 200, 201, 202, 203, 204
Christian evangelisation, 132
Colonial Office in London, 20
Companion Order of Freedom, 242
Constituency Development Committee, v, 201
Copper Harvest Foods Ltd, 216
Copperbelt, xii, 18, 19, 20, 42, 43, 55, 58, 60, 61, 75, 138, 144, 150, 158, 182, 201, 217, 228, 233, 241, 280, 304
Corrupt Practices Investigation Bureau, 86
Corruption Perceptions Index, 87